BEST

of

COVERED WAGON WOMEN

BEST

of

COVERED WAGON

WOMEN

Edited by
Kenneth L. Holmes

With a New Introduction by
Michael L. Tate

University of Oklahoma Press : Norman

Best of Covered Wagon Women is based on material drawn
from the Covered Wagon Women series (11 volumes)
originally published by
The Arthur H. Clark Company

The paper in this book meets the guidelines for pemanence and
durability of the Committee on Production Guidelines for
Book Longevity of the Council on Library Resources, Inc. ∞

1 2 3 4 5 6 7 8 9 10

Best of Covered wagon women / edited by Kenneth L. Holmes ; with a new introduc-
tion by Michael L. Tate.
    p. cm.
Includes index.
"The best of Covered wagon women is based on material drawn from the Covered
wagon women series (11 volumes) originally published by the Arthur H. Clark
Company"—T.p. verso.
ISBN 978-0-8061-3914-2 (pbk. : alk. paper)
    1. Women pioneers—West (U.S.)—Biography. 2. Women pioneers—West (U.S.)—
Diaries. 3. Women pioneers—West (U.S.)—Correspondence. 4. West (U.S.)—
History—Sources. 5. West (U.S.)—Biography. 6. Overland journeys to the Pacific—
Sources. 7. Frontier and pioneer life—West (U.S.)—Sources. I. Holmes, Kenneth L.
II. Covered wagon women.
    F591.B525 2008
    978'.020922—dc22
                                2007037677

Contents

Illustrations

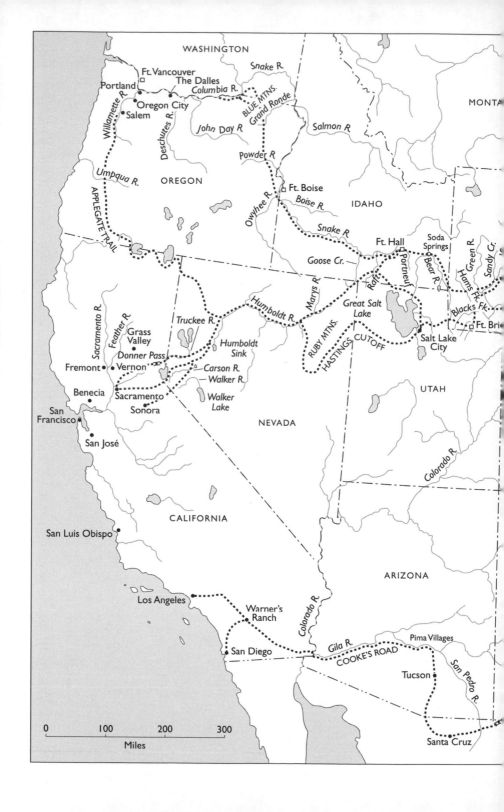

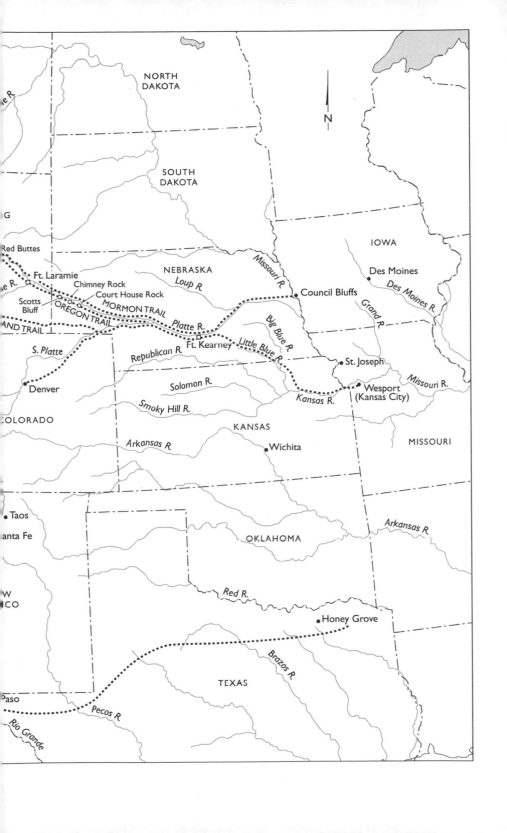

Introduction

by Michael L. Tate

Since well before the United States became a nation, its highly mobile people have sought new opportunities in unfamiliar places. Few stories of domestic migration have been as thoroughly documented as that of the transcontinental trek westward in the mid-nineteenth century. With the influx of farmers to Oregon's verdant Willamette River Valley during the early 1840s, continuing with the arrival of Mormon faithful in the Great Basin of Utah during 1847, and accelerating with the rush of miners to the California gold fields in 1849, America's most picturesque migration was well under way. In addition to the iconic Oregon, California, and Mormon trails, pathways to the Far West also crossed the southwestern territories, especially along the Gila River. At one time, it seemed everyone in the eastern states knew someone—friend, neighbor, or relative—who had succumbed to the western fever and taken up the journey.

Eyewitnesses to this remarkable phenomenon were awestruck. Margaret Frink, bound for California in 1850 with her husband, Ledyard, observed the convergence of covered wagons twenty-five miles southeast of Ft. Kearny where two branches of the trail—one from present-day Nebraska City, Nebraska, and the other from St. Joseph, Missouri—came together. Frink wrote in her journal: "It seemed to me that I had never seen so many human beings in all my life before. And, when we drew nearer to the vast multitude, and saw them in all manner of vehicles and conveyances, on horseback and on foot . . . I thought, in my excitement, that if one-tenth of these teams and these people got ahead of us, there would be nothing left in California worth picking up."[1]

American Indians also were both amazed and alarmed by the magnitude of the migration. A delegation of Pacific Northwest tribes

---

[1]Margaret A. Frink, "Adventures of a Party of Gold-Seekers," in *Covered Wagon Women: Diaries and Letters from the Western Trails, 1840–1870*, vol. 2 (Glendale, Calif.: Arthur H. Clark, 1983), 85–86.

accompanied Jesuit father Pierre-Jean De Smet to the 1851 treaty negotiations near Ft. Laramie, along what the Indians called the "Great Medicine Road," for its mysterious and incomprehensible power. Marveling at the road's width and the absence of grass because of the heavy traffic in humans and livestock, the Indians conjectured that since so many white people had crossed this large region, the lands east of the Mississippi River must be all but abandoned. When De Smet explained that the mass migration was but a small portion of the eastern population, his Indian friends were incredulous.[2]

Impressions such as these were reinforced by more reliable eyewitness tabulations. Major Osborne Cross estimated that between late April and June 1 of 1849, four thousand wagons, with an average of four persons to each wagon, had passed Ft. Kearny. He further remarked that this total did not include the substantial numbers who traversed the area along the north bank of the Platte River and had not reported to the military post.[3] Four years later, overlander Andrew McClure wrote that, according to the official registry at Ft. Kearny, as of May 20, 1853, 4,161 men, 1,030 women, 1,398 children, and 1,596 wagons had already crossed the military reservation during that year's trail season alone. Like Major Cross's estimate, McClure's did not include the emigrants who transited on the opposite side of the river.[4]

Amid all of the eyewitness accounts, partial calculations, and later attempts to study the demographics of trail life, one set of estimates remains widely accepted by today's scholars. Merrill J. Mattes, dean of the trail historians, surveyed annual migration patterns in his classic bibliography, *Platte River Road Narratives*, published in 1988.

---

[2]Pierre-Jean De Smet, Life, *Letters and Travels of Father Pierre-Jean De Smet*, vol. 2, ed. Hiram M. Chittenden and Alfred T. Richardson (New York: Francis P. Harper, 1905), 671–72. See the similar experiences of Lt. James Henry Carleton in 1845 with groups of Sioux along the Oregon Trail. J. Henry Carleton, *The Prairie Logbooks: Dragoon Campaigns to the Pawnee Villages in 1844 and the Rocky Mountains in 1845,* ed. Louis Pelzer (Chicago: Caxton Club, 1943), 250.

[3]Osborne Cross, "The Journal of Major Osborne Cross," in *The March of the Mounted Riflemen: First United States Military Expedition to Travel the Full Length of the Oregon Trail from Fort Leavenworth to Fort Vancouver, May to October 1849,* ed. Raymond W. Settle (Glendale, Calif.: Arthur H. Clark, 1940), 79–80.

[4]Andrew S. McClure, "Diary," transcript, Lane County Pioneer-Historical Society, Eugene, Oregon, 8–9.

Mattes concluded that between 1841 and 1866, approximately 500,000 people negotiated the Platte River Road to Oregon, California, Salt Lake City, and the newly settled Denver area.[5] He did not include the significant numbers that crossed the southwestern routes through New Mexico and Arizona, but even with the exclusion of those totals, the magnitude of the migration was immediately evident.

Mattes also estimated that of the half-million people who participated in this mass exodus, well over two thousand kept diaries and journals or subsequently wrote memoirs of their trip. Fortunately, many of these documents have survived, and Mattes identified the locations of 2,082 of these in original handwritten, transcript, or published form.[6]

Every person who made the transcontinental crossing, whether he or she recorded personal experiences or not, had preconceptions about what to expect. Some were optimists who voiced little regard in their diaries and letters for the dangers and privations that lay ahead. Their thoughts remained focused on the opportunities this great adventure would offer. At the other end of the spectrum were pessimists who anticipated a troubled journey from start to finish. One such poor soul was the mother of nine-year-old Barnet Simpson, who prepared burial shrouds for each member of her family before they departed for Oregon in 1846.[7] Fatalism also dominated the spirit of some of the men in Sarah Sutton's 1854 wagon train. They took along boards specially cut for constructing coffins for any unfortunates, especially sixteen-year-old Harriet Augusta, who was very ill.[8] Most, however, were simply realists who recognized that trail life contained great dangers but also believed that a successful journey was well worth the risks.

Although the overwhelming majority of migrants reached their destinations without mishap, injury and death seemed a constant

---

[5]Merrill J. Mattes, *Platte River Road Narratives: A Descriptive Bibliography of Travel over the Great Central Route* . . . (Urbana: University of Illinois Press, 1988), 2–5.

[6]Mattes, *Platte River Road Narratives,* 5 and 615.

[7]"Barnet Simpson," in Fred Lockley, *Conversations with Pioneer Men,* comp. Mike Helm (Eugene, Ore.: Rainy Day Press, 1996), 30–31.

[8]Kenneth L. Holmes, Introduction to "Sarah Sutton, A Travel Diary in 1854," in *Covered Wagon Women,* vol. 7 (Glendale, Calif.: Arthur H. Clark, 1987), 15.

companion to some, ill-fated wagon trains. Diarists often mention gunshot wounds, the result either of hunting accidents or of loaded guns discharging as they were placed in or removed from wagons. Children especially were prone to being run over by wagons or trampled by livestock as they walked during much of the journey alongside the lumbering vehicles. Likewise, drowning at river crossings proved more consequential than one might assume, as was sickness caused by poor diets, poisonous plants, and alkaline water.

Yet the most feared threats came from the diseases that plagued many overlanders, most notably cholera, whose outbreak appeared suddenly and with devastating effects. Alonzo Delano witnessed one such attack while camped on the banks of the Missouri River at St. Joseph, Missouri, in 1849. A Mr. Harris, who was traveling with the California-bound column, took sick at about 4:00 in the morning. Although he had shown no previous symptoms, the afflicted man was soon writhing in agony. His compatriots gave him laudanum and called for a local doctor. Harris's condition quickly deteriorated over the next several hours as he suffered intense pain, vomiting, cramps, and a clammy sweat. By afternoon he seemed to rally and even pronounced himself cured of the mysterious malady. Then, before day's end, he gasped for breath and was dead within five minutes.[9]

Of all the potential dangers that lay along the trail, that allegedly posed by Native Americans concerned travelers the most. Filled with stereotypical notions of Plains Indian "savages" based on artists' depictions, dime novels, and spurious newspaper articles, the majority of overlanders feared the worst from those whom Captain Randolph B. Marcy likened to Arab Bedouins.[10] Some emigrants did encounter problems with Indians, most often while defending against attempted theft of livestock, and some actually died at the hands of Indians. Yet most experienced no direct threat, and many of these actually came to sympathize with Native peoples as they traded and interacted with them.

---

[9]Alonzo Delano, *Life on the Plains and Among the Diggings: Being Scenes and Adventures of an Overland Journey to California* (Auburn, N.Y.: Miller, Orton and Mulligan, 1854), 17–18.

[10]Randolph B. Marcy, *Thirty Years of Army Life on the Border* (New York: Harper and Brothers, 1866), 4–5.

Historian John D. Unruh, Jr., in his monumental study, *The Plains Across* (1979), closely examined hundreds of diaries, journals, letter collections, and government reports to quantify as accurately as possible the magnitude of the so-called Indian threat. He noted that for the entire period 1840–1860, only 362 emigrants were killed by Indians along the central route to Oregon, California, and Salt Lake City. This represents a mere eighteen mortalities per year during a two-decade cycle. By contrast, Unruh concluded that during the same period, 426 Indians were killed by whites.[11] Even if one acknowledges the probability of nonlethal wounds in combat, unreported cases of violence, and the life-threatening consequences of losing one's livestock to raiders, the alleged Indian threat was less an issue than popular wisdom indicated. Subsequent statistical work by Glenda Riley, Lillian Schlissel, Robert Munkres, and other historians has affirmed Unruh's conclusions.[12]

Dangers, perceived and actual, occupied considerable space in overlanders' writings, and justifiably so. Yet their real fascination seemed to be with the grandeur of the land itself, places foreign to their eastern-U.S. and European experience. That sense of wonder seemed to first manifest itself along the banks of the Missouri River, where, prior to the 1854 Kansas-Nebraska Act, overlanders realized they were looking across the great river toward Indian Country, not at organized states or territories. Mary Ann Boatman stood at the river's edge in 1852 and recorded the contrast between the thriving town of Council Bluffs, Iowa, and the expanse of virtually unsettled land on the west bank. She imagined the former as "our last camping in civilization." "From now on," she lamented, "we got to face the savage."[13] The savage she alluded to was not just the expected Indian

---

[11]John D. Unruh, Jr., *The Plains Across: The Overland Emigrants and the Trans-Mississippi West, 1840–60* (Urbana: University of Illinois Press, 1979), 184–85.

[12]Glenda Riley, *Women and Indians on the Frontier, 1825–1915* (Albuquerque: University of New Mexico Press, 1984), 155; Lillian Schlissel, *Women's Diaries of the Westward Journey* (New York: Schocken Books, 1982), 154; Robert L. Munkres, "The Plains Indian Threat on the Oregon Trail before 1860," *Annals of Wyoming* 40 (October 1968): 193–94. Also see Michael L. Tate, *Indians and Emigrants: Encounters on the Overland Trails* (Norman: University of Oklahoma Press, 2006).

[13]Weldon Willis Rau, *Surviving the Oregon Trail, 1852: As Told by Mary and Willis Boatman and Augmented with Accounts by Other Overland Travelers* (Pullman: Washington State University Press, 2001), 32.

threat to follow but also the savage landscape itself, which stretched endlessly from the mighty Missouri to the Pacific Ocean.

Yet even the most reluctant of travelers came to marvel at the unfamiliar sights encountered along the way. Some found the Great Plains—stigmatized earlier by Lieutenant Zebulon Pike and Major Stephen Long as the Great American Desert—to be fascinating because of its expansiveness, broad blue skies, and oddly shaped bluffs and rock formations. Especially popular was the thirty-mile stretch, in today's Nebraska Panhandle, between Courthouse Rock and Scotts Bluff, where travelers got their first sense of mountains and the high plains. Most delightful of all was Chimney Rock, instantly recognizable from a distance. Many who camped in its shadow tried to climb the oddly shaped hill with its needlelike summit. The entire chain of buttes and hills along this section of the North Platte River resembled a wonderland of scenic delights, giving the travelers a sense of entering a new phase of their trip.

Many diarists described Chimney Rock in the most poetic of terms. Commenting in 1858, Kirk Anderson declared it "shot up like a spire in the heavens, its top gilded by the setting sun, looking like its crest was burnished with gold." Not to be outdone in supplying comparisons, Captain Philip St. George Cooke declared it to be like the Pharos Lighthouse of ancient Egypt. It struck Dr. Elijah White as similar to the envisioned Washington Monument, while to Henry S. Bloom it looked "like some vast giant leaning against the distant clouds, standing sentinal [*sic*] at the entrance to an enchanted fairyland."[14]

In similar fashion, Alonzo Delano tapped his fertile imagination to describe the east face of Scotts Bluff in 1849: "It seemed as if the wand of a magician had passed over a city, and like that in the Arabian Nights, had converted all living things to stone. Here you saw the minarets of a castle: there, the loop-holes of bastions of a fort; again the frescoes of a huge temple . . . while at other points

---

[14]These descriptions of Chimney Rock are provided in Merrill J. Mattes, *The Great Platte River Road: The Covered Wagon Mainline via Fort Kearny to Fort Laramie.* Publications of the Nebraska State Historical Society, 25 (Lincoln: Nebraska State Historical Society, 1969), 386, 394–96.

Chinese temples . . . made it appear as if by some supernatural cause we had been dropped in the suburbs of a mighty city."[15] Further west, in south-central Wyoming, Maria Parsons Belshaw stood in awe of Independence Rock. She recorded climbing to the top with her husband but becoming faint from the exertion, even though the rock was only 128 feet high. Belshaw noted the many interesting names and dates inscribed or painted on the oval-shaped formation by previous migrants, but was disappointed to discover that she did not recognize even one of them.[16] Independence Rock, dubbed by emigrants the "Register of the Desert," testified to people's ability to revel in the simplest of pleasures during their arduous journey.

More has been written about the travails experienced along the western routes and the exotic environments encountered than about another important feature of the trip—saying goodbye to friends and family in the eastern settlements. It is true that many California-bound miners intended to return to their homes after making their fortunes in the Sierras. And most Mormon emigrants expected to reunite with others of the faithful who would eventually make their own trek to the Salt Lake Valley. Yet many overlanders, especially those families that migrated to farms and small towns in the Oregon Country, had little hope of returning to the states or of seeing most of their friends and family members join them in the Pacific Northwest. It is difficult for Americans today to fully understand the emigrants' sense of finality as they began their trips. No telephones, Internet connections, or rapid transportation systems existed to maintain communication with their loved ones. Only the federal mail service served this purpose, but it was slow, unpredictable, and expensive for the average American or European emigrant family.

Men and women alike felt the melancholy moment of turning their backs on familiar people and surroundings to head for the great unknown of the West. But most were also filled with excitement and expectation. The voices of children especially echo this duality of emotions in their own diaries and later memoirs. As minors they had little

---

[15]Delano, *Life on the Plains*, 73.

[16]Maria Parsons Belshaw, *Crossing the Plains to Oregon in 1853*, ed. Michael L. Tate (Fairfield, Wash.: Ye Galleon Press, 2000), 27.

choice about whether they would accompany their parents on the trip, but they certainly had private feelings about the matter. Unlike their parents, they were concerned less about the long-term implications of the relocation than about the immediate experience. For seven-year-old Jesse Applegate, member of the famed Applegate company of 1843, "Oregon" was a word without meaning, and he refrained from bothering his parents with questions about why they were going and what they would find there.[17] For the youngster Henry Gilfry, April 1, 1852, had special meaning as "All Fool's Day." When he left home that day, some of the neighbors' said in parting that the Oregon trip was nothing but a "fool's errand" that would end in tragedy.[18] Likewise, seven-year-old Benjamin Franklin Bonney heard from friends and neighbors as he departed Illinois only a litany of warnings that his family would perish in the desert lands of the West.[19]

Leaving home also meant parting with objects that were dear to the family—clocks, chairs, beds, tables, dressers, clothes, books, toys, and a host of other items. For many children it also meant leaving their beloved pets, considered a potential burden for the journey. Fifteen-year-old Welborn Beeson was forced to shoot his pet cat Socrates "to keep him from fretting" if placed in the care of an unfamiliar family.[20]

The finality of a "last visit" was related by Keturah Belknap. Before heading west, she, her husband, and two children traveled east from their Iowa home for a month-long visit to her parents in Ohio. The reunion was cheery, mainly because Keturah withheld from her parents her one dark secret: the impending migration to Oregon that would leave her permanently separated from her Ohio-bound parents and childhood friends. She let those folks continue to believe that her family would call on them again within two years, though she knew it was a lie and she would never see them again. Keturah simply recorded that, although "it was hard for me to not

---

[17]Jesse Applegate, *Recollections of My Boyhood* (Roseburg, Ore.: Press of Review Publishing Co., 1914), 9–10.

[18]Henry H. Gilfry, "Recollections," *Transactions of the Oregon Pioneer Association* (1903): 412.

[19]Benjamin Franklin Bonney, "Recollections of Benjamin Franklin Bonney," ed. Fred Lockley, *Oregon Historical Quarterly* 24 (March 1923): 37.

[20]Welborn Beeson, *Welborn Beeson on the Oregon Trail in 1853*, ed. Bert Webber (Medford, Ore.: Smith, Smith and Smith Publishing Co., 1986), 27.

break down" when she left Ohio, she did not reveal the sad truth to her parents until after the Oregon trip was completed.[21]

For many people, feelings of isolation not only arose at the beginning of the trip but also recurred during the journey and even after they settled at their destinations. Eighteen-year-old Martha Hill was repeatedly overcome by depression and guilt feelings about having left her Tennessee home in 1853. When her wagon reached a safe location barely fifty miles from its destination of Oregon City, the sorrow struck hard again. Overhearing a man offering her father a princely sum for the livestock he had driven to Oregon, she pleaded with her father to accept the amount and immediately return to Tennessee "for I was so homesick that I would have started back that very night if father had been willing."[22]

Such recorded observations are just a small sample of the rich eyewitness accounts of the overland trail saga that have survived for more than 150 years. Although the extant trail diaries, journals, and letters have been widely used by researchers, few have been readily available to the casual reader or armchair historian. Many exist only in single-copy manuscript form in dispersed archival collections, and others are printed in academic journals not easily accessed by nonacademics. Kenneth L. Holmes recognized this access problem, as well as modern readers' voracious appetite for pioneer literature. He set about in 1979 to close the gap between supply and demand by envisioning a multivolume series of the best women's diaries, journals, memoirs, and correspondence. For much of his academic career at Oregon College of Education (today's Western Oregon University), at Monmouth, Dr. Holmes lived among people who took great pride in their Oregon Trail forefathers. With no specific goal in mind, he began to copy and transcribe rare diaries and other documents. Exercising great care, he studied the sources, compared the people's diverse experiences, and began to see the overall importance of what they had accomplished in their long-ago migrations.[23]

---

[21]"The Commentaries of Keturah Belknap," in *Covered Wagon Women*, 1, ed. Kenneth L. Holmes (Glendale, Calif.: Arthur H. Clark, 1983), 210–12.

[22]Martha Hill Gillette, *Overland to Oregon and the Indian Wars of 1853* (Ashland, Ore.: Lewis Osborne, 1971)), 57–58.

[23]Robert A. Clark, "Kenneth L. Holmes and the Development of the Covered Wagon Women Series," *Western Historical Quarterly* 28 (Winter 1997): 548–50.

The selections not only offer intrinsic value but also collectively help rebut the long-held myth of the transcontinental migrations as largely a male story. Likewise, their descriptions of daily life help us move beyond notions of women as helpmates or Madonnas of the prairie whose actions were circumscribed by prevailing notions of domesticity. Their lives on the trail certainly did include "traditional" tasks such as cooking, sewing, cleaning, child rearing, caring for the sick, and maintaining household goods, but their roles exceeded the narrow set of values embraced by the nineteenth-century Cult of True Womanhood. Among other tasks, women drove wagons, rounded up livestock, buried the dead, negotiated with Indians for trade items, repaired wagons and equipment, and entered the decision-making process with the men of their parties. The female diarists remind us again that the experiences and thoughts of emigrant women did not mirror some unified "woman's point of view," but rather demonstrated the diversity of experiences of and reactions among the writers.

When Holmes retired from teaching in 1979, he assembled the materials for possible publication. He followed archival leads to find out what happened to the individuals mentioned in the diaries and to put their unique stories into a larger context. Having examined the three volumes authored by Clifford M. Drury, *First White Women over the Rockies* (1963–66), about the overland experiences of Narcissa Whitman, Eliza Spalding, and other Pacific Northwest missionaries, he believed he would find a publisher for his own research. Holmes sent a letter of inquiry to the Arthur H. Clark Company, the celebrated firm that had published Drury's books. Renowned for its quality books about the American West, the press had released some of the most important multivolume sets in the trail diary genre—Reuben Gold Thwaites's Early Western Travels series (thirty-two volumes), Ralph P. Bieber and LeRoy R. Hafen's Southwest Historical Series (twelve volumes), LeRoy R. and Ann W. Hafen's Far West and Rockies Series (fifteen volumes), and LeRoy R. Hafen's Mountain Men and the Fur Trade of the Far West series (ten volumes).[24]

---

[24]Ibid., 549.

Holmes realized that the magnitude of his envisioned work would require a great deal of faith, paticncc, and capital from his publisher because the series would entail the release of multiple volumes over a number of years. The perfect match between editor and publisher culminated in an eleven-volume series entitled *Covered Wagon Women: Diaries and Letters from the Western Trails, 1840–1890.* The final volume included a detailed bibliography and index, as well as a large foldout map, all of which enhanced the usability of the documents.[25]

Throughout the series, Holmes purposely limited the number of bibliographical and explanatory footnotes. He was far more interested in letting the original authors speak for themselves than in overwhelming their words with his own minutiae. With each publication, however, he did include a new introduction to briefly describe trail conditions during the years covered by that volume. And he provided fairly lengthy introductory remarks at the head of each primary document to identify the people mentioned in the source and to explain some of the important themes it raised. In consultation with Robert A. Clark of the Arthur H. Clark Company, he established criteria for which items to include in the set and which items to exclude. Among these criteria were the uniqueness, entertainment value, and literary merit of the material. In other words, no diary that merely listed daily distances traveled and weather conditions would make the list. If the source had been previously published but was extremely scarce, it could be considered for publication. Also, in keeping with the original intent of letting the authors speak for themselves, errors of spelling, grammar, and punctuation were left largely intact.[26]

Despite the financial risks of publishing such a long-running series, *Covered Wagon Women* proved to be a hit with researchers and the public, and the early volumes went through subsequent printings. Many libraries and individual collectors maintained standing orders as each new volume came off the press.[27] With considerable aid from

---

[25]Ibid., 548–49.   [26]Ibid., 551.

[27]Robert A. Clark and Patrick J. Brunet, *The Arthur H. Clark Company: An Americana Century, 1902–2002* (Spokane, Wash.: Arthur H. Clark Co., 2002), 146. Sales figures through June 2006 provided by Robert A. Clark.

Arthur H. Clark, Jr., and Robert A. Clark, Dr. Holmes saw the first ten volumes to completion. The eleventh volume was being prepared at the time Holmes's health began to deteriorate, and he was able to complete work only on one of the included documents and the bibliography. The publisher finished the other introductions and series index, and Holmes saw the project completed before he died in 1995.[28]

As with the other book series published over many decades by the Arthur H. Clark Company, this one long outlived the author and achieved an even larger reading audience from a new generation of trail enthusiasts. The University of Nebraska Press republished the complete series in paperback under its successful Bison Books imprint. One by one, the volumes were issued between 1995 and 2000, complete with striking new covers, newly prepared indexes, and new introductions written by some of the best-known western historians. Sales of the new paperback format exceeded those of the original hardback editions.[29]

Holmes's important work has now undergone a third metamorphosis—a one-volume edition comprising eight of the best eyewitness accounts of overland travel. The eight documents reproduced here extend over the entire period when the overland trails witnessed their greatest human activity. We see in these women's words that conditions on these byways during the fifty-year cycle were constantly in flux. A wagon train setting out from Independence, Missouri, in 1845 would quickly have moved beyond the line of settlement as it crossed into the future state of Kansas. By 1865, however, emigrants crossing the same area of northeastern Kansas would have discovered sizable towns and farms stretching along the trail as far west as Ft. Kearny, Nebraska. These later migrants would also have encountered stage stations, telegraph offices, and other symbols of "civilization" as they traversed the entire length of the Platte River into present-day Wyoming. Four years later, they would even have seen locomotives chugging their way west over newly laid rails through the Platte River Valley. At the same time, travelers through

---

[28]Clark, "Kenneth L. Holmes," 554.
[29]Sales figures through June 2006 provided by Robert A. Clark.

this region in the 1860s would more likely have seen evidence of greater Indian problems (or at least heard more secondhand accounts of depredations) than would their predecessors of the 1840s and early 1850s. The only thing consistent in a half century of migration was the constantly changing conditions that each new year brought for Indians and overlanders alike.

Historian and essayist Bernard De Voto once labeled 1846 the "Year of Decision" because so many crucial events unfolded in those twelve months and they all pertained to American expansion into the West. Among the turning points that De Voto associated with this transcontinental thrust were the annexation of Texas, the beginning of the Mexican War, the Mormon exodus from Nauvoo, Illinois, American invasion of California, President James K. Polk's acquisition of the Oregon Country from Britain, and increased traffic on the overland trails.[30] Taking an even larger view of these and other events, one can see that the entire period from 1841 to 1869 was truly an "Era of Decision." Westward expansion, the Civil War, termination of slavery, and the move toward an industrialized and urbanized America established the mid-nineteenth century as a critical age of change for the nation. The people who made these events happen were not only presidents, congressmen, generals, industrialists, and financiers. Mixed together with prominent leaders were "average" people with less recognizable names who made the trip west to seek greater freedom and new opportunities. In this volume, we may now examine the words of eight people (nine, counting the twin sisters) who made the memorable journey and who left a legacy not only for their families but also for readers four generations removed from the events. Sometimes, it is the "little stories" that resonate with modern readers, and it is the words of the eyewitness participants that resonate best. This was the intention of Kenneth Holmes when he first prepared the Covered Wagon Women series, and this new, single-volume "best of" edition retains that philosophy.

---

[30]Bernard De Voto, *The Year of Decision: 1846* (Boston: Little, Brown, 1943).

Editorial Considerations

When the Covered Wagon Women series of eleven volumes was originally developed, the editor and publisher established certain editorial rules to guide their presentation of the transcribed diaries, journals, and letters. They were as follows:

"It is our purpose to let the diarists and correspondents tell their own story in their own words, with as little scholarly trimming as possible. The intent is to transcribe each word or phrase as accurately as possible, leaving as written whatever misspellings or grammatical errors are found. The only gestures we have made for the sake of the reader have been as follows:

"1. We have added space where phrases or sentences ended and no punctuation was to be found in the original.

"2. We have put the daily journals into diary format even though the original may have been written continuously line by line because of the original writer's shortage of paper."

The Commentaries of Keturah Belknap
1848

INTRODUCTION

No persons who told their story of the overland journey to Oregon used such an ingenious method as did Keturah Belknap.[1] Beginning with her marriage date, October 3, 1839, in Allen County, Ohio, she kept not a diary, but what she termed a "memorandum," in which she periodically recorded what had happened in the period since her last entry. Evidently later in life she added notes to the original and recorded other memories. It is even difficult, therefore, to separate out added material from her "memorandum." She records events in the past tense for several entries; then all of a sudden the present tense makes an appearance, such as, "Now we're skirting the timber on the DeMoines River and its tributaries." Then she reverts to the past tense again.

The question arises for the editor whether such a "memorandum" ought to be included in a volume of contemporary records such as diaries and letters. The answer is that the nub of her running commentary in her story is built so closely around the day-by-day or week-by-week records that they dominate and the "memorandum," therefore, has an immediacy which no reminiscence written years later can capture. This is especially true of the overland part of her record, which seems to have been written on the spot while in the wagon.

The early pages, which we have omitted, have to do with the life of

---

[1]Her given name is spelled in several ways by family and in the published literature, a common rendering being "Kitturah." She, herself, spelled it "Ketturah" in her "Chronicle of the Bellfountain Settlement," *Oregon Historical Quarterly*, XXXVIII, no. 3 (Sept. 1937), 271. The name is spelled "Keturah" in the 1870 federal census records.

The name is a biblical one. In the King James Bible, the version used by the pioneer Methodists, it appears as "Keturah" whenever used. "Keturah" was one of Abraham's wives and is mentioned in Genesis 25:1–4 and in I Chronicles 1:23–33. It is hard to believe that the parents would have named their newborn daughter for one dubbed by the biblical writer as a "concubine," nevertheless that is what happened. The meaning of the Hebrew word is "fragrance."

According to Robert Moulton Gatke, who edited the above "Chronicle," the family could not agree as to whether there should be double "t" or one. Our conclusion is to use "Keturah," under the assumption that such a devout family would have followed the Bible in usage.

the George Belknaps before they left for Oregon. In them she went into minute detail about events in Van Buren County, Iowa, during the 1840s. She tells of the births of their first four children—and the deaths of three of them. She describes the activities of devoted frontier Methodists, who often used the Belknap home, meager though it might be, as a meeting house.

On May 15, 1847, she writes, "Husband and I and two children start for Ohio to visit my father and mother." They made the journey while other Belknaps and their friends were starting for Oregon. George and Keturah and their children began their return trip from Ohio to their Iowa home in June, 1847, and she writes a vivid description of the several methods of travel, including the train. We begin her commentaries as she returned home in early summer 1847. During the next autumn she made another entry that read, "My dear little girl, Martha, was sick all summer and the 30th of October she died, one year and one month old. Now we have one little baby boy left." Jesse Walker Belknap was the child's name, born December 23, 1844, and now three years old.

Sometime during 1847 she and her husband decided to follow others of the family to Oregon during the next overland season, 1848. George's parents, Jesse and Jane Belknap, also decided to go with them. Keturah's description of the details of preparation for the long overland trek is classic, one of the best of such records that have come to light.

Her story of the journey begins with the words, "Tuesday, April 10, 1848. Daylight dawned with none awake but me." The little Jesse is "in his place with his whip starting for Oregon." From that day on she goes into great and descriptive detail about every facet of the covered wagon journey. Here again, sometimes she makes day-by-day entries, at other times making an entry after several days, or an update covering a week or more. Her last lines are two undated ones reading, "Some of the men went thru to Fort Hall on horse back and returned to meet us and say we can make it by noon." The context makes it appear that this would have been in mid-July. Her baby boy was very ill and evidently she had no time for writing. Just before the above two last lines she had told of holding her little son on her lap on a pillow and of tending him all night long. She had written, "I thot in the night we would have to leave him here and I thot if we did I would be likely to stay with him but as the daylight, we seemed to get fresh courage."

That tender little Jesse Belknap did finish the journey to Oregon. He lived on for many years after 1848. The *Pacific Christian Advocate*, the west's Methodist newspaper, later reported that he and his wife, Florence, both died in December 1871, leaving a two-year-old son.

There was another reason Keturah quit writing: In addition to having a sickly tiny boy child to care for, she was pregnant. She gave birth to another son, named Lorenzo, on August 10, 1848, somewhere in eastern Oregon. The family tradition says it was about where Vale, Oregon is today. Lorenzo also survived the journey to live a long life. He died on February 28, 1926.

Keturah's own vital dates are elusive. In another "memorandum," published in the September 1937 *Oregon Historical Quarterly,* she jotted down the words, "And now I am going to Make out A report and we will write August the 15, 1847, this is my 27 birthday." This would mean that she was born on August 5, 1820, and celebrated her 28th birthday in eastern Oregon not long after Lorenzo's birth. She lived many, many years. Her obituary appeared in the Portland *Oregonian* newspaper on August 24, 1913, with a story out of Coquille, in southwestern Oregon, dated August 23, and saying, "With the passing of Mrs. George Belknap, of this city yesterday at the age of 93 years another of the earliest pioneers of the Oregon country has departed." So her vital dates are August 15, 1820–August 22, 1913.

In addition to the one telling of her overland journey, there are several other Keturah Belknap "running commentaries." The Oregon Trail record, transcribed from a typescript in possession of the Washington State University Libraries, Pullman, Washington, has a long title which reads, "History of the Life of My Grandmother, Kitturah Penton Belknap. Copied from the Original Loaned Me by My Cousin, Walter Belknap, son of Jessie Spoken of in This Manuscript." The typist misspells Keturah, Benton, and Jesse. Another commentary telling of the later life of Belknap family was published in the *Oregon Historical Quarterly* for September, 1937, and is entitled, "Ketturah Belknap's Chronicle of the Bellfountain Settlement," edited by the late Robert Moulton Gatke of Willamette University, Salem, Oregon. The spelling reproduced by Professor Gatke reveals a manuscript not so sophisticated in its orthography as the typescript we have used. Evidently the copier of our overland commentary "straightened out" Keturah Belknap's spelling, punctuation and capitalization.

We are indebted to Mrs. Frances Milne of Pullman, Washington, for informing us of two other Keturah Belknap commentaries: One of them is a typescript labeled "Part III," which continues the Belknap story after the arrival in Oregon. In this one she says she has lost her "memorandum" and "cannot give dates, have to write from memory."

The second manuscript is labeled "Part IV," and it was written by Katherine Barrett, a granddaughter, with the help of her mother, Lovina Belknap Christian. Mrs. Barrett says near the beginning of this reminiscence that her grandmother "is now 85 but . . . is in good health and mentally alert." These two women sum up the remainder of the overland journey of 1848, according to family traditions. The key paragraphs in this reminiscence are as follows:

> We have no recollections of any thing unusual in their trip across the plains after they left Fort Hall until they reached Fort Boise. There we remember grandmother telling about camping there for several days, resting and washing their clothes in the hot springs. . . .
>
> The next event was the birth of a baby boy [Lorenzo] who was born near the present town of Vale, Oregon. They stopped a day or two and then went on. grandmother and baby quite comfortable in the bed she speaks of earlier that they had fixed up in the covered wagon.
>
> They crossed the Blue Mountains and on down the Columbia River to the Dalles. There the men took the stock and oxen by trail and Indians took the women, children, and household goods in canoes and wagon beds down the river to Portland. They had to portage around the rapids at Cascade. At Portland there were only a few houses and a trading store. They didn't like the dense timber there so went on to what is now Benton County, 20 miles from Corvallis, near Monroe, Oregon, where they established a settlement which was known as "The Belknap Settlement."
>
> It was October when they arrived and most of them were able to build log houses for shelter before winter came which was very mild in comparison with Iowa winters. Grandfather got his little family settled during the winter of '48 and in '49 he, with most of the young able bodied men, went to California to the gold fields. I think he did pretty well and was able to buy stock and necessary equipment for his farm. They took up a Government donation claim of 640 acres of land. In those days, many boys married young girls just in order to get the 320 acres of land which they could claim.
>
> The Belknaps were all Methodists and very soon had a church

in the making. At first they met at each other's as they had done in Iowa. In 1854 Bishop [Matthew] Simpson came to hold the first conference in the log school house. The church known as Simpson's Chapel today, stands near the spot where this first conference was held.

KETURAH BELKNAP'S RUNNING COMMENTARY

[June 1847] We found the folks all excitement about Oregon. Some had gone in the spring of '47; four families of the connection and many of the neighbors but they had not been heard from since crossing the Missouri River. Everything was out of place and all was excitement and commotion. Our home was sold waiting our return to make out the papers and it was all fixed up for me to live with Father Belknaps as the man wanted the house on our place. Ransom's[2] and Fathers had not been sold yet. It did not suit me to live with them so I told them it was out of the quesion so for the first time since our marriage I put my foot down and said "will and wont" so it was arranged for us to go on Rant's place and live in their home till it was sold. I knew it would use me and the little sick baby up so to be in such a tumult. There was nothing done or talked of but what had Oregon in it and the loom was banging and the wheel buzzing and trades being made from daylight till bed time so I was glad to get settled.

My dear little girl, Martha, was sick all summer and the 30th of October [1847] she died, one year and one month old. Now we have one little baby boy left.

So now I will spend what little strength I have left getting ready to cross the Rockies. Will cut out some sewing to have to pick up at all the odd moments for I will try to have clothes enough to last a year.

November 15, 1847. Have cut out four muslin shirts for George and two suits for the little boy (Jessie). With what he has that will last him (if he lives) until we will want a different pattern.

---

[2]Ransom or "Rant" Belknap was a younger brother of George. His wife was Mahala.

The material for the men's outer garments has to be woven yet. The neighbors are all very kind to come in to see me so I don't feel lonely like I would and they don't bring any work, but just pick up my sewing we think I will soon get a lot done. Then they are not the kind with long sad faces but always leave me with such a pleasant smiling faces that it does me good to think of them and I try not to think of the parting time but look forward to the time when we shall meet to part no more.

Now, I will begin to work and plan to make everything with an eye to starting out on a six month trip. The first thing is to lay plans and then work up to the program so the first thing is to make a piece of linen for a wagon cover and some sacks; will spin mostly evenings while my husband reads to me. The little wheel in the corner don't make any noise. I spin for Mother B. and Mrs. Hawley and they will weave; now that it is in the loom I must work almost day and night to get the filling ready to keep the loom busy. The men are busy making ox yokes and bows for the wagon covers and trading for oxen.

Now the New Year has come and I'll write (1848). This is my program: will start out with the New Year. My health is better and I don't spend much time with house work. Will make a muslin cover for the wagon as we will have to double cover so we can keep warm and dry; put the muslin on first and then the heavy linen one for strength. They both have to be sewed real good and strong and I have to spin the thread and sew all these long seams with my fingers, then I have to make a new feather tick for my bed. I will put the feathers of two beds into one tick and sleep on it.

February 1st, and the linen is ready to work on and six two bushel bags all ready to sew up, that I will do evenings by the light of a dip candle for I have made enough to last all winter after we get to Oregon, and now my work is all planned so I can go right along. Have cut out two pairs of pants for George (Home made jeans). A kind lady friend came in today and sewed all day on one pair; then took them home with her to finish. Another came and wanted to buy some of my dishes and she took two shirts home to make to pay for them.

And now it is March and we have our team all ready and in good condition. Three good yoke of oxen and a good wagon. The company have arranged to start the 10th of April. I expect to load up the first wagon. George is practicing with the oxen. I dont want to leave my kind friends here but they all think it best so I am anxious to get off. I have worked almost day and night this winter, have the sewing about all done but a coat and vest for George. He got some nice material for a suit and had a taylor cut it out and Aunt Betsy Starr[3] helped me two days with them so I am about ready to load up. Will wash and begin to pack and start with some old clothes on and when we can't wear them any longer will leave them on the road.

I think we are fixed very comfortable for the trip. There is quite a train of connection. Father Belknap has one wagon and 4 yoke of oxen; Hayley has two wagons and 8 yoke of oxen; Newton[4] about the same; Uncle John Starr has two wagons and 4 yoke of oxen; G. W. Bethards[5] one wagon and 3 yoke of oxen; we have the same besides 3 horses and 10 cows. Now it is the 1st of April and the stock is all in our corn field to get them used to running together; in ten days more we will be on the road.

This week I will wash and pack away everything except what we want to wear on the trip. April 5th. This week I cook up something to last us a few days till we get used to camp fare. Bake bread, make a lot of crackers and fry doughnuts, cook a chicken, boil ham, and stew some dryed fruit. There is enough to last us over the first Sunday so now we will begin to gather up the scatterings. Tomorrow is Saturday and next Tuesday we start so will put in some things today. Only one more Sunday here; some of the folks will walk to meeting. We have had our farwell meeting so I wont go; don't think I could stand it so George stays with me and we will take a rest for tomorrow will be a busy day.

Monday, April 9th, 1848 I am the first one up; breakfast is over; our wagon is backed up to the steps; we will load at the hind end and shove the things in front. The first thing is a big box that will just fit in the wagon bed. That will have the bacon, salt and various other things; then it will be covered with a cover made of light boards

[3]Betsy or Elizabeth Starr was the wife of John W. Starr.
[4]Abraham and Rachel Newton.
[5]George and Kesiah Bethards.

nailed on two pieces of inch plank about 3 inches wide. This will serve us for a table, there is a hole in each corner and we have sticks sharpened at one end so they will stick in the ground ; then we put the box cover on, slip the legs in the holes and we have a nice table, then when it is on the box George will sit on it and let his feet hang over and drive the team. It is just as high as the wagon bed. Now we will put in the old chest that is packed with our clothes and things we will want to wear and use on the way. The till is the medicine chest; then there will be cleats fastened to the bottom of the wagon bed to keep things from slipping out of place. Now there is a vacant place clear across that will be large enough to set a chair; will set it with the back against the side of wagon bed; there I will ride. On the other side will be a vacancy where little Jessie can play. He has a few toys and some marbles and some sticks for whip stocks, some blocks for oxen and I tie a string on the stick and he uses my work basket for a covered wagon and plays going to Oregon. He never seems to get tired or cross (but here I am leaving the wagon half packed and set off on the journey). The next thing is a box as high as the chest that is packed with a few dishes and things we wont need till we get thru. And now we will put in the long sacks of flour and other things. The sacks are made of home made linen and will hold 125 pounds; 4 sacks of flour and one of corn meal. Now comes the groceries. We will make a wall of smaller sacks stood on end; dried apples and peaches, beans, rice, sugar and coffee, the latter being in the green state. We will brown it in a skillet as we want to use it. Everything must be put in strong bags; no paper wrappings for the trip. There is a corner left for the wash-tub and the lunch basket will just fit in the tub. The dishes we want to use will all be in the basket. I am going to start with good earthen dishes and if they get broken have tin ones to take their place. Have made 4 nice little table cloths so am going to live just like I was at home. Now we will fill the other corner with pick-ups. The iron-ware that I will want to use every day will go in a box on the hind end of the wagon like a feed box. Now we are loaded all but the bed. I wanted to put it in and sleep out but George said I wouldn't rest any so I will level up the sacks with some extra bedding, then there is a side of sole leather that will go on first, then two comforts and we have a good enough bed for anyone to sleep on. At night I will turn my chair down and make the bed a little longer so now all we will have to do in the morning is put in the bed and make some coffee and roll out.

The wagon looks so nice, the nice white cover drawn down tight to the side boards with a good ridge to keep from saging. Its high enough for me to stand straight under the roof with a curtain to put down in front and one at the back end. Now it is all done and I get in out of the tumult. And now everything is ready I will rest a little, then we will eat a bite. Mother B. has made a pot of mush and we are all going to eat mush and milk to save the milk that otherwise would have to be thrown out. Then we have prayers and then to bed.

Tuesday, April 10, 1848. Daylight dawned with none awake but me. I try to keep quiet so as not to wake anyone but pretty soon Father Belknap's voice was heard with that well known sound "Wife, Wife, rise and flutter" and there was no more quiet for anyone. Breakfast is soon over; my dishes and food for lunch is packed away and put in its proper place, the iron things are packed in some old pieces of old thick rags. Now for the bed (feather); nicely folded the two ends together, lay it on the sacks, then I fix it. The covers are folded and the pillows laid smoothly on, reserving one for the outside so if I or the little boy get sleepy we have a good place to lie; the others are covered with a heavy blanket and now my chair and the churn and we will be all done.

Our wagon is ready to start; I get in the wagon and in my chair busy with some unfinished work. Jessie is in his place with his whip starting for Oregon. George and the boys have gone out in the field for the cattle. Dr. Walker calls at the wagon to see me and give me some good advice and give me the parting hand for neither of us could speak the word "Farewell". He told me to keep up courage and said "dont fret, whatever happens don't fret and cry; courage will do more for you then anything else". Then he took the little boy in his arms and presented to him a nice bible with his blessing and was off. The cattle have come and the rest of the train are lined up here in the lane and many of the neighbors are here to see us off. The oxen are yoked and chained together.

Uncle John Starr two are the last so they will be behind today. We will take them in after we get a mile on the road at their place. Now we roll out. Father B. is on the lead on old Nelly; Bart is driving the team; Cory[6] is on our old Lige driving the loose stock. Our wagon is No. 2. G. W. Bethers No. 3, J. W. Starr 4. Uncle Prather two wagons, Chatman Hawley two wagons and I think they all had one horse but Uncle John Starr. He had two yoke of oxen to each wagon; one wagon was a very shaky old thing. They had their provisions in it and when they get it lightened up they would put everything in one wagon and leave the old shack by the road side. They started with a family of eight and had to take in an old man to drive one team.

Now we are fairly on the road. It is one o'clock. We got started at 10; will stop for an hour and eat a lunch and let the oxen chew their cuds. We have just got out of the neighborhood; the friends that came a piece with us and we will travel on. Jessie and I have had a good nap and a good lunch and now we will ride some more. Evening we come to water and grass and plenty of wood. What hinders us from camping here? They say we have come 13 miles. Everyone seems hungry and we make fires and soon have supper fit for a king.

I will make the first call and am all the one that has a table and it has a clean white cloth on. I have my chair out. George piles in the ox yokes for him a seat and Jessie has the wash-tub turned up side down and will stand on his knees. Supper over and I fix the bed. The stock have all been looked after and are quietly chewing their quids. Some of the men take bedding and will sleep out to see that none of the stock will get up and scatter off.

April 11th.   All astir bright and early; breakfast is soon over; some of the men have gone to relieve the night watch. My work is all done up, lunch prepared for noon and all put in its proper place. Here comes the oxen; our team is soon ready. We have two yoke of well trained oxen; all there is to do is to hold up the yoke and tell Old Buck and Bright to come under and they walk up and take their places as meek as kittens. But now comes Dick and Drab a fine pair

---

[6]Bart is so-far not identified, however, Corrington G. Belknap is listed in the 1850 census as working as a farmer, 20 years old, on the farm of Alvin F. Waller, a Methodist minister in Marion County, Oregon. "Uncle Prather" is so-far unidentified.

of black matched four year olds steers; they have to be cornered. I am in the wagon sewing; Jessie is playing with his whips and now the word is "Roll out". The loose stock is started on ahead. Our wagon is in the lead today; will be behind tomorrow so now we are on the wing. It is a fine spring morning.

Noon. We stop an hour to let the teams rest and eat our lunch. We are in Missouri now; see once in a while a log hut and some half dressed children running away to hide. Every man to his team now. This afternoon we pass along a little creek with fine timber. The road is good and I am standing the ride fine. Now, we camp again. I think all days will be about the same now. Saturday evening. We have a fine start; everything seems to move along nicely.

Sunday morning. We hitch up and move on a few miles to better grass; then camp for the Sabbath. Ten o'clock we find a lovely spot; a fine little brook goes gurgling by with fine large trees and nice clean logs for seats and to spread out things on. We have cleaned up and put on clean clothes. There are some fine farms along the creek bottom; some of the ladies came out to visit us and brought some things along to sell to the immigrants but we had not been out long enough to get very hungry. I did get a nice dressed hen for 25 cents and 6 dozen eggs 6¢ a dozen. I started with quite a box of eggs and found them handy.

Now its Monday morning, April 17th. We start again; the next point is Missouri River; will cross at St. Joe. Have moved every day for a week; have had fine weather, good roads and all have been well. We have three good milch cows; milk them at night and strain the milk in little buckets and cover them up and set on ground under the wagon and in the morning I take off the nice thick cream and put it in the churn. I save the strippings from each cow in the morning milking and put in the churn also and after riding all day I have a nice roll of butter so long as we have plenty of grass and water.

The 22nd. Are nearing the Missouri River; will camp here over Sunday. Sunday. Breakfast over and the men come in from the stock and say there has been a band of sheep herded on the range for two days and they have spoiled the grass so the stock wont feed on it so some of the men get on their horses and go to look for a better place;

10 o'clock the word is "Move on". About 10 miles there is plenty of water and grass; some want to stay, others are getting their teams ready to move. Mr. Jackson's[7] voice is heard. He says if we stay it will break the Sabbath worse than if we go on so we all started but had only gone about 5 miles when a little boy was run over by the wagon and instantly killed. We then stopped and buried the child. We were near a settlement so it was not left there alone.

Monday we are on the trail again. every man at his post; made a big day's drive (20 miles they say).

Tuesday. Will get to the river tomorrow. Supper is over; we have a nice place to camp, some have gone to bed and others have gone out with the stock. They say there are some Mormons here that give us some trouble with our stock. They might want a good horse so we think it best to put a good guard out.

Wednesday. All are on the stir to get to the wharf before the other company gets here and now begins the scene of danger. The river is high and looks terrific; one wagon and two yoke of oxen are over first so as to have a team to take the wagons out of the way; it is just a rope ferry. All back safe. Now they take the wagons and the loose horses. They say it will take about all day to get us over. Next the loose cattle that go as they are in a dry lot without anything to eat. When they get the cattle on the boat they found one of our cows was sick; she had got poisoned by eating the Jimpson weeds. She staggered when she walked on the ferry and in the crowd she was knocked overboard and went under but when she came up the boat men had his rope ready and throwed it out and lassoed her and they hauled her to land but she was too far gone to travel so the boat man said he would take our wagon and stock over for the chance of her so they hauled her up to the house and the last we saw of her a woman had her wrapped in a warm blanket and had a fire and was bathing her and pouring milk and lard down her. She could stand alone the next morning so we bade farewell to the Missouri River and old Brock.

The Watts[8] company will stay here till the Jacksons get over the

---

[7]George Jackson, otherwise unidentified.

[8]Joseph Watt was the son of John and Mary Watt, who crossed the plains with this company with their other six children. They settled in Yamhill County, Oregon. They are recorded in the 1850 federal census.

river and we will move on to fresh grass and water. Our next point will be the crossing of the Platte River near old Fort Larima; there is life there now.

This is the 4th week we have been on the road and now we are among the Pawnee Indians so we must get into larger company so we can guard ourselves and stock from the prowling tribes and renegade whites that are here to keep away from the law. They seem to have their eyes on a good horse and follow for days then if they are caught they will say they got him from the Indians and by paying them something they would give the horse up, then try to make us believe that they were sent out there to protect the emigrants.

Another week has past; have had nice road; will camp here till afternoon. At the Platte River; will stay here all day and get ready to cross the river and do some work on the wagons, get tires, mend chains & etc. We will now form a company and make some laws so all will have their part. Some of the oxen are getting tender-footed; they have been trying to shoe them but gave it up. I have washed and ironed and cooked nice skillet of corn bread (enough for two dinners for George, Jessie and I). This morning the roll is called and every one is expected to answer to his name. They have quite a time with the election of officers. Every man wants an office. George Jackson and Joe Watts are pilots; they have both been over the road before and have camping places noted down so now we take the trail again. The order is for the first one hitched up "roll out" so we are ahead on the lead today then   [9] are next but tomorrow we will be behind.

Now we are getting on the Pawnee Indians' hunting ground so we must make a big show. They are out after Buffalo so we have to keep out an advance guard to keep the herd from running into our teams. The road runs between the bluff and the river and it is just the time now when the buffalo are moving to the river bottom for grass and water. A herd passed us a few days ago; the guard turned them so they crossed the road behind us; they killed a nice young heifer so we have fresh meat. It is very coarse and dark meat but when cooked right made a very good change. I cooked some and made mince pies with dried apples which was fine for lunch. During the hunt Dr.

---

[9]Unreadable word.

Baker[10] lost his nice saddle horse and a fine saddle; he jumped off
and threw down the bridle to give his game another shot and away
went the horse with the buffalo; they hunted for him but didn't find
him or the buffalo but in about two weeks the company that was
behind sent word to Dr. Baker that the horse had come to them with
the saddle still on but turned under his belly; the head part of the bridle was on him yet so old Dock got his horse and he never wanted
to leave the train again. We have been on the route till its got to be
June; all days about the same.

We will now go down the noted Ash Hollow and strike the Sweet
River, then will rest awhile. We make the trip down the hollow all
safe. Went as far as we could with the teams then took off some of
the best teams and send down so they could move the wagons out of
the way, then they would take one wagon as far as they could with
the team, then unhitch and ruff-lock both hind wheels, then fasten a
big rope to the axle of the wagon and men would hold to that to keep
the wagon iron going end over end; some were at the tongue to steer
it and others were lifting the wheels to ease them down the steps for
it was solid rock steps from six inches to two feet apart so it took all
day but we all got thru without accident.

We will stay here all night. I wash a little and cook some more,
have a ham bone and beans. This is good sweet water; we have had
alkali and nothing was good.

Just as we were ready to sit down to supper Joe Meek and his posse
of men rode into camp. They were going to Washington, D. C. to get
the government to send soldiers to protect the settlers in Oregon and
they told us all about the Indian Massacre at Walla Walla called the
"Whitman Massacre". They had traveled all winter and some of their
men had died and they had got out of food and had to eat mule meat
so we gave them all their supper and breakfast. The captain divided
them up so all could help feed them. Father B. was captain so he and
George took three so they made way with most all my stuff I had
cooked up; on the whole we are having quite a time; some want to
turn back and others are telling what they would do in case of an
attack. I sit in the wagon and write a letter as these men say if we

---

[10]This could be John and Elizabeth Baker who settled as neighbors to the George Belknaps,
according to the Oregon 1850 census.

want to send any word back they will take it and drop it in the first Post Office they come to so I'm writing a scratch to a lady friend. While I'm writing I have an exciting experience. George is out on guard and in the next wagon behind ours a man and woman are quarreling. She wants to turn back and he wont go so she says she will go and leave him with the children and he will have a good time with that crying baby, then he used some very bad words and said he would put it out of the way. Just then I heard a muffled cry and a heavy thud as tho something was thrown against the wagon box and she said "Oh you've killed it" and he swore some more and told her to keep her mouth shut or he would give her some of the same. Just then the word came, change guards. George came in and Mr. Kitridge[11] went out so he and his wife were parted for the night. The baby was not killed. I write this to show how easy we can be deceived. We have a rest and breakfast is over. Meek and his men are gathering their horses and packing, but he said he would have to transact a little business with his men so they all lined up and he courtmartialed them and found three guilty and made them think they would be shot for disobeying orders but it was only a scare "Now every man to his post and double quick till they reach the Hollow". The woman was out by the road side with a little buget [buggy?] and her baby asleep in the wagon under a strong opiate. After that we had trouble with those folks as long as they were with us; they would take things from those that did the most for them and there was others of the same stripe. They seemed to think when they got on the plains they were out of reach of the law of God or man.

It is afternoon; we will hitch up and drive till night. Here we are; it is almost sundown. We will have a cold lunch for supper, then shake up the beds and rest after the excitement of the day is over. We will leave the sweet water in the morning and have a long dry drive. Will fill our kegs and everything that will hold water so we will not suffer of thirst. We stop at noon for an hour's rest. It's very warm; the oxen all have their tongues out panting. George took the wash pan and a bucket of water and let all our team wet their tongues and he washed the dust off their noses; some laughed at him but the oxen

---

[11]George and Maria Kitrich are listed in the 1850 census as living in Washington County with their children, the youngest of whom was Eliza, 2, the one here supposedly threatened with death.

seemed very grateful. George lays down to catch a little nap; if they start before he wakes the team will start up in their places. Time is up, the word along the line is "Move up" (George sleeps on). That means 10 miles of dry hot dirt. I have a little water left yet; will have to let the thirsty ox drivers wet their parched lips. It will be hot till the sun goes down, then it will be dusk. That night we got to plenty of water. I think old Bright's feet hurt; he is standing in the water. We eat a bite and go to bed.

We are coming near to the Green River; will have to ferry it with the wagons. The cattle will be unyoked and swim over; some Mormons are here. They have fixed up a ferry and will take us over for a dollar a wagon. It will take all day to get over; it is the 4th of July. While some are getting over they have got Hawley's wagon over and have got out the anvils and are celebrating The Fourth. The Jacksons are doing their best to entertain the crowd; there is three of them. Now we are on to the Pawnee Indians. They say they are a bad set. We must pass right thru their villages; they come out by the thousands and want pay for crossing their country. They spread down some skins and wanted every wagon to give them something so they all gave them a little something and they went to dividing it amongst themselves and got into a fight. We rushed on to get as near Fort Hall as we could. There was a company of soldiers there to protect the immigrants. The scouts had been out and reported what the Indians were doing and the troops soon settled them and made them leave the road so we had no more trouble; for us it was all for the best so that was all the time we had any trouble with the Indians tho it did look a little scary for a while. The General at the Fort told us to make as big a show as possible.

For want of space I must cut these notes down; will pass over some interesting things. Watts and the sheep pulled out and fell behind. I got the blame for the split. The old Mother Watts said after they got thru "Yes, Geo. Belknaps' wife is a little woman but she wore the pants on that train" so I came into noteriety before I knew it but to return to the trail, they say we are on the last half of the journey now.

My little boy is very sick with Mountain Fever and tomorrow we will have to make a long dry drive. We will stay here at this nice water and grass till about 4 o'clock. Will cook up a lot of provisions, then will take what is known as "Green woods cut off" and travel all night. Must fill everything with water. We are on the brink of Snake River but it is such a rocky canyon we could not get to it if ones life depended on it.

It's morning. I have been awake all night watching with the little boy. He seems a little better; has dropped off to sleep. The sun is just rising and it shows a lot of the dirtiest humanity every was seen since the Creation. We just stop for an hour and eat a bite and let the teams breath again. We divide the water with the oxen. George has sat on his seat on the front of the wagon all night and I have held the little boy on my lap on a pillow and tended him as best I could. I thot in the night we would have to leave him here and I thot if we did I would be likely to stay with him but as the daylight, we seemed to get fresh courage.

Some of the men went thru to Fort Hall on horse back and returned to meet us and say we can make it by noon.

[The record ends here. The baby boy, Jesse Walker Belknap, recovered under her dilligent care and lived to a ripe old age. In her record of the journey at no point has Keturah revealed that she was pregnant. A baby boy, Lorenzo Belknap, was born on August 10, 1848, evidently somewhere in what is now called eastern Oregon. Keturah was too busy to continue to record the concluding days of their cross-country journey.]

MARGARET FRINK
Courtesy, California State Library

Adventures of a Party of Gold-Seekers
Margaret A. Frink
1850

INTRODUCTION

"There are but few women; among these thousands of men, we have not seen more than ten or twelve." *Margaret Frink, Tuesday, August 20, 1850.*

One of the classics of western history, and a very rare volume indeed, is this book published in 1897, with the lengthy title typical for the period : "JOURNAL / Of the Adventures of a Party of / California Gold-Seekers / Under the Guidance of / MR. LEDYARD FRINK / During a journey across the plains from Martinsville, / Indiana, to Sacramento, California, from March / 30, 1850, to September 7, 1850. / From the Original Diary of the trip / kept by / MRS. MARGARET A. FRINK."

The death of this lady in Oakland on January 16, 1893, was reported in the Oakland (Calif.) *Tribune*[1] and it was four years later that her husband, Ledyard Frink, thought it appropriate to publish his wife's daily journal, "owing to many requests made by relatives and friends."

Today the book is found in just a few libraries, and is one of the real rarities of western historical publication. We have been given permission of the Beinecke Rare Book and Manuscript Library of Yale University to transcribe their microfilmed copy here. We held the actual book in our hands and studied it at the California State Library in Sacramento, and from them received permission to use her portrait.

Much of the family background is given in the opening section of the diary, undoubtedly edited with the addition of these facts later, by either Mr. or Mrs. Frink.

She was born on April 25, 1818, in Frederick City, Maryland, as Margaret Ann Alsip, daughter of Joseph and Mary Alsip.[2] She was

---

[1] January 16, 1893, p. 2, col. 3.
[2] Much of the information that follows was taken from the "Pioneer Record" card in the files of the California State Library, Sacramento, and here used with their permission.

married to Ledyard Frink in Kentucky on April 17, 1839. There were
no children born to them. The Frinks lived in several eastern states
before their decision in late 1849 to follow the gold trail to California in
the spring of 1850. Their first city of residence in California was
Sacramento, where Mrs. Frink became one of the charter members of
the First Baptist Church, helping to found that institution with the
Baptist frontier pastor, Rev. O. C. Wheeler, and several others. The couple later lived in other parts of California, spending the late years of
their lives in Oakland. There Margaret Frink died at the age of 74.
Ledyard lived on until March 6, 1900.

There is a memorandum written by hand by the Frink's nephew, L.
A. Winchell, in the California State Library[3] in Sacramento saying that
Margaret often rode horseback sidesaddle on the overland journey, and
that he had given the saddle to the Sutter's Fort Museum in
Sacramento. Winchell also reminisced that with the Frinks on the over-
land journey was "a young lad about 12 years old, named Robert Parker,
and a protege of Mr. and Mrs. Frink." Robert is mentioned in Margaret
Frink's journal.

Another of L. A. Winchell's remembrances was published in the
Grizzly Bear for December, 1927, telling of the prefabricated house that
the Frinks had sent around the Horn by ship to be set up by them in
Sacramento:[4]

In the spring of 1850 my mother's older sister [Margaret
Frink], with her husband and her brother, A. B. Alsip, started
from Martinsville, Douglas County, Indiana, for the goldfields of
the West. My uncles were merchants in Martinsville and men of
ample means. Before leaving for California, having learned from
newspaper accounts that lumber was selling here for $400 a
thousand feet, while it was only worth $3 a thousand feet at
Martinsville, they decided to have materials for the home provided. Employing several carpenters, lumber of all necessary
sizes was measured, cut and fashioned ready to assemble in a
short time.

When the spring freshets came, the materials were loaded upon
a raft and floated down the White River to the Wabash, to the
Ohio, to the Mississippi and on to New Orleans, thence by ship

[3]"Pioneer Letters: Frink, Mr. & Mrs. Ledyard (Margaret Alsip)," no date.
[4]P. 28. The house stood at the corner of M and Eighth streets.

around the Horn to Sacramento, California, arriving there in March, 1851, just a year on the voyage.

The Margaret Frink Journal is, of course, a treasure of American history. It is printed here in the same style as in the 1897 original, chapter by chapter. We have also included the "Addenda," which tells "What Became of our Traveling Companions," written by Ledyard Frink.

Margaret Frink touches upon a subject that was absolutely crucial to all those traveling the western trails: the danger of scurvy. On March 31st her entry tells of a warning from a man, the landlord of a hotel east of Terre Haute, Indiana, and a former sea captain, "in regard to preparing to defend ourselves against the scurvy." They reached Terre Haute the next day and "laid in a supply of acid to take the place of vegetables." Several other times she mentioned acid, and on August 2 she tells of "pickles and acid." According to Irene D. Paden, it was customary to take along sour pickles or vinegar as antedotes to the disease.[5]

One further introductory note: Margaret Frink mentions in her *Journal* entry for Monday, May 20, 1850, "We had with us some guidebooks (Fremont's and Palmer's). . ." The first of these by John C. Fremont was printed in 1845, *The Report of the Exploring Expedition to the Rocky Mountains in the Year 1842, and to Oregon and North Califonia in the Years 1843–44.*

The second book was by Joel Palmer: *Journal of Travels over the Rocky Mountains to the Mouth of the Columbia River made during the years 1845 and 1846 containing minute descriptions of the valleys of the Willamette, Umpqua, and Clamet; a general description of Oregon Territory, its inhabitants, climate, soil, productions, etc. etc., a list of necessary outfits for emigrants; and a table of distances from camp to camp on the route* (Cincinnati, 1847). It was re-published in 1906 by the Arthur H. Clark Company as Volume XXX of Reuben G. Thwaites, *Early Western Travels.* There is a helpful article on this subject by Helen B. Kroll, called "The Books That Enlightened the Emigrants," in the *Oregon Historical Quarterly,* XLV, Number 2 (June, 1944), pp. 103–23.

---

[5]*Prairie Schooner Detours* (New York, 1949), p. 231. See also Thomas B. Hall, *Medicine on the Santa Fe Trail* (Dayton, Ohio, 1971), passim.

THE JOURNAL OF MARGARET A. FRINK

PREFACE.

Owing to the many requests made by relatives and friends for a history of our journey across the plains to California, made in the summer of 1850, the minutes of which were kept by Mrs. Frink, I have concluded, even at this late day, to issue this book.

Although there may be some errors, it is practically a correct history.

L. Frink

Oakland, California, 1897

CHAPTER I.

Ledyard Frink was born and raised in the western part of New York. I, Margaret Ann Alsip, his wife, was born in Maryland, though partly raised in Virginia, on the banks of the Potomac River. From there we moved to Kentucky, where Mr. Frink and myself were married on the seventeenth day of April, 1839. We spent that summer in Cincinnati; and in October moved to make ourselves a home at Cheviot, six miles west of that city, where we continued to live very pleasantly till 1844, when we made up our minds to try our fortunes farther west. We situated ourselves one hundred and twenty-five miles from Cheviot, in the town of Martinsville, the county seat of Morgan County, Indiana. Here Mr. Frink engaged in merchandising, in which he succeeded very well. We continued to live here nearly six years during which time we built a pleasant and convenient residence, having large grounds about it. But we were not yet satisfied. The exciting news coming back from California of the delightful climate and abundance of gold, caused us to resolve, about December, 1849, that we would commence preparing to cross the plains by the spring of 1850.

The first thing on Mr. Frink's part was to have a suitable wagon made for the trip while I hired a seamstress to make up a full supply of clothing. In addition to our finished articles of dress, I packed a trunk full of dress goods not yet made up. We proceeded in the spring to get our outfit completed. There was no one from our part of the country, so far as we knew, that intended to cross the plains that season, and we were obliged to make such preparations as our best judgment led us to do, without advice or assistance from others. We knew nothing of frontier life, nor how to prepare for it. And besides, we were met with all the discouragements and obstructions that our neighbors and the people of our county could invent or imagine, to induce us not to attempt such a perilous journey. But, nothing daunted, we kept at work in our preparations for the trip, thinking all the time that we should have to make the long journey by ourselves, as no one in all that part of the country was offering or expecting to go to California that season.

But it appeared as if there was a Providence planning for us. First, we had a boy that we had taken into our family to live with us when he was seven years of age, and now he was eleven. He was much attached to us and could not be reconciled to be left with his own friends and relatives. The child being so determined to cling to us, Mr. Frink consented to take him if his uncle and guardian, Mr. W. Wilson, would give his consent. This he very readily did, though with all his family opposed to the plan. The consent was given about four days before we started.

The wagon was packed and we were all ready to start on the twenty-seventh day of March. The wagon was designed expressly for the trip, it being built light, with everything planned for convenience. It was so arranged that when closed up, it could be used as our bedroom. The bottom was divided off into little compartments or cupboards. After putting in our provisions, and other baggage, a floor was constructed over all, on which our mattress was laid. We had an India-rubber mattress that could be filled with either air or water, making a very comfortable bed. During the day we could empty the air out, so that it took up but little room. We also had a feather bed and feather pillows. However, until we had crossed the Missouri River, we stopped at hotels and farmhouses every night, and did not use our own bedding. After that, there being no more hotels nor houses, we used it continually all the way to California.

The wagon was lined with green cloth, to make it pleasant and soft for the eye, with three or four large pockets on each side, to hold many little conveniences,—looking-glasses, combs, brushes, and so on. Mr. Frink bought, in Cincinnati, a small sheet-iron cooking-stove, which was lashed on behind the wagon. To prepare for crossing the deserts, we also had two India-rubber bottles holding five gallons each, for carrying water.

Our outfit for provisions was plenty of hams and bacon, covered with care from the dust, apples, peaches, and preserved fruits of different kinds, rice, coffee, tea, beans, flour, corn-meal, crackers, sea-biscuit, butter, and lard. The canning of fruits had not been invented yet—at least not in the west, so far as we knew.

Learning by letters published in the newspapers, that lumber was worth $400.00 per thousand in California, while it was worth only $3.00 in Indiana, Mr. Frink concluded to send the material for a small cottage by the way of Cape Horn. The lumber was purchased and several carpenters were put to work. In six days the whole material was prepared, ready for putting it together. It was then placed on board a flatboat lying in White River, to be ready for the spring rise—as boats could not pass out except at high water. The route was down White River to the Wabash, to the Ohio, to the Mississippi, to New Orleans; thence by sail vessel around Cape Horn to Sacramento, where it arrived the following March, having been just one year on the voyage.

Our team consisted of five horses and two mules. We had two saddles for the riding-horses, one for Mr. Frink and one for myself.

I believe we were all ready to start on the morning of the 27th of March. On the evening before, the whole family, including my mother, were gathered together in the parlor, looking as if we were all going to our graves the next morning, instead of our starting on a trip of pleasure, as we had drawn the picture in our imagination. There we sat in such gloom that I could not endure it any longer, and I arose and announced that we would retire for the night, and that we would not start to-morrow morning, nor until everybody could feel more cheerful. I could not bear to start with so many gloomy faces to think of. So we all retired, but I think no one slept very much that night.

I believe Mr. Frink, more than myself, began to fully realize the great undertaking we were about to embark in, almost alone. Our conversation finally turned on the likelihood that a young man of our acquaintance, named Aaron Rose, might wish to go with us. Some remark he had made led us to think he might like to join us. But Mr. Frink was of the opinion that his father and mother would never let him go, as they were already wealthy people and had but two children with them. Besides, Mr. Rose had been a confidential clerk in Frink & Alsip's store in Martinsville, during the past three years, and could not be spared from the business, as my brother, Mr. A. B. Alsip, was to remain in Martinsville and carry on the merchandising as before. But, after discussing all these objections, Mr. Frink left the house early the next morning and went to Mr. Rose's residence, where he met the young man's father, and inquired of him if he had ever heard his son say anything about wishing to go to California. "Yes," said the old gentleman, and he has thought quite hard of you that you have never spoken to him on the subject. But he says he is determined to go when he is twenty-one years old." Then the mother came in weeping, saying, "If he ever does go, I want him to go with Mr. and Mrs. Frink, for I know he will have a father and mother in them." And it was decided on, by six o'clock that morning, that we should wait a few days longer, until the young man could be fitted out for the journey. I think all the young ladies in town offered to help, as he was a general favorite. And for the next three days there was a very busy time among his young acquaintances, in making him ready for the California journey. During the meantime, we were practising the driving of our four-horse wagon, with lines in hand, and gradually educating ourselves to bear the final separation from our relatives and friends. We were all ready to leave our home on Saturday, the thirtieth day of March.

We bade farewell to all our relatives, friends, neighbors, and acquaintances. Mr. Frink and myself, having each a horse to ride, rode out of town on horseback, and with the four-horse wagon, went seven miles before stopping for lunch. It was a beautiful spring day. Our faces were not at last set westward. We arrived on the west bank of the Eel River about sundown. We were quite tired, and there being a large brick house near by, we inquired there for quarters for the night. It appeared that the landlady was, for the moment, in the stable, and, hearing our inquiry, she thrust her head out of the stable window and answered rather impatiently that she had no time to give to strangers; that she had a cow in the stable that she was going to break if it took her all night to do it; that we had better go on about three miles, where we might be accommodated with lodgings. This looked like a poor chance for us; but Mr. Frink was not to be discouraged in this manner. He went to the stable and gave the milkman such instructions as enabled him in a short time to bring the unruly cow under subjection, so that the old lady came out highly pleased, and allowed us to stay in the house all night.

Sunday, March 31.   We continued our journey to-day and struck the national road at Manhattan, where we had dinner. We lost our road, however, and had to retrace about three miles. We stopped at night about twenty miles east of Terre Haute, and were very pleasantly entertained. The landlord of the hotel had been a sea-captain, and volunteered some advice that afterwards proved very beneficial to us, in regard to preparing to defend ourselves against the scurvy, from which so many California emigrants had suffered in 1849.

Monday, April 1.   We started again in good spirits, every one at the hotel, strangers and all, wishing us good luck on our long journey. On this great "national road" the towns are near together; and whenever we stopped, even to water the horses, there would be squads of people standing about, full of curiosity, and making comments upon ourselves and our outfit, thinking we were certainly emigrants bound for California. But some would remark, "There's a lady in the party; and surely there's no man going to take a woman on such a journey as that, across the plains." Then some of them would venture to approach the wagon and cautiously peep in; then, seeing a lady, they would respectfully take off their hats, with a polite salutation; and we felt that, if there was anything in having good wishes expressed for us, we should certainly have a successful and pleasant trip. We stopped, to dine four miles east of Terre Haute. Here we heard a great many comments upon the hardihood of a woman attempting to make such a difficult journey.

We reached Terre Haute at two o'clock in the afternoon, and made some additions to our outfit. We laid in a supply of acid to take the place of vegetables after we should get out on the great plains. This is a beautiful town, situated on the east side of the Wabash

River. Our outfit attracted much attention and was greatly admired, particularly our fine horses. The first California emigrants we had seen passed us here, they having been fitted out in this neighborhood. We passed them in the afternoon. We stopped at night nine miles west of Terre Haute. The accommodations were very poor. However, we were fully prepared to board ourselves whenever the people refused to accommodate us. Here we ate our supper from our tin plates and drank coffee from our tin cups for the first time. Mr. Frink expressed regret that we had omitted to bring our tea cups, and suggested that he would buy some when we came to the next town. But for my part, I was satisfied to do as other immigrants did, and if it was the fashion to drink out of tin, I was quite content to do so. The landlady was cross and snappish, thinking, I suppose, that we were not quite worthy of her valuable attention, though I tried to adapt myself, as far as possible, to her notions. However, she gave us a nice bed, and by the time we were ready to take our leave the next morning, she seemed to have concluded that we were tolerably respectable people.

Tuesday, April 2. We had a rather late start this morning, having some fixing up to do. We reached Paris, Illinois, in time for dinner, and found it quite a pretty place. It is something smaller than Martinsville, yet quite a tastefully built town, and has a large seminary for young ladies. Here again the inhabitants had many comments to make upon the propriety of a lady undertaking a journey of two thousand miles, across deserts and mountains infested with hostile savages. But they would finally wind up and conclude by saying that I was "certainly a soldier to attempt it;" and, putting their heads inside the wagon, they would wish us all possible success in the undertaking.

Wednesday, April 3. We staid last night on Grand Prairie. Our hostess and her husband were German people, and made us very comfortable. We traveled all day on the prairie. The distance was twelve miles between houses, and no timber in sight at many times, though occasionally we passed some beautifully timbered spots. We staid all night at a house on the west side of the prairie.

Thursday, April 4. We launched out on the fourteen-mile prairie this morning, and such a time as we had,—storming, snowing, and sleeting,—and we with no place of shelter. Before we had gone far, we came to a bad-looking, muddy place, to avoid which he turned off the beaten track upon the grass, which looked firm and solid. To our astonishment, the horses broke through the sod, and, being unable to pull their feet out, they were all soon flat on the ground, and could not be gotten out until they were unhitched from the wagon. I stood in the sleet and held four horses for two hours, till I thought my feet were frozen. My cloak was frozen stiff, and I was chilled through and through.

While we were in this predicament, there came up a team with five men from Ohio, who stopped and helped us. They spaded the wagon out of the mud, and then hitched their horses to the hind axle, and we were pulled out safe; and we learned not to leave the beaten track again. I concluded after that, to ride my pony in preference to riding in the wagon. We came at last, to a half-way house of one room. They had a fire, and it was a real luxury to get warm once more. But it was a forlorn-looking set that had gathered there for shelter and a little rest. There was no woman in the company but myself. As soon as we were thawed out, we started to make the remaining seven miles of our day's journey. It was a hard day, and we did not get through till after dark. Then we found good accommodations in a large backwoods cabin. There were two large rooms with great, wide fireplaces and huge, blazing logs piled on. That great, glowing fire I shall never forget, nor the bountiful supper table, with its good, warm coffee, and, best of all, the cheerful faces that welcomed us.

Friday, April 5. We had tolerably good roads to-day, through prairies. At night we stopped at the last house before entering another lonely prairie. This was thirty miles east of Springfield, Illinois. The landlord and landlady appeared somewhat independent and a little indifferent as to whether they would accommodate travelers or not; but they finally consented, and we passed the night under their roof very comfortably.

Saturday, April 6. I felt quite unwell this morning; but we traveled steadily all day, and reached Springfield, the state capital, at nine o'clock at night. The roads were very muddy and bad, but we could not get accommodations till we reached the city; and, it being late and very dark, wc came to rather a poor hotel. But we were so tired we were glad to put up with even poor accommodations. We found considerable excitement prevailing over the report that a California emigrant had been murdered that day some ten miles west of the city, on the road we were to travel the next day. I then began to feel that we had undertaken a risky journey, even long before we came to the Indian country. We got out the Colt's revolver that night to see that it was in good order, and made ready to defend ourselves against attack; but happily we were not molested in any way. We concluded, however, that it would be prudent hereafter to answer all inquiries with the reply that we were "on a trip to the far west," and not, if we could avoid it, make it known that we had started for California.

Sunday, April 7.   We traveled only fifteen miles to-day. We found good accommodations for ourselves, but our poor horses had to stand out-of-doors, though the night air was damp and chilly. For the first time, we found that horse feed was scarce, and the neighborhood had to be ransacked to get a sufficient supply.

Monday, April 8.   We traveled through a beautiful country to-day, between Springfield and Jacksonville, and stopped at night five miles west of Jacksonville.

Tuesday, April 9.   We traveled twenty-one miles to-day, crossing the Illinois River at Naples, which is quite a business-like place, on the east side of the river. A railroad runs from Naples to Quincy.

Wednesday, April 10.   We traveled nineteen miles to-day, and stopped at a farmer's house, where we found very pleasant and agreeable folks. To-morrow we expect to cross the Mississippi River. We are now two hundred and seventy-seven miles from home.

CHAPTER II.

Thursday, April 11.   To-day we crossed the Mississippi River at Hannibal, Missouri, and traveled four miles west of the city. We got the privilege of stopping at a private farmhouse, it being then dark, where they consented to furnish us with supper and breakfast. After we had entered the house, the gentleman inquired of us what state we were from, to which we replied, "From Indiana." The gentleman and his wife then stepped aside a little, and appeared to be considering the propriety of furnishing accommodations to people from a "free state," for we were now in a "slave state," where negro slaves were everywhere to be seen. The gentleman then very politely informed us that he did not think they could accommodate us with supper and breakfast. He asked, "Have you not a supply of provisions with you?" We replied, "Yes sir, plenty of it." "Then, madam," said he, "we will furnish you with a room, with everything you may need, and a servant to wait on you." We were conducted into their parlor, where there was a large fireplace, with table and chairs, and a bed in one corner—all very good and comfortable. But some other parts of the house were not so nice as the kitchen we left in our Martinsville home.

They gave me a small negro girl to wait on me, and we had a very pleasant time all by ourselves, for we were provided with everything that the country afforded, in the way of provisions, both substantials and delicacies, so as to be prepared for all emergencies. But our prudent host and hostess did not see proper to show themselves to us any more that night. In the morning, however, as we were making our preparations for departure, the whole family made their appearance in numbers. I had put our room in good order, when the two young ladies came in, evidently curious to see a lady emigrant for California. When we were ready to get in our wagons and drive away, they all gathered around, admiring our nice outfit and our nice-looking horses.

"Dear me," said the younger lady, "and are you really going across the plains to California?" "Yes, my dear," I answered. "Are you not afraid of being burned black by the sun and wind on the plains?" "Oh, no; and if I am, I can stay in the house until I am bleached out again!" "But there are no houses in California." "Well, we have already sent our house on ahead." "How did you send your house to California?" Then I told them: "We sent it on a flat-boat down the west fork of White River to the Wabash, down the Wabash to the Ohio, down the Ohio to the Mississippi, and down the Mississippi to New Orleans. There it will be put on a sailing vessel, and go through the Gulf of Mexico into the Atlantic Ocean, and around past Cape Horn into the Pacific Ocean. Then it will go up the western coast to the 'Golden Gate,' into the Bay of San Francisco, and up the Sacramento River to the city of Sacramento, where it will meet us when we get there."

When I had told them this, the interest and excitement were such that, by the time I was seated in the wagon, the whole family, black and white, had gathered about us. We afterwards learned that our landlord had been a member of the state Legislature the preceding winter. This was our first night in Missouri.

Friday, April 12.   This was a very cold day. We traveled seventeen miles and were obliged to stop at a place with but few accommodations.

Saturday, April 13.   We stopped for our noon lunch at Clinton, in Monroe County, where we overtook the Ohio train that had helped us out of the mud. We reached Paris, the county seat, at night, and stopped at the Paris Hotel, in company with the Ohio emigrants.

Sunday, April 14.   The snow was two inches deep. We left about eleven o'clock and traveled seventeen miles over miserable roads. We got stuck in the mud again, and had to be pulled out by ox teams.

Monday, April 15.   We traveled all day and reached a place four miles west of Huntsville, the county seat of Randolph County. It rained most of the day and the roads were very bad.

Tuesday, April 16.   We remained in camp all day on account of the rain and the deep, muddy roads.

Wednesday, April 17.   We had an unusual experience to-day. We traveled twenty-three miles, and as night approached, we found it almost impossible to get accommodations at the private farmhouses along the road, and there were no hotels except in the towns, and they were far apart. Near sundown, Mr. Frink, being on horseback, rode on ahead of the wagon to procure, if possible, shelter for the night, at a place said to be the last house for six miles. But, for some unknown reason, the people, when we reached there, refused to let us stay.

I felt very indignant at such treatment. It was now almost dark, and we knew not what to do. At last we heard of a hospitable lady, a Mrs. Barker, living several miles ahead, who would probably receive us. So Mr. Frink went forward alone in the darkness, while I was left to report to the wagons, which were still behind with the Ohio Company. When they arrived, we all followed the road which Mr. Frink had taken.

It was a moonlight night, which was very much in our favor. We soon came to a fork in the road. We were now in a dilemma, not knowing which road to take. In desperation, we took the left, and traveled on and on. I remained on horseback in preference to riding in the wagon, though the night was damp and chilly, one of the company being with me.

Among the company from Ohio were two brothers named Swift. By and by we heard talking in the distance, but could see no person and no house. We began to think of all kinds of dangers. Perhaps we were going to be trapped and robbed. Finally, I determined to follow up the sound of the voices, for I thought Mr. Frink might have been waylaid and perhaps murdered. At last we came to where several negroes were sitting on a fence. I inquired the way to Mrs. Barker's house. "Why, the Lord bless you, you done come the wrong road. You got to go back three miles and take the right-hand road to get to Mrs. Barker's house." We turned back sorrowfully, and had not gone far before our wagons were caught in a bad place; but soon Mr. Frink appeared with a lantern and a guide, and, though the moon was down and the night was dark, we reached Mrs. Barker's at nine o'clock. She received us very kindly, though we were entire strangers. She had a good warm supper awaiting us, with a great rousing fire in the parlor, and plenty of darkies to wait on us and do our bidding. The explanation of her warm-hearted hospitality was this: Mrs. Barker's husband had crossed the plains to California in 1849, and she felt so much sympathy with the travelers to the land of gold, she was determined that all who stopped at her house should be well taken care of.

Thursday, April 18.   We came at night to the house of a Mr. McKinney, called "Squire McKinney," and were very hospitably welcomed. Mrs. McKinney had a nephew who went to California in 1849, and she told me of the wonderful tales of the abundance of gold that she had heard; "that they kept flour-scoops to scoop the gold out of the barrels that they kept it in, and that you could soon get all that you needed for the rest of your life. And as for a woman, if she could cook at all, she could get $16.00 per week for each man that she cooked for, and the only cooking required to be done was just to boil meat and potatoes and serve them on a big chip of wood, instead of a plate, and the boarder furnished the provisions." I began at once to figure up in my mind how many men I could cook for, if there should be no better way of making money.

Friday, April 19.   The next "squire" we fell in with was "Squire Barncs." We reached his place at nightfall and stayed all night. During the day one of the Ohio company, a Mr. Terrell, met with a serious accident, putting his shoulder out of joint. This detained us and prevented us from making a usual day's travel. We had to send eighteen miles for a doctor to reduce the dislocation.

Saturday, April 20.   We traveled twenty-one miles to-day over desperate roads. We halted before sundown, and were entertained by some very nice people.

Sunday, April 21.   We traveled twenty-two miles today and staid all night at Plattsburg. Here we heard more wonderful tales of California and the gold mines.

Monday, April 22.   We came to-day within nine miles of St. Joseph, which is situated on high bluffs, on the east side of the Missouri River.

Tuesday, April 23.   We got into St. Joseph at 10 o'clock this morning. The whole country around the town is filled with encampments of California emigrants. This is the head of the emigration at the present time. They have gathered here from the far east and south, to fit out and make final preparations for launching out on the great plains, on the other side of the Missouri River.

Every house of entertainment in the city is crowded to its full capacity. This has been a backward spring season, and thousands are patiently waiting for the grass to grow, as that will be the only feed for their stock, after crossing to the west side and getting into the Indian country.

We drove out of town two miles northward, on the road to Savannah; and, finding a comfortable log cabin, we rented it from the owner, Mr. Compton, who had built a new cabin which he had just moved into. The cabin was quite well furnished and had good beds. There was also a large fireplace, with plenty of wood close at hand. We here settled ourselves for housekeeping, until the grass should grow on the Kansas and Nebraska prairies, and remained for the next fifteen days.

We still lacked something to complete our stock of supplies; for we had neither pickles, potatoes, nor vinegar. The army of emigration was so numerous that the demand for these and many other articles could only with difficulty be fully supplied. Mr. Frink traveled sixteen miles through the farming country searching for pickled cucumbers.

He was fortunate enough to find a bushel still in the salt, which he bought and brought back with him. This, with some horseradish and one peck of potatoes, was all he could find in the way of vegetables. I prepared these very carefully, and put them up in kegs with apple vinegar; these were to be our principal defense against that dreadful disease, the scurvy, from which the overland emigrants of 1849 had suffered so severely—not only while on the journey, but long after reaching California.

We had some old friends living near Cincinnati, our former home, who came by steamer down the Ohio and up the Missouri to St. Joseph, with their outfit, horses and wagons. Among them were two brothers of the name of Carson, who were raised within six miles of Cincinnati, and twin brothers by the name of McMeans, and a Mr. Miles—making five persons in their company. There was also Mr. Silver's company from the same city. They all came and camped near our cabin, waiting, like ourselves, for the grass to grow, and making the last preparations for the final start. It gave our camping ground the appearance of a village in beautiful woods. The country surrounding St. Joseph is a delightful region. Mr. Frink and myself admired it very much; and we thought that if we were not bound for California, we should like to settle here.

Not many days had passed before we began to hear frightful tales of Indian depredations on the plains, which had a tendency, at first, to shake the resolution of some members of the party. However, we finally concluded that our arrangements were so complete that we were certain to get through safely if any one could; and so the Indian stories ceased to give us any uneasiness or anxiety.

Mr. Frink met here one day a man named Avery, who had come from the same country we had started from, without any team or company, hoping that he could find at St. Joseph some one who would be willing to take him to California. So we agreed to take him in our company—the more readily as we had begun to feel that we were hardly strong-handed enough to be perfectly safe in the Indian country. For, besides Mr. Frink and myself, the only persons in our immediate party were Mr. Aaron Rose, the confidential clerk, and a boy eleven years old, Robert Parker. This new arrangement required us now to buy another wagon, and a supply of provisions for our new associate.

Wednesday, May 8.   At last we were all rigged out for the journey. We had two wagons, one drawn by four horses, a lighter one drawn by two horses, besides two saddle-horses for Mr. Frink and myself. We were ready to start to-day, and decided that we would travel up along the east side of the Missouri River before attempting to cross over to the west side. During our very first day's journey something about one of the wagons was broken, so we only went as far as Savannah, where we stopped overnight to have the wagon repaired. Here we found some Indiana emigrants, who called on us, and had us stay in their company that night. Here we again heard alarming and discouraging accounts of deeds of violence and bloodshed that had recently been committed on the plains, along the route that we were very soon to travel over.

Thursday, May 9.   We remained all day in camp at Savannah, waiting for our wagon to be repaired.

Friday, May 10.   Our wagon having been put in good order and all made ready, we left Savannah this morning and drove twenty-three miles up the east bank of the Missouri River.

Saturday, May 11.   Starting early, we drove twenty-eight miles to-day, and stopped one mile from the stream called Big Tarchio.

Sunday, May 12.   We drove twenty miles to-day, and staid two

miles north of Linden, at a miserable place. The boys for the first
time slept in the wagon.

Monday, May 13. This day brought us to the crossing of the
Missouri River, ten miles below old Fort Kearney, which stands at
the mouth of the Platte River. Here we found a number of wagons
and the Carson boys waiting to be crossed over in an old fashioned
ferry-boat. Mr. Bullard and Mr. Bray were here with a train of wagons, loaded with merchandise for Salt Lake City. We learned that
they were old Santa Fe traders. They were registered to cross first at
the ferry, and so they went ahead, as each party must take its regular
turn as registered on the ferry-book. This was known as Bullard's
Ferry.

This was our first night in a camp. Thus far we had staid in a
house every night since we left home. We enjoyed the change very
much, and really thought we had lost a great deal of comfort in
putting up with the miserable accommodations that we so often had
met with; for here, on the banks of this majestic river, surrounded
with the freshness of the budding spring, it was a delightful change.

We are now six hundred and thirteen miles from home. The elevation of this place is nine hundred and fifty feet above the Gulf of
Mexico and about four hundred feet above our old home. So we have
already begun to climb.

CHAPTER III.

Tuesday, May 14. We were safely across the wide and muddy-
colored stream by eleven o'clock this morning. Now that we are over,
and the wide expanse of the great plains is before us, we feel like
mere specks on the face of the earth.

I think none of us have realized until now the perils of this undertaking. During the past week not much has been discussed but the
Indians and their doings. Printed circulars have been distributed
informing the emigrants of many Indian depredations. Now I begin
to think that three men, one woman, and one eleven-year old boy,
only armed with one gun and one Colt's revolver, are but a small
force to defend themselves against many hostile Indian tribes, along
a journey of two thousand miles.

The Carson company of five men were crossed over at the same time that we were. They confidently talked as if they had studied everything pertaining to Indians and their tactics, and had nothing to fear from them. I had a very strong feeling at the same time, that these men would have felt more at ease if there had not been a woman in the party, to be taken care of in case of danger. However, each company was wholly independent of the others, and our wagons became separated from the other trains. During the day I began to feel, and so expressed myself to the rest of the company, that for greater safety it would be well if we could fall in with some strong company and unite with them for mutual protection; but when camping time came, late in the afternoon, and night was drawing nigh, our little party was all alone. We picked out a camping-ground on a rolling knoll, so that we could the better defend ourselves in case we were attacked during the night. But no one except myself expressed any fear of the savages; it was all nonsense to think they would attack us. But the first thing I did after we halted, was to get out the field telescope which we carried, to see if I could find any Indians; and sure enough I soon espied a party of them riding on an elevated ridge a long way off.

I announced my discovery to the camp. Other glasses were got out and leveled in that direction. All agreed that I was right. Then every one went quickly to work to put our camp in the best condition for defense.

A few minutes later, to our great delight, a company of five fine-looking men from Michigan drove up and asked the privilege of camping with us that night. We were more than glad to have our force increased by the addition of a party of such resolute-looking men, and readily gave our consent. We informed them of our discovery of Indians scouting at a distance. The wagons were then placed in position to form a corral, or circular inclosure, and picket-pins or stakes were driven down in the center, to tie our horses to after they had done grazing. All our ropes and lariats were made ready for the same purpose. After our supper was over and it was fairly dark, all the horses were brought in from their grazing ground and tied and doubly tied to the picket-pins and stakes inside the corral. The wagons were then securely fastened together, to form a solid barrier against a stampede, and every precaution was adopted that would increase our safety. The next thing was to see that our firearms were in good order. Then the guards for the night were appointed for the different watches. Finally the camp-fires were extinguished and the little circular village on the knoll was left in darkness. But no one was inclined to sleep, and I do not think any one retired but Mr. Frink. He evidently thought that the others were pretty badly scared, and therefore there would be enough to watch, so he could sleep undisturbed. For my part, I did not change my clothing during the entire night, neither shoes nor bonnet.

I sat up all night in the wagon to see that the guards kept awake, though it was too dark to see any distance. Once in a while, however, one of the guards would step up to the wagon and cautiously whisper that "no Indians had been seen yet." This, in a measure, would relieve my apprehensions; but still I was in such a state of anxiety and suspense that when I thought Mr. Frink was sleeping too soundly and breathing too heavily, I would arouse him; I could not understand how he could sleep soundly when there was so much danger. In this manner passed our first night on those vast, uninhabited plains. But by the time the day dawned and the guards came in, I was out and had a fire made and breakfast under way.

Wednesday, May 15.   When we drove out from our fortified camp on the elevated knoll, and reached the main traveled road again, we met a large train of wagons from Ohio and Michigan. We kept in company with them during the day and encamped with them at night. Our party was now increased to fifty or more. We all traveled together for the next week.

Thursday, May 16.   It was about half past six when we started this morning, but we traveled nearly twenty-five miles before night.

The Ohio and Michigan trains who were with us were fitted out with hardy Canadian ponies, small but tough, and capable of enduring greater hardships than ordinary horses. But the drivers were in too great a hurry to get to California before all the gold was dug out, and traveled too fast. Many of our party being young, inexperienced men, thought it necessary for us to pass all the ox teams and loose cattle on the road, fearing there would be no feed left for our own stock. They would whip up furiously and try to pass every train they overtook.

This did not accord with Mr. Frink's best judgment. Our own horses, like most of the western horses, were large and had been accustomed all their lives to be fed on corn. And now, to get nothing to eat but the scanty new grass of the plains, they could not endure what the sturdy Canadians could, and so after the first week had passed we traveled more slowly.

We encamped at night on Salt Creek, which runs northeast into the Platte River. Here Mr. Avery, the man who had joined our party at the camp below Savannah, caught a fine lot of catfish, which we enjoyed very much for supper.

Friday, May 17. This morning we started again at half past six, following, in a westerly direction, the well-traveled road which had been used for many years by teams hauling supplies to the frontier forts. Fort Kearney, at the head of Grand Island, is two hundred miles from the Missouri River. Fort Laramie, at the foot of the Black Hills, is about three hundred and fifty miles further; and Fort Hall, once an English trading post, is about five hundred and thirty miles still beyond. The road along here was in good condition, all the bad streams being bridged.

Saturday, May 18. To-day we traveled about twenty miles, descending the steep bluffs from the high plains, over which we have been marching ever since we crossed the Missouri River, to the low bottom of the Platte River, and coming for the first time to its south bank. Here we encamped for the night, finding grass and fire-wood very scarce.

This river differs from all those we have been accustomed to. A shallow groove, or flat, low valley, from ten to twenty miles wide, has been scooped out of the sandy plains for four hundred miles from the "Black Hills" to the Missouri. Along each side are bold, sandy bluffs, one hundred and fifty feet high. In the bottom of this valley the Platte River has cut out for itself a winding channel from six to ten feet deep and from one to two miles wide.

The valley, as well as the extensive plains on each side, is totally devoid of timber or undergrowth of any kind, except where a few straggling cottonwoods and willow thickets, long distances apart, stand close to the water's edge. In four hundred miles the descent of the stream is twenty-four hundred feet, or six feet to the mile, producing a swift current that plows out deep pools in its bed, and piles up high bars of quicksand, so that the volume of water is constantly changing from one to six feet in depth.

Our road from this point follows the south bank of the main stream and of its northern branch for four hundred and fifty miles. Fifty miles beyond it meets the Sweetwater, which leads two hundred miles further, to the South Pass.

Sunday, May 19.   We are resting to-day, remaining in camp by the river. Near us are a few cottonwoods. There are no groves or forests in sight. We left all forests behind us at the Missouri River. Here the whole earth, as far as the eye can reach, is naked and bare except that a thin growth of grass partly hides the sandy ground.

During the day we thought it prudent to organize our forces for protection against the Indians, and to insure the safety of our stock at night. Something like a military system was adopted, with proper officers. In case of an attack by Indians, each man was expected to be at his appointed post. Mr. Frink was elected captain. Four men were to be detailed every night to stand guard over the horses, and bring them in the next morning. As there were now nearly fifty men in the party, no one person would have to stand guard oftener than once in ten or twelve days.

We had passed through the lands of the Pottawattamies, but without seeing any, and without molestation. The Kickapoos and Nemahas were sixty miles south, on the Blue Rivers. But ahead of us were many oher tribes,—the Pawnees, Sioux, Cheyennes, Blackfeet, and others, not supposed to be very friendly. We therefore thought it best to be fully prepared for them.

Monday, May 20.   It was about six o'clock when we started this morning. We had with us some guidebooks [Fremont's and Palmer's], from which we learned that to-day we would pass the village of the Pawnee Indians, who had the name of being very warlike. In anticipation, every gun and pistol was put in good order, and regular military tactics were observed. At ten o'clock we came to the village, which was situated on a ridge extending nearly to the river. But instead of a bloody fight, which some expected, we took the village without firing a gun. From appearances, the place had not been occupied for years. There was nothing to indicate a village, except some tent-poles and a quantity of buffalo bones and those of other animals, that may have been killed for food. Our military prowess all disappeared in a twinkling. Up to this time we had seen but a single Indian, and he was a long way off. We learned afterwards that the tribe had removed about one hundred miles to the northward, to the Loup Fork of the Platte, where their chief village is, and where they raise considerable corn, during the times when they are not hunting or fighting.

In the afternoon we came to the junction of the emigrant road from St. Joseph with our road, about twenty-five miles below New Fort Kearney. That road ran westward from St. Joseph to the Blue Rivers, and up the Little Blue to its head, where it turned to the northward across the high plains to the Platte. Here the two roads met. Both roads were thickly crowded with emigrants. It was a grand spectacle when we came, for the first time, in view of the vast emigration, slowly winding its way westward over the broad plain.

The country was so level that we could see the long trains of white-topped wagons for many miles. Finally, when the two roads came together, and the army which had crossed the Missouri River at St. Joseph joined our army, which had crossed the river above Savannah, it appeared to me that none of the population had been left behind. It seemed to me that I had never seen so many human beings in all my life before. And, when we drew nearer to the vast multitude, and saw them in all manner of vehicles and conveyances, on horseback and on foot, all eagerly driving and hurrying forward, I thought, in my excitement, that if one-tenth of these teams and these people got ahead of us, there would be nothing left for us in California worth picking up.

Mr. Frink was not with our wagons just at this moment; he had either ridden ahead to look for grass, or was with some one behind. So I took the responsibility, and gave orders to the drivers to whip up, to drive fast and get ahead of that countless throng of wagons.

But in a little while Mr. Frink appeared, and wanted to know of the drivers what they had got in such a hurry about. Already the horses were showing signs of being fretted; and Mr. Frink at once instructed the drivers that it would not do to attempt to travel at that rate of speed if we expected ever to reach California. But I was half frantic over the idea that every blade of grass for miles on each side of the road would be eaten off by the hundreds and thousands of horses, mules, and oxen ahead of us. And, worse than all, there would only be a few barrels of gold left for us when we got to California.

Mrs. McKinney, at whose house in Missouri we stopped on the night of the 18th of April, was responsible for my belief that it would be an easy thing to collect barrels of gold. And when, looking forward or backward at this place on the Platte, it seemed as if a number of cities had gathered here with all their people, on the same errand of seeking for gold, I was impatient at our slow progress, but we gradually toned down. In a few days the crowd strung out more evenly along the road, and was not gathered in such great masses.

There were all conceivable kinds of conveyances. There was a cart drawn by two cows, a cart drawn by one ox, and a man on horseback drove along an ox packed with his provisions and blankets. There was a man with a hand cart, another with a wheelbarrow loaded with supplies. And we were not yet two hundred miles from the Missouri River. The journey was only fairly commenced.

Tuesday, May 21.   Leaving our camp in the Platte bottom at the usual hour, we traveled all day up the broad valley. With the exception of a muddy creek, or slough, now and then, the road was very good. During the day we passed New Fort Kearney, a small United States military station near the bank of the river, the walls of which were constructed largely of sods cut out in large blocks, and laid up as adobes are laid in California. This is the first human habitation we have seen since crossing the Missouri, two hundred miles distant. From that point we have been steadily climbing up hill, the altitude here being twenty-one hundred and fifty feet, which is twelve hundred feet higher than Bullard's Ferry. We camped to-night on the bank of the river.

Wednesday, May 22.   After we had started this morning, there was great excitement over a buffalo chase, opposite the head of Grand Island in Platte River. Some of our men partook of the excitement. As far as we could see, every one that was on horseback went flying in the direction of the buffalo. Our men gave the saddle-horses a fatiguing run, but not without a reprimand from Mr. Frink when they returned. He informed them very distinctly that he had not started for California to hunt Buffalo. But I really could not blame the men very much, though the chase was bad for the horses. The animation and excitement of the moment beat anything I ever saw, and I would not, for a good deal, have missed the sight of that great chase over that grand plain. Some one brought us a piece of buffalo steak, so that we were not without a share of the prize.

The road to-day continued level and good, with exception of some muddy places and small gullies, which gave us no trouble. Fire-wood is scarce, there being none except along the river bank. Every stray piece we find we pick up and carry with us. The camp to-night presented the appearance of a village of tents and white-topped wagons.

Thursday, May 23.   We are now in the midst of the buffalo country; but to our disappointment, we have seen only the small herd that came in sight yesterday. There are hundreds of thousands of them on these plains; but the emigration has frightened them to the right and to the left, away from the road, so that they are seldom seen. We often pass the bones and skulls in great numbers, where they have been killed by the Indians.

Friday, May 24.   We left camp at the usual hour. The road often leaves the river to cross a large bend, and does not reach it again at camping-time. In such cases, the only resource for water is by digging wells a few feet deep. But the well water is usually muddy and warm. The soil is a kind of sandy loam, through which the river water makes its way, under the entire bottom.

Our chief inconvenience here is the want of firewood. There being no timber except the few cottonwoods and willows along the river, it often happens that we find hardly enough to cook our meals. But Mr. Frink adopted the plan of gathering up all the fragments we found and hauling them until time of need.

To-day the line of white wagons reaches out to the front and to the rear farther than we can see. Among such an army, we have little fear of trouble from Indians.

Saturday, May 25.   Still traveling up the Platte. The road is a little monotonous. The scenery does not change much. The river has a winding course, and contains many islands. Some are little more than sand bars, others are covered with low willows. The road is at times along the river bank, and again near the bluffs on our left. The bluffs are getting higher. The face is gullied with deep ravines, in which cedar shrubs are growing, the first we have seen.

From our guide-books we learn that in a few days we shall reach the South Fork of the Platte, beyond which the face of the country changes.

Sunday, May 26.   This is the day of rest, but there is not much rest crossing the plains. If our camp is at a place where there is neither grass nor water, we are compelled to travel on until we find them. And in camp there is no end of necessary work. Wagons, harness, and clothing have to be mended, washing to be done, animals to be changed on the pasture and guarded, innumerable small things to be looked after.

There is no time for reading, and there are neither newspapers nor letters to read. We have not heard from home since we left, nearly two months ago, and do not expect to until we arrive at Sutter's Fort, three months hence.

Monday, May 27.   To-morrow will bring us to the South Fork, which we are told we must ford. From what we have seen of the river so far, it looks rather dangerous to cross, and we have some apprehensions of difficulty. But it may not so bad when we come to it. If we get safely over, we expect to reach a more interesting country to travel through.

The South Fork heads in a southwest direction from here, among the highest peaks of the Rocky Mountains. Our road will lead us up the North Fork of the Platte, and up its main branch, the Sweetwater, to the South Pass.

Our military organization has fallen to pieces. Those who were in so much of a hurry have driven ahead, reducing our number to about twenty-five. Mr. Frink thought the only sure way to get to California with our animals was to drive slowly. We have found, too, that it is best to travel in small parties, on account of the scarcity, in many places, of grass and water. Many camping places that would afford enough for a small train, would not supply a large company.

Tuesday, May 28.   We left our camp near the river about half past six, and in a few miles came to the South Fork, a short distance above the junction, where we were to cross. A great crowd of emigrants was encamped here, making all preparations, though a great many of them were undecided what was best to do. We heard all kinds of reports as to the best route to take, for every one was ignorant. Some thought they would follow up the valley of the South Platte, on the south side; but the majority decided to ford the river at this point. On the whole long journey to California there were neither ferries nor bridges, except a ferry at North Platte and one at Green River, and the small bridges back near Salt River, and a little one in Carson Cañon.

The stream we had now reached was fearful to look at,—rushing and boiling and yellow with mud, a mile wide, and in many places of unknown depth. The bed was of quicksand—this was the worst difficulty. But there was no way to do but to ford it. So we started down the bank and into the raging water.

From a guide-book we had with us, we learned that the proper way to cross the stream was to take a diagonal course,—first down the stream, then up again. Accordingly, after driving into the water, we turned down at an angle of forty-five degrees till we had reached the middle of the river; then, turning up stream at the same angle, we arrived safely at the northern bank, nearly opposite our point of entrance.

Of all the excitements that I ever experienced or thought of, the crossing of that river was the greatest. A great many other wagons and people were crossing at the same time—mule teams, horse teams, ox teams, men on horseback, men wading and struggling against the quicksands and current, many of them with long poles in their hands, feeling their way. Sometimes they would be in shallow water only up to their knees; then, all at once, some unlucky one would plunge in where it was three or four feet deep.

The deafening noise and halloing that this army of people kept up, made the alarm in the river more intense. The quicksand and the uncertainty of depth of water kept all in a state of anxiety. Our horses would sometimes be in water no more than a foot deep; then, in a moment, they would go down up to their collars. On one occasion I was considerably alarmed. Several other wagons, in their haste, had crowded in ahead of us on both sides, and we were compelled to stop for several minutes. Our wagon at once began to settle in the quicksand, and it required the assistance of three or four men lifting at the wheels, to enable the horses to pull out.

Where we crossed, the river was a mile wide, and we were just three-quarters of an hour in getting over. I here date one of the happiest and most thankful moments of my life to have been when we landed safe on the north side. The danger in the crossing consisted in the continual shifting of the sandy bed, so that a safe ford to-day might be a dangerous one to-morrow.

We were now nine-hundred and thirteen miles from home.

The next excitement we met with was some day after, when the rumor came back from the front that the grass ahead was all burned off. What was to become of us, with nothing for our horses to eat, and we unable to go either forward or backward?

But we out-traveled this rumor in a day. We were journeying, of course, in the dark all the time, and never knew what was in store for us ahead.

The elevation of this point is two thousand seven hundred and ninety feet above the Gulf of Mexico.

CHAPTER IV.

Wednesday, May 29.   A broad mass of high, rugged mountains filled most of the space between the two forks of the Platte. The point comes down opposite the ford. Many of the emigrants turned to the left, up the South Fork for six miles, then crossed over the hills to the North Fork valley. Our party bore to the right at the ford, and in half an hour came to the low point of the great promontory. This was the outer-most spur of the Rocky Mountain chain, and here, for the first time, our wheels and horses' hoofs struck its solid granite ledges. We crossed without difficulty, and drove up the valley of the

North Fork for several miles, before going into camp. The valley here is about five miles wide, level, but more sandy than below. High, rocky ridges border it on both sides. There is some undergrowth in the side canons, but generally timber is scarce. Sometimes we find no firewood, and have to draw from our stock in the wagon.

Thursday, May 30.   The road continues up the valley, along the south side of the river. Occasionally it leaves the river, to pass over and around the bluffs. In the cañons the heat is oppressive. This valley is claimed by the Sioux Indians, a large tribe once hostile to the whites. We are now getting near the sagebrush region, that we have heard so much about. The roads continue heavy and very dusty.

Friday, May 31.   We expect to reach in a few days some great natural curiosities. One is a large rock in shape like a court-house, or a church without a steeple. The other is a tall, square tower or chimney, which can be seen for a long distance. We are also on the lookout for Indians, though they are thought to be friendly. Our large company is reduced to but a few persons, and our horses are strictly guarded every night.

Saturday, June 1.   To-day the bluffs came to the river and cut off our passage along the bank. We had to climb a long hill to go around. We descended to the river again through a deep ravine called Ash Hollow, where Colonel Harney, with a detachment of United States Regulars, had a severe fight with the Sioux, several years ago.

The heavy sand and hard climbing begin to tell on the strength of our horses. Feed is often scarce and they suffer in consequence.

Sunday, June 2.   We remained in camp all day, repairing our small wagon. The hind axle was broken. Mr. Frink had seen a wagon abandoned, near the road at Ash Hollow. He went back with a man to-day, and took out the bolts and brought the hind axle and wheels to camp. It was then fitted to the small wagon in place of the old axle, and did very well.

Monday, June 3.   We traveled ten miles to-day and stopped on good grass. In the afternoon we passed an Indian encampment numbering seventy tents. They belonged to the Sioux tribe, but were quite friendly. The squaws were much pleased to see the "white squaw" in our party, as they called me. I had brought a supply of needles and thread, some of which I gave them. We also had some small mirrors in gilt frames, and a number of other trinkets, with which we could buy fish and fresh buffalo, deer, and antelope meat. But money they would not look at.

A heavy storm of wind and rain came up afterwards, which we prepared ourselves for by picketing down the wagons with ropes fastened to stakes, and tying the horses securely.

Tuesday, June 4.   In the morning it was raining some and Mr. Frink got breakfast. We had been closely on the lookout, and at three o'clock we came in sight of the famous "Court-house Rock," eighteen miles distant, and many miles south of the road. It presented a very imposing appearance. "Chimney Rock" also came in sight, about thirty miles further on. Our camp at night was made nearly opposite the Court-house Rock, and six miles distant; but the atmosphere was so clear that it did not seem to be more than a mile away. Many persons, thinking they could walk to the rock in a few minutes, would start out on foot to examine it more closely; but after walking for an hour, finding it to be as far off as ever, apparently, would give up the attempt.

Wednesday, June 5.   The weather to-day was quite hot and oppressive. We had to cross a long stretch without water. The road we took led us close to the base of Chimney Rock, where we stopped for some time to satisfy our curiosity. The base is shaped like a large cone, from the top of which rises a tall tower or chimney, resembling the chimney of a manufacturing establishment. According to Fremont, it was once five hundred feet high, but has been worn down by the winds and rains until it is no more than two hundred and fifty feet in height. It is composed of marl and soft sandstone, which is easily worn away. Mr. Frink carved our names upon the chimney, where are hundreds of others.

Thursday, June 6.   We came to Scott's Bluffs to-day. When we reached there, we found water in a deep gully on the left side of the road, where a great many thirsty people were waiting for water. There was a very small weeping spring, where we caught the water in a cup, as it wept out from under the rocks.

Friday, June 7. To-day we crossed over the bluffs, and encamped near the Platte River, not far from Horse Creek.

Saturday, June 8. The mail-carriers passed us on a trot this morning, going to the summit of the Rocky Mountains, where a post-office for the accommodation of the emigrants was established. When we came to the Laramie River, the water was very high, and ran into our wagon. This is a dangerous ford, where a number of persons have been drowned.

At four o'clock we arrived at the place we have so long been anxious to reach,—Fort Laramie. This outpost formerly belonged to the American Fur Company, who built it as a protection against the savages, then very numerous and hostile. After the United States Government bought it, they sent regular troops to protect the emigration.

The fort is one hundred and eighty feet square, having adobe walls fifteen feet high, on the inside of which are rooms built against the walls all around, of the same material. The parade-ground in the center is one hundred and thirty feet square. On top of the wall are wooden palisades. Over the front gateway is a square tower with loopholes for rifles.

As it is not our intention to go by Salt Lake, this is the last human habitation we shall see until we reach Fort Hall, five hundred and thirty miles further on.

The altitude of Fort Laramie is four thousand four hundred and seventy feet. This is almost four thousand feet higher than our starting-point. But we are not yet half way up to the highest point of our road, and have traveled not half its length. Our camp last night was on the forty-second parallel of north latitude,—two and a half degrees north of that of Martinsville.

We should have been glad to stop here and rest a while, before starting out on the next stretch of our long, mountainous journey. But it was necessary to find a good camping-place for the night, and we tarried but a short time. Three miles beyond, we found good feed and there made our camp.

Sunday, June 9. We remained in this camp all day, resting as much as is possible on such a journey and under such circumstances. But it was a very different Sunday from those we had been always accustomed to at home.

Monday, June 10.   It was at this camp that we had to leave our cooking stove, which we had found so useful ever since crossing the Missouri. It being light, we had always carried it lashed on the hind end of the wagon. Some careless person, in a hurry, drove his team up too close behind, and the pole of his wagon ran into the stove, smashing and ruining it. After that, we had to cook in the open air. We adopted a plan which was very fashionable on the plains. We would excavate a narrow trench in the ground, a foot deep and three feet long, in which we built the fire. The cooking vessels were set over this, and upon trial we found it a very good substitute for a stove.

We started at twelve o'clock to-day, traveled fifteen miles, and went into camp at five o'clock. The road was among and over the spurs of the Black Hills, and very rough. I rode horseback the most of the day. Many wagons are being abandoned. Every day we pass good wagons that have been left for any one that might want them.

The Black Hills are so named from the fact that they are covered with pine, hemlock, spruce, cedar, and other evergreen trees, which give them, at a distance, a dark and gloomy appearance.

Tuesday, June 11.   Our road keeps on westward up the valley of the North Fork—the river on our right, the Black Hills on our left, bordering the valley. They appear to be about seven or eight miles distant. Among them we can see Laramie Peak, twenty-five miles to the south. It is six thousand five hundred feet high.

In six miles we came to Poplar Creek, which is well timbered with poplars. The bottom is rich and produces good grass, but it is now nearly all eaten off. Seventeen miles further we came to Horseshoe Creek, which runs from the Black Hills to the river. This is a fine stream, having groves of poplars along its banks. It is next to the largest creek between Fort Laramie and the crossing of the North Fork. Seven miles beyond here we came again to the bank of the Platte, where we found the feed to be very scarce. This region is said to produce clouds of grasshoppers in dry seasons.

Wednesday, June 12.   The road sometimes follows near the river, then goes over the bluffs, then across deep sand. The hills and bottoms are mostly covered with sage-brush. It grows in dense, tangled thickets, and to break a road through it is hard work for the heaviest and strongest teams. It is about four feet high, with stems two inches thick at the ground, and often matted close together. It is of a dull gray color and gives the country a gloomy appearance. Very little grass grows among it. And yet it is said the soil is rich, and would produce well if cleared and cultivated.

Thursday, June 13.   To-day we passed near where an old fort was built by some hunters or trappers, to protect themselves from Indians, who were very troublesome some years ago. The remains of the fort have nearly disappeared. We are coming into the range of the Arapahoes, who are reputed to be fighting Indians, but we have not seen any of them. They are supposed to be on the trail of the buffaloes, that have been frightened away by the crowds of emigration. The buffaloes are the chief means of subsistence of the Indian tribes over hundreds of thousands of square miles of this region.

To-morrow we expect to reach Deer Creek, and hope to find plenty of feed for our horses, who have a hard time of it over the rough and sandy roads, with only a scanty supply of food.

Friday, June 14.   In six miles we came to Wood Creek. The grass, abundant in the spring, was now mostly eaten off. A fine growth of poplars lined the banks of the stream, and we were told that when feed is scarce the Indians chop down the young saplings and feed their horses on the leaves and tender branches.

It was three o'clock in the afternoon when we reached Deer Creek, thirteen miles beyond Wood Creek. This is the largest of the many streams running into the Platte, above the Laramie Fork. Along the bottom is considerable timber. With Robert's assistance, I did the washing this afternoon. During the night a heavy storm of wind came up, but passed over without doing any serious damage.

Saturday, June 15.   This morning we started at eight o'clock. Our friends, the Carson boys from Cincinnati, came up with us here. We made a long drive to-day of twenty-six miles and camped within three miles of the crossing of the North Platte. For several days past we have been traveling among extensive thickets of sage-brush, or artemisia. It has the odor of turpentine mixed with camphor, which fills the air.

Sunday, June 16.   We remained in camp at this place all day. A great many emigrants are gathered here and above, preparatory to crossing the river. The water is too deep to ford and the ferry charges are very high. Some are making ferry-boats of their wagon bodies taken off the wheels, and launched in the water, with long ropes to haul them back and forth across the river. In some cases, empty casks are tied to the four corners of the wagon body, to keep it from sinking. This plan is very dangerous in the swift current, and we hear of many persons who have lost their lives in these attempts.

Monday, June 17.   A great crowd was waiting to cross the ferry. But by starting early, we were not delayed, and got over by six o'clock. This ferry was established by Kit Carson, the famous hunter and trapper, one of Fremont's guides. There were several ferry-boats. The water was deep and swift. The boats were attached to strong ropes stretched across the river, and were driven quickly from shore to shore by the strong current. We paid $5.00 each for our two wagons, and $1.00 each for our seven horses.

   The Platte River at this place comes out of the mountains from the southward, making a sharp bend at the above. Our road here leaves the Platte, which we have followed for four hundred and fifty miles, and strikes across to the Sweetwater, fifty miles further west. The space between the rivers is mostly a desert, covered with sage-brush, and producing but little grass. There are pools of alkali water and beds of dried-up ponds, crusted with soda or salt, several inches thick. The wheels and horses' hoofs break through the crust as if it were ice.

   We started early to cross this long, bad stretch. On our left were some high, red cliffs called the "Red Bluffs." After traveling twenty-two miles without water, we stopped all night by the only good spring. This is called Willow Springs; it lies in a deep, narrow gully, where the water is dipped by the cupful to fill the kegs and water vessels. At dark, while I was cooking supper, a heavy storm of wind and snow came up. There was no shelter, and we ate our supper while it was snowing and blowing. During the night, the men took turns guarding the horses in the snow, Mr. Frink being with them part of the time.

Tuesday, June 18. This was a bright June morning. We snowballed each other till ten o'clock, when the sun got too warm for the snow to remain. We traveled twenty-two miles, and came to the Sweetwater River, up which our road follows for one hundred and thirty miles, to the South Pass.

Wednesday, June 19. We traveled ten miles and came to "Independence Rock," a famous landmark in the Sweetwater Valley. The road runs close to it. It received its name from a party of emigrants on their way to Oregon, several years ago, who celebrated the anniversary of the Declaration of Independence at this point, on the Fourth of July. This singular rock is a granite boulder, about nineteen hundred feet long, two hundred feet wide, and one hundred and twenty feet high, standing on a level plain, entirely detached from the mountains near by. The sides and front, to the height of six or eight feet, contain hundreds of names painted with black paint made of gunpowder and bacon grease.

Thursday, June 20. Five miles above "Independence Rock" we came to the "Devil's Gate," where the river breaks through a spur of the mountains. The gap is nine hundred feet long, four hundred feet high, and one hundred and five feet wide. The road passes through another break a few hundred yards to the left. This opens into another beautiful valley about five miles wide, hemmed in by mountains that rise abruptly from the plain to a height of fifteen hundred or two thousand feet. There are scattering lines of pine timber on the tops, among which we could see patches of snow.

The valley is nearly level, and mostly covered with sage-brush. On the south side of some sand hillocks there are clums of sage six feet high, with stems six inches in diameter. Along the river are narrow borders of good grass. The elevation of this valley is six thousand forty feet.

We only traveled fifteen miles to-day. Our Cincinnati friends, the Carsons, who have been with us for some days, left us this morning and drove ahead, being in a hurry to get to the end of the journey. We had the novelty of camping alone for the first time.

Friday, June 21. Our fellow-passenger, Mr. Avery, also left us this morning, concluding he could walk to California sooner than we could get there, at the rate we were traveling. We gave him all the provisions he could carry, and he started, with blankets, clothing, and provisions strapped on his back, to walk fifteen hundred miles to California.

Six miles from our camp we came to the canon of the Sweetwater, and crossed the river by the difficult fords three times in less than a mile. Eight miles beyond the cañon we encamped on the Sweetwater by ourselves again.

Saturday, June 22. This morning we crossed ford number four of the Sweetwater, and then crossed a desert of sixteen miles without water. About midway was an extensive marsh, said to be underlaid with ice, but to what depth was not known. It is supposed that the marsh is frozen to great depth in winter, and that only a thin surface is thawed in summer.

During the forenoon we ascended a long, sloping hill, at the top of which, looking across a wide stretch of rough country covered with sage-brush, we got our first sight of the Wind River range of the Rocky Mountains. They were covered with snow, and appeared to be about fifty miles distant. We now realize that we are getting near the South Pass, which lies at the left of the snowy chain, where the mountains are broken away.

A few miles further we came to Sweetwater ford number five. The great number of fords on this stream are made necessary by the crooked course of the river, and the rough nature of the country. At this place we fell in with a company from Independence, Missouri, among whom were several emigrants from Kentucky and Indiana. A young Kentuckian, Mr. Thomas Wand, had ridden on ahead that day, and found a good camping place. He invited us to join them and to place our horses and mules with theirs on the pasture, which offer we readily accepted. One of the party, Mr. Johnson, proved to be from our own county.

Sunday, June 23. To-day we traveled twenty-three miles, crossing Sweetwater three times. We then left the river and went around the mountains. After crossing a small rivulet, we came to the Strawberry branch, and a few miles beyond reached what was known as the Quaking Asp branch of the Sweetwater, where we encamped for the night. The days are warm and pleasant, but after sunset the air cools rapidly, and heavy frosts whiten the ground in the morning.

Monday, June 24.   This was a day long to be remembered. At five o'clock we drove out of camp, and, in two miles, crossed the east branch of the Sweetwater. Five miles further we came to the main and last branch of the stream, which we had no difficulty in crossing. On the mountains near the road there were deep banks of snow in the gulches.

We then traveled up a long, gradual slope, or plain, free of rocks, trees, or gullies, and came at half past eleven o'clock to the summit of the South Pass of the Rocky Mountains. We could hardly realize that we were crossing the great backbone of the North American Continent at an altitude of seven thousand four hundred and ninety feet. The ascent was so smooth and gentle, and the level ground at the summit so much like a prairie region, that it was not easy to tell when we had reached the exact line of the divide. But it is here that after every shower the little rivulets separate, some to flow into the Atlantic, the others into the Pacific.

It was a beautiful, warm, hazy day. Near the summit, on each side of the road, was an encampment, at one of which the American flag was flying, to mark the private post-office or express office established by Gen. James Estelle, for the accommodation of emigrants wishing to send letters to friends at home. The last post-office on our way was at St. Joseph, on the Missouri River. West of that stream were neither states, counties, cities, towns, villages, nor white men's habitations. The two mud forts we had passed were the only signs of civilization. The entire region between the Missouri River and the Rocky Mountains was then called by the official name of the Indian Territory; and as it was only a hunting-ground for the tribes we had passed, and for the Cheyennes, Blackfeet, Snakes, Arapahoes, Oglallahs, and Crows, its name was appropriate.

To see the old flag once more strongly reminded us of home. There was a hail-storm at noon, but that did not prevent the assembled company from having an off-hand celebration of our arrival at

the summit. Music from a violin with tin-pan accompaniment, contributed to the general merriment of a grand frolic. In the afternoon
we spent some time in writing letters to our friends, to be sent back
by the express. On each letter we paid as express charges $1.00. The
returning messengers delivered the letters to the postmaster at St.
Joseph, and in due time they reached their destination, one thousand
four hundred thirty-eight miles distant.

Then we set out to begin the long descent to the Pacific Ocean,
bidding farewell to everything on the Atlantic side. We drove down
a ravine for eight miles and encamped for the night at Pacific
Springs. There being no grass here, the animals were taken into the
hills two miles to the north, where the men guarded them all night.
In the morning Mr. Frink found a field of bunch grass, not far from
the camp, which he estimated would yield two tons per acre.

CHAPTER V.

Tuesday, June 25. We are now on the borders of the desert
region. Between here and Green River extends a barren plain seventy
miles wide, with only two streams and but scanty grass. We remained
in camp until half past five o'clock in the afternoon. We then started
across the first stretch of twenty-one miles, prepared to travel in the
night to avoid the heat and lessen the thirst of our animals. The road
was level and good. In ten miles we reached the dry bed of a small
creek called "Dry Sandy." The moon shone bright as day, and our
party was in good spirits. The violinist played while others sang, and
the long night passed off very pleasantly. We reached the first water,
at Little Sandy, at two o'clock in the morning, pretty well fatigued.
Here we halted, put our horses out to feed, and staid till morning.

Wednesday, June 26. All around is a plain thinly covered with sage-
brush and grease-wood. A few miles to our right commence the
foot-hills of the Wind River chain, and beyond them the Snowy
Mountains rise abrupty to great height. They extend in a northwest
direction farther than we can see. About fifty miles north is
Fremont's Peak, thirteen thousand five hundred seventy feet high,
the loftiest of the Rocky Mountains. Fremont planted the American
flag on the summit in August, 1842, being probably the first human
being to scale the mountain.

At fifteen minutes before ten o'clock in the morning, we started again, and after traveling six miles came to the Big Sandy, where we remained until half past six in the afternoon. We passed, on the way, the forks of the road, the left hand of which runs southwest to Salt Lake City, two hundred miles distant. We took the right-hand road, which is supposed to be shorter, and is known as Sublette's Cut-off.

Having now a forty-mile desert to cross without water, we filled our water-bottles, containing five gallons each. Starting a little before sunset, we traveled during the night twenty miles and stopped at four o'clock in the morning at a place where we found feed for the animals.

Thursday, June 27. From this camp Fremont's Peak can be distinctly seen, rising above all others. A few miles west of its base, in the valley, are the ruins of an old fort built by Captain Bonneville, of the U.S. Army, who explored this region in 1832.

There was no water on the desert, but our bottles supplied us with all that we needed. At six o'clock we started on, being anxious to get to Green River as soon as possible. After traveling twelve miles, we halted for our noon lunch, but as soon as this was over, we hastened forward. Fifteen miles brought us to the bluffs on the western edge of the desert, about four o'clock. From here we could see the bright waters of the river, several miles away. The bluffs were high, steep, and rocky, and we had to let the wagons down cautiously with ropes. The narrow gorges through which we passed down, were filled with clouds of blinding dust. At the foot of the bluffs the dust was from twelve to twenty inches deep. The river bottom was a plain of dust, crowded with wagons and animals, and thickly populated with emigrants waiting their regular turn to be ferried over. Each of the two ferries had a small flatboat rowed with oars.

Many of the animals had already been swum across; but the water was high, deep, swift, blue, and cold as ice, heading in the ice mountains on our right. The poor horses were reluctant to venture in. One of our animals utterly refused to swim. The ferryman was loath to take him on the boat but at last consented. By leading one or two of our horses behind the boat, the others were induced to follow. Mr. Rose crossed at the same time and took the animals seven miles further to pasture.

Mr. Frink had been taken sick during the day, and when he got to the foot of the bluffs, he was no longer able to walk, and with difficulty climbed into the wagon. As our wagons could not be taken over that night, we had to stop in that miserable desert of dust until late the next day, waiting our turn to cross. Our boy, Robert, remained with us; but, excepting him, Mr. Frink and I were entirely alone. The situation was a serious one. I was frightened at feeling we were almost helpless, a thousand miles from civilization.

Friday, June 28.   This morning we heard that a gentleman by the name of Redwine, who had crossed the plains the year previous, was encamped near us with his family. At Mr. Frink's suggestion I called at their camp to learn, if possible, something of the road ahead of us; for our guide-books did not cover this part of the route. Mr. Redwine's reply was that he knew no more about the road than if he had never traveled it; that everything seemed new to him, but he thought it was yet a thousand miles to California. He could give us no information of any value.

Fortunately, Mr. Frink improved so much that he was enabled to cross the river with us in the afternoon.

Green River runs southward to the Colorado, which empties into the Gulf of California. The Spaniards, long ago, named it the "Rio Verde." The Crow Indians call it "Prairie Chicken River," from the quantities of grouse to be found on its upper branches.

Saturday, June 29.   Mr. Rose was now taken sick with mountain fever. Mr. Frink was still confined to his bed. The outlook for the future became, for a time, quite dark and discouraging. But at this critical moment Mr. Thomas Wand, whom we had met on the Sweetwater, volunteered to take charge of our horses and to pasture and guard them for us. This was a great relief, for which I felt very thankful. But we had no way of showing our gratitude except by sending to him a present of a few delicacies from our stock on hand. This was the darkest period of our whole journey, and the assistance he gave us was highly appreciated.

Sunday, June 30.   This is our third day in this dismal camp on the west bank of Green River. But Mr. Frink and Mr. Rose are both improving, and matters look more hopeful. There were frost and ice in camp last night, though to-day, at ten o'clock, the thermometer shows eighty degrees in the shade.

Monday, July I. Mr. Wand and his company have left their wagons here and made pack-saddles, intending to pack their clothing, blankets, provisions, and cooking utensils on their animals, in order to travel faster. They stopped here two days for that purpose, and are now ready to start. Mr. Johnson, of Morgan County, Indiana, had been with Mr. Wand's party up to this time, but preferring not to pack through, made arrangements with Mr. Frink to travel with us. His horse, a good animal, was harnessed to our wagon and proved quite useful.

This morning some packers overtook us and brought the alarming tidings that cholera had appeared on the Platte River, behind us. This was the first that we had heard of its being on the road.

Mr. Frink and Mr. Rose are much improved. At twelve o'clock we started and traveled twelve miles. We hope in a few days to reach Bear River, where grass is said to be abundant.

Tuesday, June 2. Our sick people are still improving. We traveled to-day twenty miles over hills and valleys, and encamped alone by a mountain brook.

Wednesday, June 3. This morning Mr. Rose was not quite so well. In the afternoon he grew much worse, having a severe attack of mountain fever. At two o'clock a company from Illinois overtook us. I rode on horseback most of the day. We traveled thirteen miles and encamped on Ham's Fork, which runs southward into Green River. This is a beautiful stream of clear water, in a narrow, grassy valley.

Thursday, July 4. At six o'clock we started and after going a short distance down the stream, turned to the right and climbed up a long, narrow spur, to the top of a high mountain. We continued to ascend one after another, until we had reached a great height. This was the Bear River Range of the Rock Mountains. On the summit the road wound through a dense grove of tall young aspens and pines. We were delighted to be among trees once more, but they were soon passed by. This ridge is eight thousand two hundred thirty feet high, being seven hundred forty feet higher than the South Pass.

From this high point the road ran rapidly down, through a long, dusty, rocky ravine, or cañon, to a small valley within three miles of Bear River, where we encamped for the night, after a very hard day's drive. Mr. Rose was very sick all day. At one time his condition was alarming, but about sunset, to our great relief, there was a change for the better.

Notwithstanding our anxiety and fatigue, our dinner, in honor of the national anniversary, was the best we could provide. The last of our potatoes, which had long been saved for the occasion, made it a rare feast.

Since crossing the high ridge, we had descended, in less than half a day, one thousand eight hundred thirty feet, the elevation of this Fourth-of-July camp being six thousand four hundred feet.

Friday, July 5.   We started at six o'clock and traveled northward, down the valley of Bear River—the mountains on our right, the river on our left. About three miles from the camp, we came to a rapid stream called Smith's Fork, issuing from the high mountains on our right, and divided into four separate creeks that ran across our road to the river. The second one being very narrow and deep, with perpendicular banks, had been bridged in a novel manner. A log had been split in the center and laid across with the flat sides up, at the proper distance to fit the wagon wheels; so that, by using a little care, the wagons could be safely crossed.

From here we drove on to the bank of Bear River, some distance to the left, and took our noon lunch. Then we traveled on to Thomas Fork, which is a fine stream, coming from the northeast, where we encamped for the night. Here we found good grass. Mr. Rose was some better during the day. The thermometer at noon showed eighty degrees.

Saturday, July 6.   We started at six o'clock, forded Thomas Fork, and, turning to the west, came to a high, steep spur that extends to the river. Over this high spur we were compelled to climb. The distance is seven miles, and we were five hours in crossing. Part of the way I rode on horseback, the rest I walked. The descent was very long and steep. All the wheels of the wagon were tied fast, and it slid along the ground. At one place the men held it back with ropes and let it down slowly.

After coming to the valley, we drove to the river and rested some time for dinner. In the afternoon we went seven miles further, down the valley, and encamped at sundown on a beautiful stream lined with shrubs, running from the mountains to the river. Here we intend to stay over Sunday.

Sunday, July 7.   We are remaining in camp to-day, resting from the severe labors and anxieties of the past week, as far as the pressing duties of camp life on the plains permit us to do so.

Monday, July 8.   It rained considerably during the night. Mr. Frink was on guard until two o'clock, when he returned to camp bringing the startling news that, from some unknown cause, the horses had stampeded. We had no means of knowing whether it was the work of Indians or not, but it was useless to hunt for them in the darkness, Mr. Frink lay down and slept till daylight. Then a search was commenced, which resulted in the animals being soon found, not for from camp, very much to our relief.

When we arose, we found the range of mountains covered with new-fallen snow. This is a beautiful valley, and when under settlement and cultivation, will be a delightful region. Wild flax is growing in many places, as thickly as if sowed by the hand of man.

At half past ten we passed a village of Snake River Indians. Soon after, we crossed six beautiful mountain streams. Mr. Rose was much improved to-day, and able to drive the small wagon part of the time.

I visited a lady to-day at a train which had halted not far from ours—an unusual incident on this journey. We traveled ten miles and encamped on the bank of the river.

Tuesday, July 9.   At half past five we set out, and in two hours and a half reached the far-famed Soda Springs and Steamboat Spring, at the big bend of Bear River. At this point the stream—along which for five days we have been traveling northward—suddenly bends to the left around a high, steep mountain, and, reversing its course, runs directly southward for one hundred twenty-five miles, to lose itself in the Great Salt Lake.

The Soda Springs are on the right of the road and boil up from the ground in many places, forming mounds of earth with a little cup or hollow on the top. Some of the mounds are several feet in height, the water bubbling over the top on all sides. By some they are called Beer Springs, from their peculiar taste.

About a mile further on is the Steamboat Spring, on the left of the road near the river. It derives its name from the ebullition of the water at regular intervals of about thirty seconds, which produces a sound similar to that of a steamboat. About three feet from the spring is a constant discharge of steam through a small crevice in the rock.

This region abounds in rare curiosities. I have never visited a place where there was so much of an interesting character to be seen. The whole country seems to have been curiously formed. I left this spot very reluctantly. Everything I saw was full of interest. But a party of Michigan men, who were at this time traveling with us, claimed that they could neither see nor feel an interest in anything this side of the gold of California.

There was an Indian village here of considerable size. The Indians seemed to be well-disposed. Our boy, Robert Parker, made a trade with them, exchanging his worn shoes for a pair of new moccasins.

The emigration was very thin on this part of the route, the heaviest portion of it having gone by way of the Salt Lake road, that turned off a few miles east of the Little Sandy.

Driving on a mile from the Steamboat Spring, we came to the forks of the road, the left-hand one, called Myer's Cut-off, going westerly over the plains and hills to Raft River, the right-hand one taking a northwest direction, and crossing the northern rim of the Great Salt Lake Basin, to Fort Hall, on the Snake River, or Lewis Fork of the Columbia.

We have now traveled sixteen hundred twenty-two miles from home. The elevation of this place is five thousand eight hundred forty feet, indicating that we have descended only one hundred sixty feet in our journey of seventy miles down the Bear River Valley.

CHAPTER VI.

Tuesday, July 9, Continued.   When we came to the forks of the road, we decided to take the right-hand one, leading to Fort Hall, because of the advice and illustration given us by an old Indian at the Soda Springs. He raised up the bail of a bucket to signify a high mountain, and passing his hand over the top, said, "This is Myer's Cut-off." Then, laying the bail down and passing his hand around it, said, "This is the Fort Hall road." We were told afterwards that this was correct.

The whole plain, fifteen miles wide, west and northwest of the forks, seemed to have once been the mouth or interior of an immense volcanic crater. It was a level floor of hardened lava, seamed with chasms of great depth.

We soon came to a soda pool, on top of a mound five feet high. We drove by the side of it and I dipped a cupful without leaving my seat in the wagon. Its taste was that of ordinary soda water. I learned afterwards from those who had used it that it made very light biscuit. We had no chance to give it a trial in this way.

In the afternoon we traveled twelve miles, passing many curious objects and crossing one small stream. During the night it rained.

Wednesday, July 10.   Five of our horses were missing this morning, but after a short search they were found and brought into camp. After breakfast, we traveled northward for ten miles, crossing to the west side of a stream of water, where we halted for dinner. While there, a party of Snake Indians came into the camp, begging flour, coffee, and bread, of each of which we gave them a little.

About half past twelve we started to ascend the mountain chain which separates the Great Salt Lake basin from the valley of the Columbia. The road was very rough, but we had crossed the main ridge by four o'clock, and soon after came to a small spring branch flowing northward into Snake River, where we made our encampment for the night, in view of banks of snow from five to ten feet deep.

This is the road that was followed by Peter Lassen, one of the earliest pioneers of California, long before the gold was discovered. It is now the main road followed by emigrants to Oregon.

Thursday, July 11.   The road to-day was very hilly and rough. At night we encamped within one mile of Fort Hall. Mosquitoes were as thick as flakes in a snow-storm. The poor horses whinnied all night, from their bites, and in the morning the blood was streaming down their sides. At our noon camp we found a thicket of wild currant bushes, from which we gathered currants enough to furnish pies for the next two or three days. They were a great luxury to people who had been without fruit of any kind for three months.

In the afternoon we came to a creek that appeared to be deep and bad to cross. Just as we were beginning to examine for a safe place to ford it, three Indians on horseback came toward us. They rode across the creek before us, apparently to show us the best way. We crossed without difficulty, and they afterwards accompanied us to where we encamped for the night. One of them, much older than the others, informed us that he had traveled as far east as St. Louis; and in order to make us understand, he imitated with his mouth the puffing of a steamboat. He rode onwards after we had reached camp; but the other two turned their horses loose, and stayed near us all night. They told us that this was the Indian's country.

Friday, July 12.   We left our camp at half past five in the morning, and at seven o'clock reached a former trading-post of the Hudson's Bay Company, established many years ago, when the English people made claim to all this part of our territory. It was in charge of Captain Grant, a Canadian, who had been here for nine years, and had entertained Colonel Fremont and his party, in September, 1843, while on their way to the mouth of the Columbia River.

We stopped here for a short time, and were hospitably received by Captain Grant, who treated us in a very gentlemanly manner, and formally introduced us to his wife, an Indian woman, of middle age, quite good-looking, and dressed in true American syle.

Before we left, he very kindly presented us with a supply of fresh lettuce and onions, expressing regret that because of the lateness of the season, he had no other varieties to offer us. We thankfully accepted them as a very unusual luxury.

We did not visit the United States Government post, Fort Hall, as it was a mile off the road, though it was in full view on our right as we passed along.

We have now reached the most northerly point of our wearisome journey. The latitude of Fort Hall is forty-three degrees one minute and thirty seconds north, according to Colonel Fremont's calculation. This is three and a half degrees north of Martinsville. The altitude of Fort Hall is four thousand five hundred feet.

We are now to turn to the left at a right angle, and travel the rest of the way in a nearly southwest direction, until we reach Sutter's Fort, which is still seven hundred miles distant; and from all accounts, the worst part of the road is yet to be passed over.

During our halt at the fort, our company had gone on; so we set forward alone. In two miles we came to a stream, which, though deep, we crossed without much trouble. But three miles beyond, a considerable stream running to our right was found to be much deeper. Here, in crossing, we got our things wet, for the first time on the journey. We could not ford in the usual way, but had to draw the wagons across by ropes stretched to the other bank. The next slough was also deep, but we got over safe.

After traveling about ten miles further, we came to Snake River, which here runs in a southwest direction, and encamped for the night on the southeast bank.

Saturday, July 13.   We started at five o'clock this morning, and soon came to the American Falls of Snake River. This stream, which is nine hundred feet wide, is inclosed between high walls of black, volcanic rock, and has a perpendicular fall of fifty feet. Beyond it is a wide plain of black lava, so broken and split with deep chasms that it can hardly be crossed by a man on foot. Fifty miles distant, northwest, the "Three Buttes" rise high and bold out of the lava-plain, and can be seen for a long distance. Our first view of them was from the high ridge south of Fort Hall.

We halted for dinner in sight of the falls, and were visited by a party of five Crow Indians, who brought some fine fish into camp, for which we traded. Soon after dinner, we came to a beautiful creek—a long succession of dashing falls. The rock over which it ran had something of the appearance of the soda formations near the Steamboat Spring.

We traveled all the afternoon down Snake River, and encamped at night on Beaver Creek, which comes from the south.

Sunday, July 14.   If we could have had our own way, this would have been a day of rest in reality, as well as in name; but such it was not to be. Not only the customary duties of camp life, but the weekly laundry, had to be attended to, although the day was excessively warm, the mercury marking one hundred and twenty degrees inside our wagon. The dryness of the air, and the high altitude, made the heat more endurable than it would have been in a moist climate, at a low elevation.

Monday, July 15.   We left Beaver Creek at six o'clock, still traveling down Snake River, and in eight miles came to Raft River, a small stream that flowed from mountains on our left. Here the roads fork again, the right-hand one turning off northwesterly towards Oregon, while we took the left-hand one, going south-westerly towards California, leaving Snake River, and traveling up Raft River. We crossed it three times during the day, and at dark drove into camp on a branch of this stream, not far from the junction of the Myer's Cut-off, which we had passed near the Steamboat Spring. We are now coming again into a hilly country.

Tuesday, July 16.   It was half past five when we left our camp. The company we were with drove too fast for us to-day, and when we halted at noon, we found ourselves alone. But Mr. Cole and his party came up with us just as we were starting after dinner, traveled with us during the afternoon, and when we stopped at a beautiful nook in the mountains for our night camp, they remained in our company until morning.

Wednesday, July 17.   This morning we started early, at half past five o'clock, and nearly all day traveled over rough roads. During the forenoon we passed through a stone village composed of huge, iso-lated rocks of various and singular shapes, some resembling cottages, others steeples and domes. It is called the "City of Rocks," but I think the name "Pyramid City" more suitable. It is a sublime, strange, and wonderful scene—one of nature's most interesting works. The Salt Lake road, which turned off between Dry Sandy and Little Sandy, and which we passed on the twenty-sixth day of June, rejoins our road at this point.

The altitude of Pyramid City is five thousand nine hundred sev-enty-five feet, being the highest point between the top of the Bear River Range and where the emigrant road crosses the Sierra Nevada.

Eight miles from Pyramid City we recrossed, going southwest, the forty-second parallel of latitude, which we had crossed, going north, on the eighth day of June, near Fort Laramie.

At noon we halted for lunch in company with Mr. Cole's party. But they were quite anxious to travel on and started out before us. During the afternoon the road was very rough—a continual succession of mountains. We only traveled seven miles. The Goose Creek Indians are said to be warlike and troublesome, but we have not found them so up to this time. Our horses, however, are closely guarded every night. We reached the little valley of Goose Creek this afternoon, and encamped near the bank of the stream about sunset, in company with some ox teams.

Thursday, July 18.   We traveled up Goose Creek in a southwesterly direction all day. We fell in company with a train that had come by way of the Salt Lake road, and encamped with them at night. This was a cloudy day, with slight indications of rain.

Friday, July 19.   We started at half past six in the morning, and continued to travel up Goose Creek. The road was very rough. The face of the country presents volcanic appearances. At the last crossing of Goose Creek we broke our small wagon, which detained us an hour and a half. It was fourteen miles from this place to the next water. We reached it at five o'clock, at the entrance to Thousand Spring Valley. The spring was a beautiful one, flowing out from beneath a large rock. Four miles beyond this rock we encamped for the night. Here we traded some gun-powder for an antelope ham, with some friendly Indians of the Snake tribe. To-day, like yesterday, has been cloudy, with some sprinkling of rain.

The Thousand Spring Valley, which we have just come into, takes its name from the great number of springs, both hot and cold, to be found in it. If all the tales we hear about it are true, it is an interesting place. At the farther end we expect to reach the head of the Humboldt River, which we have been told extends nearly to the California mountains.

When we encamped in the evening, there being no grass near, the horses were taken some distance to the mountains, where good feed had been found.

Saturday, July 20.   It was seven o'clock when we started this morning. We traveled down the Thousand Spring Valley for twenty miles. A party of Indians encamped with us at noon, but gave no signs of being unfriendly. The ox teams that stayed with us last night, came up and camped with us again. It is seldom that we are without company on this part of the journey.

Sunday, July 21.   This morning we started at eight o'clock, and soon came to springs that were boiling hot. Only five feet from them was another as cold as ice. Here were men engaged in washing their clothing. Their position was such that, after washing a garment in the boiling springs, they could take it by the waistband and fling it across into the cold spring, and vice versa, with perfect ease. There were said to be creeks of running water too hot to bathe in, but we did not have leisure to visit them.

We continued to travel down the valley, in a southwest direction, until three o'clock, when we stopped for the night—this time by ourselves—near the western end of the valley.

Monday, July 22.   We started over a ridge, or bluff, at half past six o'clock, still traveling in a southwesterly direction. During the day we reached Cañon Creek, one of the small tributaries of the Humboldt, and encamped on the bottom, where we found abundant grass.

Tuesday, July 23.   This day brought us to the far-famed Humboldt River. We had left camp at five o'clock, and after traveling five hours, came to the stream which many said reached nearly to California. Others said that it ran into the ground at the edge of a great desert which the emigrants had to cross; and after that, they would have to cross the highest mountains on the route, covered with snow and ice. Rumors of all kinds passed up and down the line, for very few knew anything about the country ahead of us.

Near this place we met a party of men with pack-mules returning to the Atlantic states. It was a rare thing to see any one going that way. The emigrants were anxious for information. They asked hundreds of questions of the packers. Had they stopped to answer, they would have been kept all summer. They kept their mules going at a rapid gait, and shouted back their answers as long as they could be heard.

At noon we stopped for lunch on the bank of the river, but had to swim the horses across to find pasturage. In the afternoon we traveled ten miles and encamped again on the river, in company with a Missouri train.

We have now traveled eighteen hundred thirty-five miles. The altitude here is five thousand six hundred twenty-eight feet.

CHAPTER VII.

Wednesday, July 24.   At six o'clock we started and crossed over some bluffs. We stopped for dinner near Dr. Miller's company. The river passed through a canon near by. This upper portion of the Humboldt Valley produced fine grass in great quantity. The great herds of the emigration have already consumed a large portion of it. The water is bright and clear, cool and refreshing. At night we encamped with a party from Cincinnati, some of them being of McFarland's company.

Thursday, July 25.   This morning we were on the road by six o'clock, and soon fell in company with Mrs. Foshee. We saw our friend Miss Cole to-day. Near the crossing of the Humboldt we stopped for the night. The river was too high and we could not cross. In the early part of the day we had taken what is called the "Greenhorn Cut-off," which required fifteen miles' travel to gain six miles on our journey. What is called a "cut-off" is a shorter road across a bend. A "greenhorn cut-off" is a road which a stranger or new traveler takes believing it to be shorter, but which turns out to be longer than the regular road. There were many such on the plains.

Mr. Cole's party caught up with us as we were all starting out of camp at half past four the next morning.

Friday, July 26.   After traveling about five miles this morning, we came to the mountains. We had a long drive over them. I walked seven miles during the morning. Mr. Clarke's company and Mr. Cole's was fifteen miles, all the way without water.

Saturday, July 27.   Traveled down the river four miles, then came to the mountains, the roughest road we have gone over thus far—a seventeen-mile stretch without water.

Mrs. Foshee rode with us to-day until noon, and took dinner with us, their team not coming up. Our boy Robert took up a horse near the road, it having the appearance of being lost, and by so doing got separated from us. During the afternoon we became quite anxious about him, but reconciled ourselves with the thought that we should find him at the river. But when we reached the river, Robert was not there, and it was getting late. Every one, being tired, wished to get to where we could camp. I was almost frantic for fear the Indians had caught him, and to increase my agony, a company of packers came along, just starting out to travel all night, who informed us that there were some five hundred Indians encamped very near us. I suffered the agony almost of death in a few minutes. I besought them to turn back and help us look for our lost boy, but they had not time, and were, besides, on short rations. But Aaron Rose had unhitched the best horse, and started back over the hills. Never can I forget those minutes. The thought of leaving the boy, never to hear of him again! But just at dark, Aaron came in sight, having the lost boy with him. My joy turned into tears. It was some time after dark before we got into our camp for the night.

Sunday, July 28. We started at seven o'clock, traveled fourteen miles, and stopped for the day. After that we were engaged with our usual Sunday duties, from which there was no escape.

Monday, July 29. We are traveling in a southwest direction. The river makes a great bend to the northwest. Sometimes our road runs near it, but often at a distance across the bends.

Tuesday, July 3o. To-day we traveled twenty-five miles. This is a long day's drive, as our animals seldom go out of a walk. If they were urged faster, they would soon fall exhausted. This is the condition of all the stock on the road.

Wednesday, July 31. We started at six o'clock, and soon came up with Mr. Clarke's company. The valley is from ten to twenty miles wide here, much of it rough and covered with sage-brush. The river bottoms are narrow, but we are told they widen towards the "sink." A few cottonwoods and low willows grow along the stream. There is no other timber.

Thursday, August 1. We crossed the slough as soon as we started. Then we had a very bad hill to climb, though it was short. William Johnson went hunting. We came to the river, but could not cross it. Took to the bluffs. Found the road good with the exception of two very rough places. Started again at three o'clock, but did not proceed far before our small wagon broke down, and we had to stop. Mr. Cole's party stopped with us, and we rigged a cart out of the wagon. Mr. Clarke's wagon being ahead, they did not hear of our accident. We encamped in the neighborhood of several boiling springs.

Friday, August 2.   We were ready to start at six o'clock. We are now traveling on the south side of the Humboldt River, with only Mr. Cole's party in company. We encamped on a salt plain not far from the river. We found a well near by, but it proved to be salty.

The Arkansas train camped near us. We traded pickles and acid with them for tea and sugar.

Saturday, August 3.   After a twenty-five-mile drive, we encamped at evening on the bank of the river. Feed is becoming scarcer than ever. Whenever we come to grass that can be mowed, Mr. Frink has the men cut a good supply of it with the scythe, and it is then hauled in the wagon for future use. In this hot, dry air, it cures very quickly, adding but little weight to the load.

Away from the river, the soil is hard and dry, void of any vegetation except sage-brush, which is worthless for any purpose but fuel. When it is dry, it makes a hot fire, from the oil it contains, but burns out very soon. Much of the level land of this valley is barren, from the salt and alkali in it.

Sunday, August 4.   This day we remained in camp to recuperate ourselves and animals. Constant travel over rough roads, through suffocating dust, makes a rest welcome whenever we can take it. Mr. Cole, having a broken wagon to mend, must repair it to-day or lose to-morrow.

Monday, August 5.   We started at six o'clock, following a rough, hard road over bluffs. The way along the river is often shut off by the cliffs, forcing us over low, rocky spurs. The heat is sometimes oppressive. The dust is intolerable. Many wear silk handkerchiefs over their faces; others wear goggles. It is a strange-looking army.

Tuesday, August 6.   We found the grass at this place very good, but we could not remain longer. Just as we were starting out, our friends the Carson boys and their party drove up. Their animals had been suffering from want of feed, and were losing strength every day.

Their provisions were also running short, and it was yet three hundred and fifty miles to Sutter's Fort, over bad roads. The long, hard journey was not the pleasure trip they had looked for. Some of the company were contrary, and all of them had become, like hundreds of others, much disheartened at the discouraging prospect ahead of them. But we endeavored to put the matter in the best light we could, and rendered them such little assistance as was in our power. We were able, among other things, to contribute from our reduced stock a supply of those two great luxuries on the plains, acid and sugar, which they fully appreciated. And, having found here plenty of good feed for their stock, and seeing that there was no immediate danger of starvation, the spirits of the party were in great degree restored. So we drove off and left them in camp, promising to let them know of our whereabouts in case we got through first.

It was a hard road we traveled to-day, fifteen miles without water. We broke a new road across a dried-up lake, having an incrustation like ice. It was either borax or soda or salt, probably some of each. Then we came to the river and went into our night camp.

Wednesday, August 7. Starting at seven o'clock, we drove over a spur of the rocky hills, a difficult road. We finally came to the south bank of the river, which here had a westerly course. There was neither bridge nor ferry, and the water was too deep to ford. Some people had made a boat of a large wagon bed, which they had turned bottom upward in the river, with an empty keg lashed under each corner to keep it afloat. A long rope was tied to each end and men on opposite banks pulled it back and forth. When they had finished their crossing, they permitted us to use the boat. We piled our provisions, bedding, cooking utensils, hay, and all other stuff, upon it, and after many trips got everything safely over. When I crossed, I sat with my feet in the wash-tub to keep them dry. The horses swam over, and the empty wagons were pulled through the water by means of long ropes attached to the tongues.

A few days before this Mr. Johnson swam over the river, carrying with him the end of a long rope. At the other end was tied a mowing scythe, which he dragged across after landing. Having cut all the grass we needed, he tied it in bundles, which were hauled over to our side. The scythe was returned in the same way, and then Mr. Johnson swam safely back.

After getting everything landed on the north side, we harnessed up, loaded our wagons again, and traveled four or five miles down the river in search of grass. Finding none, we fed our animals from the hay that had been hauled in the wagon.

Thursday, August 8.   Our horses had nothing to eat this morning. A boat was rigged, by means of which Mr. Johnson crossed the river and cut hay, which was ferried over the river to feed with. By two o'clock we were ready to start again. Some Hungarians passed us to-day who had eaten nothing for two days. I encouraged them all I could, but the situation looked gloomy to every one of us. There was nothing but sand-hills as far as we could see, without a spear of herbage. We traveled on again for ten miles and about sundown came to the river, where we met the Carson boys crossing from the south side to the north side of the stream. We did not stop but traveled along ten miles further, and at ten o'clock at night came to the first water. Around us was a terrible scene; the earth was strewn with dead horses and cattle.

Those whose duty it was to stand guard last night, went to sleep through excessive fatigue, and the horses got to the wagon containing our provisions, and ate all the beans and dried fruit. The animals had had nothing to eat except a short allowance of the hay we had hauled with us.

Friday, August 9.   We started at six o'clock and traveled eight miles, to a place where we watered for the last time, there being no water after that for twelve miles. At the end of that distance, we came to a spring in a deep ravine, where we found many of our former traveling companions. It was a pleasant meeting in that desert place. We exchanged congratulations and experiences, each narrating the hardships they had met. Then, for a time, we traveled on together.

One of the Carson's mules gave out to-day. Mr. Frink let them have one of our horses in its place. During the day we passed many dead animals. Just as the sun was going down, we came to a wide tract of marsh land covered with coarse swamp grass, and called the "big meadows" or "Humboldt meadows." Finding no good place for our animals, Mr. Frink bought some hay tied up in small bundles, for which he paid twenty cents each.

Saturday, August 10.   The horses were taken across a slough for grass. Here we found many more of our old road acquaintances, whom we were glad to meet. Hearing of better grass ahead, we went on for four or five miles. All the way, both sides of the road were thickly settled with campers. They are resting and feeding their stock, lightening their wagons, cutting grass and making hay, and preparing the best they can for crossing the Humboldt Desert—the worst on all the route—now only two or three days' travel ahead.

We encamped near the edge of the marsh, between Bennett's and Hall's passenger trains. It was Mr. Frink's plan to remain here until enough of the coarse grass had been cut and cured into hay to feed our horses across the desert. On the other side, in Carson Valley, we hope to find good grass again.

The reports which came from the desert of the loss of horses, mules, and oxen were very distressing and caused much uneasiness. We did not know but that our own animals might meet the same fate.

The river is the only water to be had, as there are no brooks, springs, or wells in the valley except at the head, where we first came to it. But we had not traveled fifty miles down the stream before we found the water gradually becoming brackish and discolored from the salt and alkali in the soil. The farther we traveled the worse it became. During the last eight or ten days it seems to have been mixed up with everything nauseous, but we do not expect anything better until we get to the Carson River, about seventy-five miles distant, on the other side of the Great Desert.

Sunday, August 11.   Mr. Clarke's company came up and camped beside us. Also part of the Mount Morris company, whom we met on Bear River—William Bryant, Mr. Sharp, the two Coffman brothers, and our lady friend, Mrs. Foshee. The Indians had stolen all their horses except two nice ponies. The whole party were now in sad plight, on short rations, with only two horses, and a lady in the company, whom the young men felt it to be their bounden duty to see safely in California. The young men were willing to walk and carry their own provisions if they could find some one who would take Mrs. Foshee to Sacramento, and accept the two horses for pay. For herself, she had no fear, for she felt sure that God would provide her some way to get there safely, for he had already, in a miraculous manner, saved their company from starvation.

We had met them several days previously, near the Humboldt River, and I had gone to their camp, where I found them entirely out of provisions. They had just eaten the last food they had. But Mrs. Foshee was not dismayed, and was pleading with the young men not to despair, to still put their trust in God, for she was sure they would be provided for. And so it actually turned out. They had not traveled far that afternoon when one of the young men came across a young cow tied to some willow bushes, with a card fastened to her horns, on which was written the statement that nothing was the matter with the cow, that she was only footsore and not able to travel fast, and that any one in want of provisions would be at liberty to kill her for food. This being their desperate case, they stopped, killed the animal, cut the meat into small strips to dry, and traveled on with lightened hearts.

The next day they found a sack of flour with a card attached, on which was written permission to anyone in need of food to appropriate it to his own use. As this applied to their own party, they gladly took it with them. Mrs. Foshee's prediction was fulfilled to the letter.

And now here they were at our camp to-day, the young men offering their two horses to any one who would furnish to Mrs. Foshee a safe passage to California.

While we were all talking the matter over, there came into camp the Rev. Mr. Morrow, a Methodist clergyman, to give us notice that he would preach in a tent near by at two o'clock. We had had some previous acquaintance with him, and I suggested to him that here was an opportunity to put in practise the teachings of Jesus Christ, by giving up to Mrs. Foshee his comfortable seat in the passenger carriage he was traveling in. A train to carry passengers across the plains had been fitted out in St. Louis by McPike and Strother, and Mr. Morrow was with them. The situation was fully explained to him. The four young men, all that remained of the Mount Morris company, with whom Mrs. Foshee had set out from home, now offered to the minister to give him their only two remaining horses, by which he could reach California sooner than by the slow passenger train, if he would give his seat in the carriage to Mrs. Foshee. He could take with him either his own supply of provisions, or her share of the dried beef and flour which the young men had found, and she would accept in return what provision he had on hand.

After discussing and considering the matter a little further, Mr. Morrow consented. The exchange was made. And the next morning we all said good-by to Mrs. Foshee, as she sat in her carriage, smiling and happy, ready to continue her journey. At the same time the Rev. Mr. Morrow, riding one of the two horses and leading the other, packed with his clothing, blanket, and provisions, passed out of sight and we saw him no more.

And so the four young men who had given up their ponies, were left to travel the rest of the journey on foot, each with his bundle of flour and dried meat, which had so fortunately been found a few days previously. They were happy to be relieved of their responsibility for the safety and welfare of Mrs. Foshee. They had to leave behind them, when they started out, a complete outfit of new clothing, blankets, and comforts, with all the little articles which their mothers, sisters, and sweethearts had, with so much care, fitted up for them, as, without their horses, they could carry but little save the bare necessities of life. Mr. Bryant, however, carried his pick, with which to dig gold when he got to California.

Monday, August 12.   It being Mr. Frink's intention to make enough hay here to last us across the desert, the men have been at work most of the day mowing grass in the wet meadow and spreading it out on the hot sand to dry.

Many people are passing to-day begging for food. The Carson company came up, but only stopped a short time, being anxious to push forward. Mrs. Cook, a traveling acquaintance, reached here in the afternoon. Among the crowds on foot, a negro woman came tramping along through the heat and dust, carrying a cast-iron bake oven on her head, with her provisions and blanket piled on top—all she possessed in the world—bravely pushing on for California.

Tuesday, August 13.   The grass that was cut the day before cured rapidly in the hot sun and dry air. In the afternoon it was tied up in small bundles and piled on the wagon. There was a large load of it. We spent the day in making everything ready for the start toward the desert the next morning. The rumors that came back from there were very distressing—animals dying without number, and people suffering from prolonged thirst.

Wednesday, August 14.   This was a pleasant morning, and we got an early start. We had gone but a few miles when we came to a man who was just unhitching his two-horse wagon to abandon it, his horses being unable to haul it any further. Mr. Frink gave him $5.00 for it, and left our cart by the roadside, for any one who might want it. We could carry more hay in the wagon, and it was large enough for some of the men to sleep in at night. It lasted us all the way through to Sacramento, where Mr. Frink was offered $40.00 for it and sold it.

After this the road turned nearly south, and brought us opposite to the end or point of the mountains on our left, on the east side of the river. A broad, sandy desert opened and extended beyond them to the east and also to the south, farther than we could see. On the west, forty miles away, we could distinguish the long-looked-for California mountains, the Sierra Nevada, lying in a northwest and southeast direction. They were dark with heavy pine forests. On the plain was neither tree, shrub, nor blade of grass.

In a few miles we came to where the river, along which we have been traveling for the last three weeks, spreads out on the level plain, and forms a broad, shallow lake. This lake is called the "sink of the Humboldt." One-half of it sinks into the sand, the other half rises into the sky. This is the end of the most miserable river on the face of the earth. The water of the lake, as well as that of the river for the last one hundred miles above, is strong with salt and alkali, and has the color and taste of dirty soap-suds. It is unfit for the use of either animals or human beings; but thousands of both have had to drink it to save life.

We stopped near the margin of the sink, fed our horses from the grass in the wagon, and took dinner. The elevation here is three thousand nine hundred twenty-nine feet, which is two thousand forty-six feet lower than "Pyramid City," and is the lowest altitude we have reached since leaving "Chimney Rock," one thousand two hundred fifty miles distant, on Platte River. The total distance we have traveled thus far is two thousand one hundred fifty-eight miles.

After lunch we set forward again, and about one o'clock passed a party of emigrants who were burying a man in the sand-hills, a most desolate place.

Intending to travel in the night as much as we could, we drove on until eleven o'clock. Here we came to the last slough, or bayou, that we had to cross, and remained for the night. The water was horrible. The next morning we were to launch out into the dreadful desert, forty miles wide, with neither grass nor water on the way, and our horses ready to drop from fatigue and hunger.

CHAPTER VIII.

Thursday, August 15. We made our final preparations and crossed the muddy slough by ten o'clock in the morning, expecting soon to enter the confines of the desert. I walked most of the way for the next six miles, to relieve the animals as much as possible. About one o'clock p.m. we stopped to rest and to feed the horses. At three o'clock we started again. A few miles further we came to the last of the sloughs or bayous, that connect the river with the sink. Here we filled our five-gallon water bottles, and other vessels, it being our last opportunity of doing so. The men waded into the middle of the slough to fill them, hoping the water there might be better than near the bank. We then drove onward until dark, when we stopped for a short time to refresh ourselves and our weary horses. As night came on, the air grew cool and invigorating, which was an advantage. Our next drive continued until midnight, when we halted again, fed and watered our animals, and took lunch. Then we slept until three o'clock in the morning.

Friday, August 16. It was long before sunrise when we left camp. Our plan was to travel by easy stages, stopping often to feed and rest our horses. The early morning was cool and pleasant. At six o'clock we halted and rested four hours.

We set forward again at ten o'clock and soon began to realize what might be before us. For many weeks we had been accustomed to see property abandoned and animals dead or dying. But those scenes were here doubled and trebled. Horses, mules, and oxen, suffering from heat, thirst, and starvation, staggered along until they fell and died on every rod of the way. Both sides of the road for miles were lined with dead animals and abandoned wagons. Around them were strewed yokes, chains, harness, guns, tools, bedding, clothing, cooking-utensils, and many other articles, in utter confusion. The owners had left everything, except what provisions they could carry on their backs, and hurried on to save themselves.

In many cases the animals were saved by unhitching them and driving them on to the river. After resting, they were taken back to the wagons, which in this way were brought out.

But no one stopped to gaze or to help. The living procession marched steadily onward, giving little heed to the destruction going on, in their own anxiety to reach a place of safety. In fact, the situation was so desperate that, in most cases, no one could help another. Each had all he could do to save himself and his animals.

As we advanced, the scenes became more dreadful. The heat of the day increased, and the road became heavy with deep sand. The dead animals seemed to become at every step of the way more numerous. They lay so thick on the ground that the carcasses, if placed together, would have reached across many miles of that desert. The stench arising was continuous and terrible.

The fault lay, in many cases, with the emigrants themselves. They acted injudiciously. Their fears caused them to drive too fast, in order to get over quickly. Their animals were too weak to be urged in this way. If the people generally had cut grass and made hay at the "big meadows" above the "sink," as Mr. Frink did, and hauled it with them into the desert, and brought a few gallons of water for each animal, traveling slowly and resting often, much of the stock and property that was lost could have been saved, and much distress and suffering avoided.

Towards noon we came to a carriage by the side of the road in which sat our friend Mrs. Foshee. The horses having become exhausted, had been unharnessed and led forward to the river. She was awaiting their return with her usual composure.

A few miles beyond we met a wagon drawn by strong, fresh horses, loaded with barrels of pure, sweet water for sale. It had been hauled from a newly discovered spring, four or five miles southeast of the road. Mr. Frink bought a gallon of it, for which he paid $1.00. After the nauseous stuff of the Humboldt "sink," this spring water was more than an ordinary luxury.

Traveling slowly onward, we came to a halt at one o'clock and rested several hours, sending Mr. Rose, during the meantime, to water the horses at the spring. When he returned, which was about four o'clock, we resumed our journey. Before night we came to the wagons of the Carson boys, standing idly by the road. They told us that they had taken their mules to the spring, and having given them water, were returning to the wagons. On the way back the mules, unwilling to leave the water, became stubborn, refused to travel, pulled away from the men, ran off into the desert, and never were seen again. Part of their company, when we came up, had already gone on to the Carson River to buy more animals to bring the wagons out.

It was eleven o'clock at night when we reached the river. We had been thirty-seven hours on that frightful desert. But we came through all well and without loss of animals or property. We were completely tired out, but having eaten nothing since four o'clock, we had to get supper before going to bed.

Saturday, August 17.   The Carson River comes close to the south edge of the desert. This stream was named after the famous hunter and explorer, Kit Carson, the guide of Fremont. Its source is one hundred and seventy miles southwest, among the snows and granite of the Sierra Nevada. Its water was clear, cool, and pure, free from salt or alkali, as different from the Humboldt soap-suds is from night.

We were informed that the Carson Valley was a beautiful region, abounding in rich pastures, and that our road would follow up the valley for one hundred miles or more, gradually approaching the California Mountains on our right to where the river issued from Carson Cañon. There it would enter the cañon to cross the mountains to Sutter's Fort, only one hundred miles further. Our hopes revived on hearing we were so near the end of our journey. We knew but little of what was ahead of us.

By the side of the river, where we came to it, was a collection of dirty tents and cloth shanties called "Rag-town." California traders had brought supplies here to sell to the emigrants. Beef was sold at twenty-five cents per pound, bacon $1.00, and flour $2.00 per pound. We bought some beefsteak for breakfast, our first fresh meat since trading with the Goose Creek Indians for antelope ham, on the 19th of July.

It was at this point that we reached, in our southward journeying, the latitude of our old home in Indiana, thirty-nine degrees and thirty minutes north. The altitude is the same as that of the "sink." But from here the road begins to ascend, at first with gentle inclination, but afterwards more rapidly till we reached the highest point on our journey, the crest of the Snow Mountains.

After breakfast we traveled six miles up the Carson River in search of feed for the animals. We were compelled to camp where the grass was very poor, but, fortunately, enough of the hay remained that had been cut at the Humboldt meadows, to feed the horses that night.

Sunday, August 18. We remained in camp near the river all day, resting after the severe toil of crossing the desert. The valley is about twenty miles wide. On the east side is a low range of hills. The California Mountains, on the west, are the grandest we have seen. The sides are covered with pine forests. Above them are the white snow beds. We expect to strike the foot of the mountains soon and follow it along to the Carson Cañon, the gateway through which the road runs to cross the Sierras.

We are disappointed not to find the rich pastures that we heard about. Thousands of animals have fed them off. Mr. Frink has had the men cut grass wherever we can find it, to take with us. But for this, our stock would often fare badly. Much of the slope between the mountains and the river is covered with sage-brush.

Monday, August 19. We started on our journey very much disheartened, our horses having had but little to eat and being in sad condition. Myself and Robert picked every spear of grass growing between the clumps of bushes, and tied it up in small bunches, to try to keep up the strength and courage of the animals. After traveling three miles we stopped to water the horses, the road here leaving the river, which ran through an impassable cañon. When we had traveled four or five miles beyond the cañon, we became convinced that there must be grass on the river, as we had not seen any wagon tracks leading that way. So Mr. Frink sent Aaron Rose and one of Mr. Cole's men to prospect, while we kept on at a snail's pace; for the animals were so weak they could hardly walk. We soon saw Aaron's signal, and driving out to the side of the road, we unhitched the horses and sent them to the river. To our great joy, the men had found a fine meadow untouched, there never having been an animal in it.

Mr. Frink and I remained with the large wagon by the roadside all day, the men having taken the small wagon with them to the meadow to fill it with grass. The men came up with a big load by sundown, at which time I had supper ready. It was a campful of happy people, to know that our half-starved animals had had so good a feed. At dark we were ready to start on a long night journey across another desert. There was a bright moon shining and we traveled steadily on. We did not find any water until we reached the river again, at three o'clock the next morning. I walked most of the way over the rough and dusty road.

Tuesday, August 20.   This morning we traveled up the Carson River bottom, about ten miles, and at noon dined alone. Usually we have plenty of company. The road runs nearly parallel with the mountains on our right, gradually getting nearer. The emigrants are a woe-begone, sorry-looking crowd. The men, with long hair and matted beards, in soiled and ragged clothes, covered with alkali dust, have a half-savage appearance. There are but few women; among these thousands of men, we have not seen more than ten or twelve.

The horses, cattle, and mules are getting gaunt, thin, and weak, almost ready to drop in their tracks, as hundreds of them have already done. The hoofs of many cattle wear out, so they can no longer travel, and are left to starve. The once clean, white wagon tops are soiled and tattered, and grimy with two thousand miles of gray dust. Many wagon beds have been cut off short to lighten them, or sawed in two to make carts. The spokes of the wagons left behind have been cut out to make pack-saddles. The rickety wheels are often braced up with sticks, the hubs wound with wet rags to keep the spokes in, the tires bound with wire, or wedged with chips of wood, to hold them from dropping off. They go creaking along the dusty roads, seeming ready to fall to pieces, drawn by weary beasts hardly able to travel, making up a beggardly-looking caravan, such as never was seen before. The great, splendid trains of fifteen, twenty, or thirty wagons have shrunk to three, four, or at most half a dozen, with three-fourths of their animals missing. Their former owners now trudge along on foot, packing on their backs the scant provisions left, with maybe a blanket, or leading skeleton horses that stagger under their light burdens. One of the "passenger trains" left most of its carriages by the side of the road, the passengers having to finish their journey on foot.

One only hope sustains all these unhappy pilgrims, that they will be able to get into California alive, where they can take a rest, and where the gold which they feel sure of finding will repay them for all their hardships and suffering.

Wednesday, August 21.   Our road to-day continued to follow southward up the Carson. Part of the way was very rough, over volcanic beds of lava. The low hills push down near the river, leaving only a narrow passage for the wagons. We have seen no Indians for several weeks. There are no signs of game, though some of the emigrants have killed sage-hens, and it is said there are deer in the mountains. The sage-hens resemble prairie-chickens, though considerably larger. We never tire of looking at the great mountains that we are soon to climb over. They are so close now that the thick forests hide from view the snow fields above them.

Thursday, August 22.   Our horse Mark mired down this morning and had to be dug out. This detained us for some time. We traveled eight miles in the forenoon, and then stopped to rest and feed the horses, as we have fifteen miles of desert road ahead. The roads have been very rough to-day. Mr. Frink had a short interview with some Californians who have come over to this side to prospect for gold. They are looking for a hidden lake in the mountains called "Gold Lake," where the gold is said to exist in great quantities.

The men cut plenty of grass to take with us, and we made everything ready to start early in the morning, to cross another of the many Carson deserts. But these are small as compared with the "Humboldt desert."

Friday, August 23.   At sunrise we were ready to start. After traveling several hours, we stopped in the middle of the desert for dinner.
Here we met several gold-hunters. Two of them had already found
gold. The largest piece was thought to weigh $4.00.

(I have been over this part of the road since 1850. The gold these
people had found is where "Gold Hill" is situated, near Virginia City,
Nevada.)

In four miles we came to the river. Four miles beyond that place
we encamped for the night by ourselves, our traveling companions,
Mr. Cole and his party, having gone on further. While we were at
supper, two men came up afoot, each leading a mule. After picketing
the animals, they sat down on the ground near us. They told us they
had no provisions left, but having had their dinner to-day, they felt
quite satisfied. They had started from Ohio with a good outfit, but
the Indians had stolen their animals, and they had to leave their wagons and nearly everything else. We happened to have two biscuits
left, and I handed one to each of them as I would to children. Our
stock of provisions was low and we were living on short rations; but
their condition was so much worse than our own that we resolved to
give them their breakfast in the morning.

Saturday, August 24.   We started at six o'clock and in four miles
came into what was called the "Carson meadows." During the
forenoon we crossed two beautiful streams running from the snow-
covered mountains now close at hand on our right. One of the gentlemen to whom we gave breakfast this morning, Mr. Russell,
applied to have Mr. Frink bring him through to California, offering
his mule for pay. As we were coming soon to where we could buy
meat and flour, Mr. Frink consented to take him. The other man,
having some money, went on by himself. We overtook Mr. Cole's
party, who had decided to remain in camp for a while. We now met
many gold-hunters, "prospectors," as they are called. The trading
posts became more frequent. Finding at one place some fresh beef
just brought over the mountains from California, we bought five
pounds, for which we paid $1.25.

Sunday, August 25.   For several days we have been traveling along
the foot of the Sierra Nevada, in a southerly direction. We drove ten

miles to-day, and encamped near a meadow, in order to cut grass to take with us going over the mountains. There is no time for rest, even on Sunday.

Monday, August 26.   We remained at our camp all the morning, waiting for our hay to dry in the hot sun, and tying it up in bundles ready for use on the mountains. This delayed us until three o'clock, when we started on our way. At a trading post we bought two pounds of rice for one dollar and a half. At night we had got within ten miles of the Carson Cañon, and encamped on a beautiful ice-cold rivulet that ran out of the mountains and across our road. There are hot rivulets, too, which burn the mouths of unsuspecting drinkers. The great forests of immense trees come down the steep side of the mountains to the edge of the road.

Tuesday, August 27.   We rose early this morning, fully prepared to expect a hard day's travel. After tugging over a heavy, sandy road for ten miles, we came, about eleven o'clock, to the mouth of the famous Carson Cañon, where the road turns abruptly to the right, to enter it. This is a great, rocky gorge opening into the granite mountain, out of which rushes the west branch of Carson River, foaming, dashing, and tumbling over the huge rocks that have fallen into it from the high cliffs. It was six miles through this cañon over these rocks. The road, if it can be called a road, lay along the river, once or twice crossing it. The river was nothing but a chain of wild cascades. The road was but a track over and among piles of huge rocks. The teams were sometimes taken off and the wagons pried up and raised by levers, to get them over impassable places.

At noon we stopped in the cañon and took our lunch. Here we met some emigrants, among whom was a lady who had lost or left her husband behind. Their horses had been stolen by the Indians, and he went after them, but never returned. The mother, with seven children, had been brought thus far by strangers, and upon them she depended to get through to California.

In the afternoon we resumed our scrambling over the rocks and boulders that constituted the road, and continued until sundown, when, to our great relief, we had gotten out of the granite jaws of the mountain and had come to an open, level, beautiful valley, sprinkled over with trees. This is known as Hope Valley, which we thought an appropriate name. We went a mile further and camped in sight of the snow-covered mountains now near at hand. The night was very cold. There was heavy frost in the morning, and ice was formed in the water bucket. In preparation for a still colder climate, we got out our winter clothing to wear.

We are now in the state of Califonia. The line dividing it from Utah territory runs across the Carson Cañon, which we came through this morning. But we have the high Sierras to cross before we get to where they are taking out the gold.

Hope Valley is two thousand three hundred eighteen miles from Martinsville.

CHAPTER IX.

Wednesday, August 28. It was seven o'clock before we started. About a mile before reaching the foot of the "one-mile mountain," we stopped for lunch. The horse Mark got mired down again in a marsh, and we had a good deal of trouble in getting him dug out. At three o'clock in the afternoon we started up the mountain with the small wagon. We first put on four horses, then six. After getting that up, we went back for the large wagon. Most of the load was packed on the horses' backs. But still we could not get the large wagon up the steep road. At last we tied the wagon securely on a large, flat, slippery rock, and left Aaron Rose and William Johnson to sleep in it. Then we packed all the baggage we could on five horses, and harnessed the remaining horses to the small wagon. As it was now dark, we lit the lantern. I led four of the horses. Robert Parker had one, with a camp kettle and some provisions.

I went ahead with the lantern. Mr. Frink drove the wagon. The going down the mountain appeared to be only step by step, over shelving rocks. I tried to keep in front of Mr. Frink, to guide the wagon after the lantern. In this way we finally got to camp, one mile down from the top of the mountain, at ten o'clock at night. Here the mountain was lighted up with many burning trees. We found that one of our horses had been left behind. Mr. Frink went back with the lantern and found him half a mile back. We had crackers and tea for supper, and went to bed between twelve and one o'clock in the morning.

Fortunately, we here met a Mr. Hutton, from Illinois, who loaned us a tent for the night,—a style of shelter we now slept in for the first time on our journey.

Thursday, August 29.   Mr. Frink got up by daylight to go back for the big wagon. He took Mr. Russell and Robert with him, leaving me by myself at the camp. When he reached the place, he rigged up some kind of a machine, and drew up the wagon by hand. They all returned to the camp by ten o'clock, by which time I had breakfast ready for them. Then they started off to hunt feed for the hungry horses, leaving me again at the camp.

Mr. Frink found good grass not very far away, and sent Mr. Russell back to camp for some bags, intending to fill them with grass for our horses on the next big mountain. When he was returning to where he had left Mr. Frink, he got lost, and in his wanderings came upon the body of a dead man with a whip in his hand; and he was so much frightened, he did not stop to examine him, or find out who he might be.

While I was in camp, there came along a man who had lost everything. He had one pint of corn meal left. He was without shoes, and his feet were tied up in rags. I made a dish of gruel, into which I put a little butter, with some other nourishing things. I encouraged him to keep up his spirits and try to go forward. By the time the men came in with the horses, I had dinner ready; and by half past four o'clock we were ready to be off. Just as we were about starting, the Carsons came along with some Cincinnati people and their wagon.

We all went on together about four miles to Red Lake, which lies in a valley between the two summits. After we had encamped, the man to whom I had given the gruel came again to the wagon, having nothing to eat and no other place of shelter. I went to a trading post near by, and begged some meat for him. We remained at Red Lake that night.

Friday, August 30.   It is five months this morning since we left home. We are now about to climb the main ridge of the snowy mountains, called the Sierra Nevada. From the base to the top the distance is five miles.

The snow is from ten to fifteen feet deep. We had been advised to start early in the morning, while the snow was frozen hard, before the sun would melt it. We had four horses harnessed to the big wagon, and two horses to the small wagon. The Carsons had two wagons, with four horses to each, having bought more horses at Ragtown, after losing their mules on the desert. Mr. Russell had his mules, but no wagon.

After traveling one mile from the edge of the lake, we came to the foot of the mountain. It was very steep and high, and looked impassable.

The road turned to the left and went up slanting, which was an advantage. But it was a hard struggle for the weak horses. Though the wagons were nearly empty, we had to stop often and let the animals rest.

After great toil, we had climbed by noon to the steepest part of the road, where it seemed impossible to go any further. Here the road turned directly south, and the sun at noon could shine right into it. The snow in the road was melted down to the ground, leaving the bare rocks to travel over. The snow walls on each side of this passage were twelve or fifteen feet high. From the foot of this steep place to the top was half or three-quarters of a mile.

We halted here and took our lunch, and fed to the tired horses the last of the hay that Mr. Frink had provided for them. So many teams were ahead of us, and climbing so slowly, that we could not start again till two o'clock. We first took everything we could out of the wagons, in order to lighten them, and packed them on Mr. Russell's mules. Then Mr. Frink unharnessed the two horses from the small wagon, and hitched them with the four horses on the large wagon. Then he tied long ropes to the tongue, and strung them out in front. Four or five men put these ropes over their shoulders and pulled with the horses. Others lifted at the wheels, and when the horses stopped, they held the wheels to keep the wagon from rolling back. Robert and I went ahead leading the pack mules. We found it all we could do to get up this steep place. We had to stop often and take breath. The air was getting lighter at every step, and the climbing was hard work.

At last Robert and I got to the top with the mules and their burdens.

I was utterly exhausted. I took a buffalo robe from the packs and wrapped myself in it, and lay down by the side of the road on top of the mountain and went to sleep. I told Robert to keep watch over me and the mules.

After a long time Mr. Frink with the men and the six horses got to the top with the large wagon. Then they unhitched the horses and took them down to the foot of the steep place, and brought up the small wagon. The Carsons doubled their teams the same way, and Mr. Frink helped them get their wagons to the top. By five o'clock, after nine or ten hours of hard toil, struggle, and scramble, we were all safe on top of the main ridge of the Sierra Nevada. Thanks that the worst is now over.

We were above where all vegetation grew. When I awoke from my nap, my voice was gone. When Mr. Frink reached the top, he was almost worn out. He was more fatigued than at any other time during the journey. We had to go a mile further to encamp. There was some bare ground on the south side, but between the rocks there was plenty of snow. I gathered some of the snow for use in cooking supper. The horses were taken down a cañon a short distance, where was found plenty of good bunch-grass.

It was not far from this place that Col. John C. Fremont and his party of explorers crossed, in February, 1844, six years and six months before we did. He gave the height where he crossed as nine thousand three hundred thirty-eight feet above the sea, which is nearly two thousand feet higher than the summit of the South Pass, which we had crossed on the twenty-fourth day of June, and eleven hundred eight feet higher than the Bear River Range, which we had crossed on the Fourth of July.

During the night I was seized with a severe chill, the result of over-fatigue, from which I was only relieved by having some rocks heated in the fire, which served to restore warmth. Thus passed our first day and night on the Sierra Nevada.

Saturday, August 31.   The men on guard with the horses had a frosty night of it, and came in early to breakfast. Some wild onions, or "leeks," had been found, which, at dinner, we enjoyed very much. These were the first vegetables we had tasted since receiving the lettuce and onions from Captain Grant at Fort Hall, seven weeks before.

This was another hard day. We had expected an easier road down the mountains after crossing the main ridge, but were disappointed. Our road to-day was very rough, up and down mountains all the way.

To make matters worse, our white horse gave out today, he having fallen and hurt himself while he were coming up the one-mile mountain. He was a favorite horse, and we gave fifty cents a pound for flour to mix in water for him to drink, thinking it would strengthen him; but we only managed to get him as far as Tragedy Springs, where we had to leave him for the night. It was two miles further before we could find a camping-place, and the next morning, when Mr. Frink sent Russell back for him, he found the faithful animal dead.

These springs were named from a tragical affair occuring in 1849, in which two men, intoxicated, got into a fight with each other, in which one of them was killed.

Sunday, September 1.   We are still in the midst of rough mountains. They are covered with heavy forests of pine and fir. Many of the trees are of great size and very tall. Much of the time we are traveling in the shade. We have got below the snow fields, but not beyond the frost at night. In the sunshine at midday it is very warm. The dust is as deep as it was on the hot plains, and there is no wind to blow it away. It settles thick on everything along the road. The road is rough and the hills are often steep and rocky.

Before noon we came to a notice on a tree by the side of the road, saying that the Carson boys had turned off here to find feed, and inviting us to follow. We did so, and in a short distance came to a fine meadow. This style of telegraph was in general use on the plains. Notes were, often seen stuck in a split rod planted by the side of the road, where every one could see them. By this means news was conveyed to friends coming up behind.

We remained here all day. The men cut as much grass as we could well carry. We never knew when feed might be scarce. We had kept up this plan for three hundred miles down the Humboldt and one hundred miles up the Carson. By this means every animal came through, except the one lost by accident.

To-day we reached the region of oak timber. We had seen nothing but willows, cottonwoods, and pines for so long that the oaks seemed like old friends. Near our camp some black oak trees had been cut down, the leaves of which our horses ate greedily.

Before night the Carsons left us and drove on a few miles further to Leak Springs.

Monday, September 2.   This morning we started early. There was no change for the better in the roads. The dust was very annoying. The only pleasant thing was the forest we were passing through.

An amusing incident occurred which might have proved serious but only produced a little fun. Robert had picked up a pair of Spanish spurs, and of course had put them on. He then attempted to ride our smartest mule, but had no sooner got on than he stuck his spurs into his sides, and then Billy sent him flying. I thought for a moment he must be seriously hurt, though I couldn't help laughing, he looked so ridiculous flying over the mule's head. We heard no more of Spanish spurs.

We got to Leak Springs early in the forenoon. Here a small stream of water leaked or trickled out from the rocks, but it was so full of mineral that it was not fit for man or beast. There was a trading post here, kept by a California trader, who had supplies to sell to the emigrants. His fresh beef hanging on a hook, not being protected, seemed likely to be eaten up by yellow jackets, which swarmed upon it like bees.

We met here the barefooted man to whom I had given the gruel at Red Lake. He knew our wagon from the name on the side. They had taken him in here until he recruited. He told us the most distressing tale. He had left Red Lake by a cut-off through the mountains, only a pathway, and he was very weak from having so little to eat. He said he found himself at what he called a cave, by the side of the mountain, where the side of the mountain was rock, straight up and down. He was so weak he could not climb, so he wandered around trying to find a place where he could get over; and in his travels he found five dead men, and several others that were, like himself, looking for a place to climb the mountains, and all weak for want of food. He finally got out with some of the others, and, by hearing cow-bells, he had got assistance to a place where he was taken care of by the relief committee, sent out from Sacramento to assist suffering emigrants.

We bought flour at this place at thirty-seven cents per pound. From this time on to the end of our journey, trading posts were more frequent and prices more moderate. They generally kept a small supply of what the emigrants needed most,—beef, flour, bacon, beans, cheese, rice, ship-bread, dried herring, etc., etc.

Tuesday, September 3.   This day we reached Dusty Ridge, which was well named. The dust was over our shoe-tops. Mr. Russell was very sick to-night, with symptoms like those of the cholera. In the morning, however, he was much improved and able to continue on the journey.

Wednesday, September 4.   At noon we arrived at Pleasant Valley, where we stopped for lunch. Afterwards we concluded to remain all night. There were two or three miners here, but the diggings did not seem to be very rich.

We prospected a little for gold, through curiosity, but found none.

Thursday, September 5.   Early this morning we reached Ringgold, which was the first regular mining-camp we came to. Here was another trading post. We bought a supply of potatoes at forty cents per pound. By this time we had found that in California all vegetables, fruits, and grain were sold by the pound, instead of the bushel, as at home.

They inquired of us of we had any flat-irons to sell. I had the very article, had brought them across the plains with remonstrance, and now thought there was a chance to make something, freight-money at least. But when I asked the man five dollars apiece, he only laughed at me, saying, "I guess you have learned all about California prices." So there was no trade and the laugh turned on me. We were afterwards informed that flat-irons were plentier than cobble-stones in San Francisco, having been shipped from the eastern cities in great quantities.

We drove twenty-five miles to-day, and stopped for the night at a place where a shingle-mill had been set up, to make shingles from the pine timber. It is now a railroad station and called. Shingle Springs. It is thirty-eight miles from Sacramento.

Friday, September 6.   The roads to-day and yesterday are much improved. We are getting out of the high mountains, and descending into the Sacramento Valley. Our drive to-day was twenty-five miles, and brought us to the Rio de los Americanos, or American River, about fifteen miles above Sacramento, where we encamped for the night. The Carsons came up and joined us and also encamped here. Our journey is rapidly drawing to an end.

Saturday, September 7. This is our last day on the plains. We started early and at twelve o'clock passed Sutter's Fort, two miles east of the city. We stopped a few moments to examine the place which had become famous as the home of Captain Sutter, the owner of the mill where the first lump of gold was found, and the owner of the land on which Sacramento City was built. He was no longer living here, having moved to his ranch on Feather River, called Hock Farm, thirty miles from the city. The fort was deserted and going to decay, its walls and buildings being constructed of large bricks dried in the sun, and called by the Mexicans, adobes.

Being anxious to finish our journey and encamp for the night, we soon drove on; we did not enter the city, but turned southward to a place called Sutterville, on the east bank of the Sacramento River, three miles south of the city, and here made our last camp.

We had now traveled two thousand four hundred eighteen miles, to a point just one degree south of our starting-place, and four and a half degrees south of our northernmost camp at Fort Hall. The road we followed diverged three hundred miles from a direct line.

During the last eight days of the journey, we had descended, in traveling ninety miles, from a height of nine thousand three hundred thirty-eight feet, to within thirty feet of the tide-level of the Pacific Ocean.

We had left home just five months and seven days before. Our friends the Carsons came into camp with us. They had crossed the Missouri River with us on the fourteenth of May, at Bullard's Ferry, ten miles below Council Bluffs, but after that were separated from us for weeks and months at a time. They were strongly of the opinion that Mr. Frink would never get through, because he brought his wife with him. Yet here we are, all together once more, safe at the end of our long and eventful journey.

[We end the account of Margaret Frink at this point. Her book contained one additional chapter describing her early experiences in the Sacramento, California, area. Mrs. Frink and her husband opened a make-shift hotel, suffered through a cholera epidemic, relocated their hotel, and began purchasing milk cows that eventually became a dairy. Mr. Frink appended a short summation of the fate of some of their travelling companions.]

Journal of Travails to Oregon
Amelia Hadley
1851

INTRODUCTION

Sigmund Freud would not be born until 1856, but that did not stop Amelia Hadley from using a Freudian slip in the title of her overland diary in 1851. She really intended it to be "Journal of Travels," but somehow it came out "Travails." She has special talent for variety in misspelling the word "travel" all through her diary, and many other words as well.

She was born Amelia Hammond near Cleveland, Ohio, on September 21, 1825. On April 10, 1851, she married Samuel B. Hadley, a man from Maine, in Galesburg, Illinois, on his 30th birthday. Four days later, on Monday, April 14, they left by wagon train for Oregon and Amelia made the first entry in her daily diary. So Samuel and Amelia Hadley's overland journey was a honeymoon trip lasting some 130 days. There was another Hadley who accompanied them on the wagon trek— Sam's younger brother, Melville.

The early part of the diary reveals a very cheerful young lady. On May 29 she wrote, "It is amuseing [sic] and delightful to travel over these plains, and is not such a task as many imagine perhaps I may sing another song before I get through. . ." On June 2 she gazed upon the beauty of Courthouse Rock and emoted, "I for one never enjoyed myself better and never had better health." She blamed the bad luck of others on "carelessness and Miss-management." Then the "travails" begin to make their appearance: On July 15, while chasing an Indian who had stolen a horse from the camp, Melville Hadley, her husband's younger brother, received a gunshot wound in his right side, "the ball passing in between his ribs and out within an inch of his back bone." If it had not been for the presence of a medical man in the party, Dr. James C. Cole, who went out with a group of men and brought him in, Melville might well have died. As it was, he lay in the wagon for a number of days suffering repeated bumps and jolts.

Then, on July 20 she wrote, "Do not feel verry well my self," and for the next three days she did not improve, and on July 23 she added, "I am no better   will have to give up journal for few days." She did not add more until August 10 when she wrote, "After striking the Columbia I again resume my journal. I have been verry sick for the past 2 weeks and not able to wait on my self and of course my book neglected." By the time she wrote her last entry on August 23 in Oregon City, the final words were, "This is the end of a long and tedious journey."

One noteworthy feature of the Hadley's overland journey was its speed. The very idea of reaching the Willamette Valley as early as August 23 is unusual. More often, it took other travelers another month or two. The main reason for this was that the Hadleys used horses. Amelia constantly refers to passing the ox teams of others all along the way.

For the first few months in Oregon, they lived in the little town at the confluence of the Willamette and Columbia rivers: Portland. Then they moved south to the valley of the Umpqua River and settled a claim near what was to become Roseburg, which, at that time, was being founded by their cohorts on the cross country trek, Aaron and Sarah Rose.[1] The claim record indicates that the Hadleys took up their claim on December 1, 1851. That richly timbered part of Oregon was to be the main center of their activities for the rest of their lives. There were two short periods away, one near Yreka in northern California's Siskiyou County, the other in eastern Oregon on the banks of Summer Lake. Dr. James Cole, who had attended Melville's wound on the westward journey, settled with his family a short distance away in what became known as Coles Valley.[2]

Over the years following, the Hadleys had eight children, generally speaking every two years: Albert in 1852, Margaret in 1854, Samuel in 1856. Then in Siskiyou County, California, on April 22, 1858, there came twins: Melvina and Melville. Later children were Kitty in 1862 and Henry in 1866.

But there was a ninth child, one whom the others remembered vividly. Melvina F. (Hadley) Hayes, one of the twins, told Fred Lockley of the *Oregon Journal* about this child in the issue of July 1, 1938:

> When I was a little tot my parents adopted a Siskiyou Indian boy, 5 years old. His mother was blind and couldn't take care of him. Father named him Joe Bowers. He grew up with the rest of us and was like one of the family. He idolized Mother. He was one of the finest Indians I have ever known. He was perfectly dependable and

---

[1]Howard M. Corning, ed., *Dictionary of Oregon History.* (Portland, Ore., 1956), p. 212.
[2]O. Larsell, *The Doctor in Oregon* (Portland, Ore., 1947), pp. 267–68.

everyone liked him. Father was a stockman and usually had 300 to 400 horses. Joe Bowers and my brothers, Albert, Melville and Hank, rode the range and were expert horse wranglers. They would break horses to ride, before Father sold them.

The Hadleys were Methodists. Although she did not deplore traveling on Sunday, as some other covered wagon women did, Amelia did mention it several times. In Oregon, their home became a center of Methodist activities. A friend of theirs, William Grandison Hill, remembered in later years that "Sam Hadley kept a meeting house and some of the worst blue rum a man ever got outside of."[3]

In its issue of October 8, 1886, the Roseburg *Plaindealer* newspaper reported the death of Amelia Hadley, and with a segment of the obituary we close our summary of her life. Her first name is spelled wrong, but the rest of the story is authentic:

> Mrs. Emelia A. Hadley was born near Cleveland, Ohio, September 21, 1825, and departed this life at Myrtle Creek, Or., Oct. 3, 1886. She was married to Mr. S. B. Hadley at Galesburg, April 10, 1851. Together they crossed the plains the same year and remained a while in Portland. They settled in the Umpqua Valley in the fall of 1851 where, with the exception of a few years spent East of the mountains, they have remained ever since. For many years her life has been that of an earnest and consistant Christian and she died in full fellowship with the M. E. Church South. Her hands were ready to every good work and the hearty sympathy and help of the community during her last painful sickness and the large number of friends who followed her to her last resting place fully attest the high esteem in which she was held by the entire community.

We have been unable to locate the original copy of Amelia Hadley's diary. We have used, with permission, a mimeographed copy in possession of the Corvallis Public Library in Oregon. There are identical copies in other Oregon libraries as well. The time we have spent with the manuscript convinces us that it is a fairly accurate copy made by someone who was careful to transcribe Amelia's style and spelling as accurately as possible. Amelia Hadley's "Journal of Travails" has to be one of the finest records of frontier life extant and an item of rare significance as a document of American history.

---

[3] "A Pioneer in Oregon"—The Story of William Grandison Hill as told to his daughter, Ella Hill (Douglas County Museum-Roseburg, Ore.), p. 8.

THE JOURNAL OF AMELIA HADLEY

Monday May 5   Left Mr. Hustons, and traveled about eight miles which brought us to Kanesville, or Council Bluffs. This is quite a town some larger than Henderson in Ill.   the houses are mostly hewed log, 2 story and on main street they have sided them up and they present quite a fine appearance   Here we lay in our provisions to cross the plains, flour 2½ hundred which is reasonable for this place, here you can get everything you want, crossed the Missouri which is a wide mudy looking river   ferried over in a small flat boat, which they rowed, saw several Indians up and down the river which are the first I ever saw, The bluffs are surely romantic and beautiful presenting them in huge collums and if I may so speak in various kinds of architecture. Some of them are verry high while others are still lower reminding us of the work of nature and of the creation when every thing was formed as the creator best saw fit. We are now in the Indian Territory and a more wild barren place I never saw. The sand on the west side up the Mo, is almost insurmountable while each side of the road rushes, are abundant, and you may [see] a vast sea of them, traveled about eight miles from the river and camped on a small stream. There are the tribe of Omahaws the first tribe we pass through, they are the most filthy thevish set and are mostly naked, Their cheif can talk verry good American, also his daughter   she has lived 2 years in St. Louis and had been to school, tried to buy a dress said she wanted to dress like white woman.

Tuesday May 6th   Lay by to day for the purpose of organizing a company. There are a good many camped with us, some with ox, and some with horse teams, The wind blows verry hard and the sand and dust is flying in clouds and put me in mind of a monsoon, they say that on this river there are always clouds of sand flying. It is indeed disagreeable. No timber this side of the river of any account   plenty of willows.

Wednesday May 7th   Traveled 12 miles and found a good camping place, grass about 2 hands high, good water no timber, & great many Indians. Of the Potowatamie tribe which is the 2 tribe we pass through. They are a filthy tribe and barbaroic similar to the former tribe. They follow us up from one camping place to another, and were it not for our number they would, be down upon us. Our company consists of 23 waggons horse teams and some 50 men and 11 women besides a number of children   passsd the old Morman burrying ground, and town as the ruins where they were, there burrying ground covers an acre and were just as thick as they could dig the graves, It beat anything I ever saw, This place was called Winter Quarters, It lies on both sides of the Mo. and the buildings are log. I should think there were about 2 hundred of them. They have all left the west side of the river and gone to Salt Lake, and it looks from appearance, like the riuins of Sodom. The old burrying yards stands open and look[s] lonely and solemn. One cannot but help drop a tear to see how providence will order everry thing. True, how short & fleeting is life, we cannot but reflect what frail creatures we are. We will muse no longer on the past but call our thoughts to the present.

Thursday May 8   Here we cross the Elk horn, have to ferry it, plenty of Indians   travelled 21 miles which brings us to the platte river, camp on the platte, this is a mudy sandy stream like Mo. It covers considerable surface, and is cut up with sand bars. It is the whitest sand I ever saw, and finest and is disagreeable when the wind blows, which is almost constant, find verry little timber and that is a mixture of oak, elm, and a verry little walnut   have seen 2 or 3 cotton woods, passed by an old Indian grave which had the appearance of a wigwam and supposed it was untill reaching it,   It is constructed of sodds and built pyramid stile, and has a hole at the side about a foot acros

Fryday, May 9   Travelled, 22 miles to day   crossed Shell creek. 12 ft wide, 2 ft deep. We are now traveling on what is termed plains, they are beautiful, but the land differs verry little from what we have been traveling over   find little or no timber principaly Willow and this serves for fuel, that is the dead ones, good camping places so far, our teams look fine haveing plenty of good grass. The water of the platte is verry good when settled which we do by throwing in a little alumn, and let it stand for a while. The water is as soft as rain water. camp to night on the banks of the platte. We form a currelle with our waggons, and at bed time put our horses in side and tents and then

have a guard stationed. We are a merry crowd, while I am journalize-
ing one of the company is playing the violin which sounds delightful
way out here. My accordian is also good, as I carry it in the carrige
and play as we travel, had a verry hard rain this evening, and everry
thing seems affloat.

Saturday May 10.   Travelled 19 miles   come to Loup Fork of Platte,
it is verry high on account, of the rain and we cannot either ferry or ford
it.

Sunday May 11.   Camped on the Loup Fork on account of crossing   verry rainy and cloudy, and considerable cold, find plenty of
grass, and little timber have had no trouble with the indians as yet,
they are affraid to tackel us   an ox train back of us they atacked and
took 2 oxen and 2 sacks of meal. Have seen some antelope and plenty
of wolves.

Monday May 12.   Still camped, high water and high washes

Tuesday May 13   Still camped, prospects no better.

Wednesday May 14   Try to ferry this morning. The boat is an awful
constructed thing and is not fit to ferry with. It sank yesterday with
12, or 15 men on it, no lives lost, some of our company has crossed,
and we still remain here, an awful thunder storm accompanied with
hail, and heavy wind, is on hand. The waves run high, have to camp
again with nothing to eat or sleep uppon our waggons being on the
other side, and nothing with us except the carrige, some of our company on the same side and better of[f] than us brought us something
to eat and sleep uppon, so we fared verry well.

Thursday May 15   Crossed this morning   looking rather rough,
but came accross safe   a beautiful sun and rainbow presents itself to
our view this morning and we feel fresh and invigorated after the
storm, a great deal of thunder and lightning we have and terrible
storm everry one says that has travelled here on the Platte river, we
have some 2 hundred miles to travel on it, camp to night about 2
miles from the fork grass not very good, rather short, plenty of timber for camping purposes. Another thunder shower has come and
heavy wind.

Fryday May 16   The light of another day has dawned and with it an awful storm. It seems it never rained harder, But at this we will not complain for we shall soon reach where it seldom or ever rains. Pass a good many Indians, camp grounds and their little wigwams no timber but popple [poplar], and willow which makes when dry verry good fuel   I beleive willow grows everry where, and where nothing else will grow, see a good many antelope. Traveled 25 miles, found a good camping place   water soft and good, rolling land, good grass and fine scenery.

Saturday May 17   Had another hard rain last night accompanied with hail. The soil is so verry sandy that these heavy rains does not make it mudy. Find in most places excellent grass. Mushrooms in abundance, and also a great variety of flowers, here also are a number of old Buffalo trails, looking a good deal like furrows. We are now in the Pawnees country have not seen any of them yet, traveled 24 miles and camped on the bare plain   no timbers, nor no water, seem, as though we should perish for the want of it, tolerable grass, and some dew, which made it better for our horses.

Sunday May 18th   Started very early, and traveled to where there was water and breakfasted   good grass, no timber. This place is called prarie creek, and is excellent water. here are two graves, on the bank of the creek, one was in memory of A. Kellog, died June 12, 49 aged 23 years, the other the name Edgebert, cut out on a peice of board, serving as tomb stones. They look verry lonesome, away here To day is the sabbath but does not seem much like it, has to travel to where we could get timber, traveled 16 miles and struck wood river about 1 o'clock and camped for the night, found plenty of timber but it is cottonwood some dry willow excellent grass, to day has been verry fogy, and a good deal of thunder and lightining. The wind is cold   have not had but one or two days that might be called warm. I hardly can see how the grass can grow, when it is so cold. It is nothing for it to storm on the Platte, they are frequent and verry hard. saw 2 antelope   was near enough to see them. They resemble a deer verry much but are lighter collered, and some larger. Their meat is called better than deer.

Monday May 19th   Traveled 15 miles   good water tolerable grass, and tolerable camp, saw a grave but had no inscription on it.

Tuesday May 20th   Traveled 20 miles and camped   camp not verry good, saw several antelope, and an animal called prarie dogs, which resemble a puppy There are acres of them so by speaking I mean that they are like the meadow mole   they plough the ground up and form little knolls all over the ground and also eat the grass of[f] so that the ground looks almost bare. They dig a hole in the ground, and throw it up around like an ant heap, grass in abundance timber cotton wood and but very little of that.

Wednesday May 21   Traveled 16 miles   found a good camping place   camped on elm creek, had one of the worst storms that I ever experienced   hail as large as quils eggs. face of the country level, plenty of grass, and game.

Thursday May 22   Traveled 21 miles camped on the banks of the Platte. The river is about a mile wide where we now are. In it are a great many sand bars which makes the river very shallow and verry much cut up but verry wide, timber popple   we are now at the head of grand Island, and in the Buffalo country, on the south side of the river, is fort Kearny about a half a mile from the river land flat and wet. The air is cold almost enough to freeze. It seems as though summer would never make its appeared. Water poor white with clay of which the Platte and Mo. are alike   But by taking a pail full, and putting in a little alum, and it will settle in a short time. This water is verry soft. One of our company killed an antelope and gave us some. It is verry sweet and tender, a good dead like veal. much better than venson.

Fryday May 23 51   traveled 25 miles   grass the most of the day verry short, and poor I think from the appearance that it has been tread out by the bufalo for it looks just like an old barn yard more than anything else, crossed Buffalo creek, and passed Willow and Tetah Lake. They are south side of the road long and verry crooked soil sandy, passed 2 graves   camped again on the banks of the Platte, our road some times cuts of[f] a bend in the river and we do not camp on it for 2 or 3 nights, find good grass on an Island in the river, have no corn for our horses and they have to subsist entirely upon grass which seems hard and work them hard all day and then turn them out on grass and that sometimes not very good. We left

Kanesville with 12 bush shelled corn, and fed each horse 2 quarts a piece as long as it lasted.

May 24 Saturday   Traveled 20 miles   crossed the Platte, and travelled on an Island, which was about 6 miles and crossed back which shortened our distance about 8 miles. saw a good many buffalo. One of the company shot eight balls into 3 of them and killed none   they are tremendours hard thing to kill you can't kill them to shoot them in the head. passed graves to day, one was a fresh one, buryed 5 day ago. This name Ezekiel Clifton from Michigan. grass not verry good timber willows and Popple. plenty deer & antelope   There are any quantity of scorpions and resemble Lissards on these sand bluffs which look disagreeable, though perfectly harmless. There are three kinds of them   one is a kind of pink one nearly black and one brown, the brown one is rather different from the others being nearly round while the others are long. This round one looks some like a toad head like a toad and has a sharp tail about 4 inches long the querest looking thing you ever saw,   Prickely pears grow spontaneous and 3 kinds of cactus,   they look beautiful. The Platte is a delightful stream all though back from the stream on each [bank?] in most places they are huge sand bluffs which look like snow drifts being so white and not an atom of vegetation on them but on the banks of the river plenty of grass and some little skirts of timber. It is in most places some 5 or 6 miles to these bluffs but does not look more than half a mile, It is deceiving like any prarie country. The road leads along the north side of the river some times near the river and then we near the bluffs. there is also a road on the south side   There is a kind of grass called Buffalo grass which grows thick like our blue grass and looks like it at first sight but I think that It never grows over 4 inches high, you will see patches of this where you will see grass of no other kind excellent feed, camped on the Platte while we were driving in camp one of our companys horses ran away with their waggon   tiped it over   cleared themselves from it and ran themselves down.

Sunday May 25   Waggon repaired and everry thing to rights   traveled 25 miles   camped on the platte the river here is about a mile wide, here is the last timber we find for the next 2 hundred miles pass a large company   they are driving about two hundred head of cattle, look well, passed one grave to day   the name Gordon from Dubuque Iowa, died last May 1850, aged 27 yrs   Henry, and wife are acquainted with him. Our company to day have killed 2 deer and 4 buffalo, plenty of fresh meat. It is good and quite a luxury after liveing on salt meat so long.

Monday May 26   Camp to day to prepare for the 2 hundred miles where we have no wood   shall be about 10 days crossing.

Tuesday May 27   Traveled 13 miles, find the best of grass verry heavy sandy, road. These sandy bluffs are tremenduous hard traveling for we sometimes cross them in small ravines, which are sultry hot, beating directly upon the sand. There is however now and then a good cold spring isueing from the hillside which gladdens us poor weary travelers, the water is verry clear the bottom being pure white sand, in some of the ravines where there is water there is verry good grass. It looked almost impossible for grass to grow in such verry deep sand. Saw 3 or 4 head of Buffalo, fording the river had a good view of them   Our curiosity is pretty much satisfied as to Buffalo, haveing had some to eat, you could not tell it from beef. If you were not told and had It set before you, come to examine closely you will perceive that it is a little coarser grain and a little darker. Crossed bluff creek, reproduce as 10 rods and 2 ft, deep water clear sand bottom, some quick sand as also in the Platte, which causes these streams to change greatly and make them dificult to cross   camped on the river   had to cook with buffalo chips for the first time   It makes verry good fuel when dry, and is more prefforable than wood for the verry good reason, (can't get it.)

Wednesday May 28   Traveled 21 miles   some verry sandy and some swamp road, about 2 miles was so mirey that we could hardly get through it   The heat is almost intense in these blufs, crossed Duck weed creek   10 feet wide   here is an abundance of good cold spring water, which was verry palitable, crossed shoal stream, 3 ft wide, On the oposite side of the river from us there is plenty of cedar, which looks rather inviting as we have no wood, camp on rattle snake creek 20 ft wide 1½ ft deep   swift current, sandy bottom, not verry hard to cross, now at what is called cedar bluffs, grass about ½ foot high and good water. We have had no misfortunes as yet   our company are all well and teams look fine. See a good many buffalo, they are not as fleet as I had supposed. you can easily ride up to them, the same as cattle. They do not mind you at all and will not run at the sight of you but as soon as they get the scent they are off, you can get up to them on the windward side.

Thursday May 29   Traveled 17 miles   had some heavy sandy road 4 buffaloes came down to our camp this morning. It so happened that our horses did not see them and had no trouble. Some of the company crossed the river and got some cedar for wood, red cedar, verry nice. It is amuseing and delightful to travel over these plains, and is not such a task as many imagine   perhaps I may sing another song before I get through, a person wants to take a great deal of care of their teams, and take a moderate walk and average about 18 or 20 miles a day and they will stand it verry well.

Fryday May 30   Traveled 19 miles over some of the heaviest sandy road that I ever saw   as much as our teams can do to drag over it, traveled along side of the river today, passed one Lone tree, which was cedar, about 100 yds from the river   looks verry singular there being no tree nor shrub for a hundred miles, remind me of the Charter oak, scenery delightful, find some of the most beautiful flowers none that we see in the states except wild roses, I love to walk along and gather them, came to an Indian camp about noon where they had quite a little village of wigwams & a great many poneys. They are the tribe of Soos. They are kind and hospitable and are the most polite and cleanest tribe on the road. They are whiter, to than any that we have seen. They are well dressed and make a fine appearance, went in one of their houses made of dressed skins sewed to gether and verry large. They are all busy some of them jerking Buffalo, some painting skins for boxes which looked very nice. The old chief came out shook hands with me invited me in, and seemed almost tickled to death to see a white woman, quite a curiosity.

Saturday May 31   Traveled 21 miles had good roads and verry good grass. over took an ox train for Oregon, which had just crossed the Platte, comeing this far on the south side   passed two graves to day & one yesterday, one a lady the name Margarett Hawk from Ill, died Aug 6, 1849, aged 46 years, camped on a little lake south side of the road   tolerable grass, and an excelent spring, cold and clear   road lays along the bank of the river, river here not verry wide but quite deep, weather fine but air quite cold.

Sunday June 1st   Traveled 20 miles   had the best of roads equal to Mcademised road. This road leads over the bluff called Cobble Hills, and one would certainly think from their rude construction they were rightly named, after leaveing these and traveling some miles farther we discover some more hills, or bluffs, Called Ancient Bluffs ruins which are decidely grand and beautiful for such as love such a scenery. It looks like ruins of old castles and buildings of all sises and descriptions   one in particular runs up some 100 ft and almost square, and the top of it covered with grass, the ruins being princi-paly rocks, makes it look more strange, here is part of a company who are the most delightful of any thing I have seen   visitors have to be verry careful on account of the many rattlesnakes lurking among the clefts of the rocks   camped again on the river   verry poor grass, have to be verry careful with our horses on account of alkali water It is to be seen only in places standing in puddles. The ground seems covered with this salt, as potash, and this lye looks and smells as strong as I ever saw in an ashery.[4] It has the same taste and produces the same effect   some of our company went up among the ruins and found a quarry of chalk perfectly white and pure as chalk can be look very white from the road

Monday June 2   road runs along the river   to day passed court house rock, south side the river   It is on the top of the ridge of bluffs, and accends up in a square form 2 thirds of its height and then forms another square on the top   looks as much like a court house as anything can. I will give you a draft in the back of the book. It is about 2 hundred ft high above the main ridge   verry romantic. see a company on the other side of the river, stop to dine in sight of chimney rock. I seated myself this day noon to scetch it as near as I can from so great a distance and from observation you with this also in the back part of the book. It is from the level of the river 2 hun-dred ft high and runs up to a spire similar to a steple. It looks like an old doby house and great big clay chimney, it is a kind of yellow clay,

---

[4]An ashery was a shop where soap was made by combining lye and grease.

so that It crumbles and washes   In 3 or 4 years you will hardly
notice it at all, hardly looks like the work of nature, traveled 23 miles
good grass considerable of this alkali; stake out our horses with a long
rope around in places where they cannot get it   Weather fine to day,
air warm verry windy, the sand flyes verry bad, makeing it verry disagreeable, Traveling has become a second nature on these plains, but
is not so bad after all. It is true that a great deal suffer during this
long journey, but It is one half owing to carelessness and
Mismanagement, little or no sickness as yet as I know of, health is a
great blessing on this road. I for one never enjoyed myself better and
never had better health   saw 7 buffalo before us in the road. This
road is better than any laid out road in the states, looks like an old
road in an old setled country, But not much to be wondered at for
there is a continual trail all the time and onley the one road, we surely
wont loose our way

Tuesday June 3   Traveled 23 miles to day   had verry good road,
passed a number of ox trains   some of their cattle are dying from
drinking alkali water   Some of them think they are making great
head way, but have about killed their teams off   they drive some
days over thirty miles and no team can stand it, on this route passed
2 indians of the soo tribe   said they were a going to fight the
pawnees   were on horseback had great long spears, and other weap-
pons. As they passed us they said to me, Soo, and then point their
spears at us saying   me for, Pawnees   and rode off as fast as they
could. Saw some cactus on the bluffs and mountains some of them
in blossom   they were the prettyest things I ever saw   plenty of
mountain moss and a beautiful variety of stones or pebles, a great
many curiosityes to attract the traveler   passed Scotts bluffs on the
south side of the river, they are grand more so than any we have seen
named from a man by the name of Scott that starved to death on top
of them   should like to have drawn them had we camped where I
could have had a chance   camped on spring creek which was said to
produce trout but saw none   the creek is clear and cold coming from
the mountain formed from spring I suppose. The road considerably
distance from the river   grass is verry good but later than at this
time of the year in the states. We are, still rising and on a much

higher elevation than the states   grass here now as in April there &
it is now June.

Wednesday June 4   We are now 46 miles from fort Larrimi   all
well in body and spirits   over took another ox team which were
driving considerable stock. See a number of waggons on the other
side   travelled 20 miles   found good road   runs considerable close
to river. We are now on the North Fork of Platte. It is quite small in
some places and then again it covers considerably surface and form a
good many Islands, camped on the Platte plenty of timber such as it
is, it is mostly cotton wood, but in the states we would not call it
plenty but It seems plenty to us after doing without any   plenty for
camping purposes   found on the bank of the river a log of pine,
which I supposed had drifted there which was delightful wood. It
was so full of pitch that little of it done our cooking verry well, we
carried some of it a number of days.

Thursday June 5   Travelled 22 miles   had some verry sandy road,
road still near the river, cotton wood plenty, good grass, within 6 miles
of Fort Larimi, camped here and lay by a day. plenty of timber. There
is an Indian village where we are camped where the Sioux wintered last
winter, cut nearly all the trees off about as high as their heads   here
we had a hard hail storm   hailed about an hour as hard as I ever saw
it so that the ground was perfectly white   hailled also last night not so
much but considerable larger   see nothing much worthy of note to
day but expect to when we arrive at the fort. It is over 900 miles from
home to fort Larimie shall soon be half our distance.

Fryday June 6   Lay by to day   plenty of grass and wood on the
bank of the platte   Indians around our camp all day   bought some
moccasins of them which are made verry nice. Some of our company
did not lay by and have gone on   they are anxious to see the elephant[5] I suppose.

Saturday June 7   travelled 20 miles   came to the fort which was
beyond all expectation   about as large a town as henderson and much

---

[5]The term "to see the elephant" was used by some overlanders to sum up in one phrase the
whole dangerous enterprise. The entire third chapter of Merrill J. Mattes' *The Great Platte River
Road* (Lincoln, Neb., 1969), is devoted to "Elephants of the Platte." His short definition is, "It was
the poetic imagery of all the deadly perils that threatened a westering emigrant" (p. 61).

handsomer   on main street the building are brick 3 story high stores in the lower stories   here you can get almost any thing you want. It seems as though I could hardly contrive how they could get goods there   the town is a square, block, and brick side walks   It is on the south side of platte there are quite a number of frame buildings. here is a good blacksmith shop   here are any quantity of wigwams and Indians about 5 or 6 hundred, soil sandy there are only about 80 soldiers here now   some of them have their wives with them. This town is at the foot of the mountains in a bend of the river, here we now begin to accend the Rocky mountains   these mountains are covered with wild sage pine & cedar. These pines and cedar are scruby some about 1½ ft through and 20 ft high which is the largest   you may ask I wonder where they got their lumber to build those frame houses, I answer They have a sawmill, about 10 miles from the fort, which is strange for this place. They have a good ferry at or oposite the fort, we are not obliged to cross   we still go up on the north side. some of our boys went over to put some letters in the office. This road up on the north side of the river is a new one and comes into the old one about 80 miles above the fort. these mountains look verry high and almost insurmountable   the road follows up ravines and round among them so as not to be verry bad, plenty of rocks as you may suppose look like Iron ore, camp 15 miles in the mountains to night   dismal enough, and pleasant to, feel some timid, here is a spring of cold clear water side of the road. 2 waggons joined our company from the fort. There are over a hundred good waggons at the fort which the emigrants have left pretty good grass on the mountains. There are about 3 hundred crow Indians in these mountains   they do not show themselves   I wish they would   I should not be affraid of them   as long as you can see them there is not much danger.

Sunday June 8   Traveled 21 miles   camp within 8 miles of the platte,   as you must know that It heads up in these mountains. We have had a verry hard road to day steep long hills and enormous rocks and caverns. I never saw such ledges on rocks and so awful high and steep   I think sure they are Rocky mountains   This part is called black hills range, of Rocky mountains   quite a romantic scenery after all   what gave them the name of black hills is they look like

burnt ruins   black   the soil and rocks is preasely [precisely] the collar of snuff Macabay[6]   you can take up a rock and it will all scale and
crumble in your hands, and the earth is the same   looks as though
it would cullar, good springs of water, from the mountain side.

Monday June 9,   Travelled 23 miles   good though hilly road   good
watering places at suitable distances the farthest 14 miles. Traveled up
the platte which is here not verry wide   came to a place in the mountains where the platte runs as cuts a place, not over 20 ft wide through
which is worthy a travellers notice   The water is deep and swift being
in such a narrow Kanyon. camp on the river plenty of wood, grass &
water, had some antelop to night   see some hens called sage hens, I
have heard say that they were good to eat, some of our company killed
some, and I think a skunk, prefarable, their meat tastes of this abom-
inable mountain sage, which I have got so tired of that I cant bear to
smell it, they live wholly upon it and it scents their flesh.

Tuesday June 10   Traveled 22 miles   found verry good road and no
water except touching the river occasionaly. camp to night on the
Platte in a nice little cotton wood grove with awful great mountains
all around us, the most romantic place I ever saw, overtook and
passed 2 ox trains to day.

Wednesday June 11   Traveled 25 miles   had some very heavy sandy
road and some bad hills, Though our road winds around through the
mountains at an astonishing rate and is more lined than I should suppose it could be. It is the most natural road I ever saw. We see almost
all kinds of plants and roots that grow in our garden and green houses
of which is Cactus 2 kinds, Prickely Pear, Wormwood, Southernwood,
and Chamoile and an abundance of sage of which the latter is not like
our garden sage. Flowers of which are Larkspur Sundials, China asters
and roses in abundance 3 kinds, of them one kind are nearly as large
as a tea saucer   I never saw the like and just as red as blood, most
beautiful indeed. plenty of peas which look like our sweet pea have just
such a blossom, here are a great variety of flowers that you do not have
in the states   plenty of wild sunflowers and I do not know where that
does not grow, Our road has run to the river at intervals to day which
has afforded water for our teams   at one of these watering places there

---

[6]Maccaboy was a special snuff scented with attar of roses.

stood a large lone cotton wood tree, with an indian grave in it, which was quite a curiosity, could not think at first what it was. It was a small child from appearance, the skull was lying on the ground, the crows had picked it all to pieces and left the bones. It was first put in a blanket and then rapt in a buffalo robe, and I should think there were about a quart of beads about it which they had ornamented it with. its scull was painted   corpse was lashed to the limbs of the tree with a number of little sticks layed across under it, saw also a buffalo to day, and another ox train camp to night within half a mile of the river in an awful sandy place   no wood and have to burn sage for the first time. Any quantity of locusts on our journey to day the first we have seen—

Thursday June 12   Traveled 20 miles   have found a most beautiful camping ground on the river   our road has been verry hilly and sandy this afternoon. We are now 130 miles from fort Larimie   We have cool winds and a constant breeze here in the mountains   have good grass which you will probably think strange but their are small valleys that afford plenty of grass. I can tell you that we are in sight of snow, on the top of these mountains. It looks verry strange to me having seen It so before. This snow lies principaly in the deep narrow ravines and is some 20 or 30 ft deep and from that to 50 ft which is not so easily melted, and more than that I should think from the air now that It never would get warm enough up there to melt it much.

Fryday June 13   road runs near the river occasionaly touching the bluffs with awful heavy sand at these points. Our road mostly to day has been delightful runing through a nice grove along the river. You may know that it seemed good to get into timber again enough to make any shade. came to a grave his name Glenette died 1849, was burried in a canoe. The wolves had made a den down in his grave. They dig up everyone that is buried on the plains as soon as they are left. It looks so cruel I should hate to have my friends or myself burried here. which all may be. The weather is verry changeable nights verry cold and verry warm in the middle of the day. some times it will turn cold in an hour so that from shirt sleeves, you will be cold with the heaviest of winter clothing. It beats anything I ever saw. travelled 25 miles had not water except what little we carried in our canteens.

Saturday June 14   Travelled 20 miles   passed one grave and a great deal alkali water. About 25 head of cattle which had died from drinking it lay around   people are not half careful enough. Passed through a plane called rock avenue which was a curiosity one which I cannot describe any more than for you to look at some quarry here are ledges which look as though some one had cut the stone square and layed them up in a wall. I can tell you how it came here is where the Free Massons done their first work. (now you know) camped at Willow Spring   plenty of grass, and good water   willows for fuel.

Sunday June 15   Travelled 25 miles, about one mile from the spring is Prospect hill   It is a delightful view, and here you can see the range of Sweet water mountains   we then had a bad slugh to cross, which smelled awful   nooned at Greese wood creek, 6 ft wide, 1 deep; this takes its name from a shrub which grows upon it and resembles the gooseberry bush but the leaves look like hemlock. It is called Greesewood, we next came to alkali lakes, which were 3 or 4 rods wide the water dried up and the ground just as white as snow and this is 3 or 4 inches deep and you can get chunks of salaratus as large as a pint cup just as pure as that you buy   here I gathered some, and I send you some   It has got durty. We have now left the platte entirely   we had travelled on it so long that it seemed like an acquaintance   camp to night on the Sweet water river 200 miles from fort Larimie   passed a grade to day. This river is 8 rods wide 2 ft deep swift current good water as soft as snow water which it is coming from melted snow from the mountains. This water tastes like sap which gave it this name. I always had a curiosity to taste of it have to cross the river for grass, so many have camped here that they have eat it all up on this side.

Monday June 16   Lay by to day on this river. There is independence rock, about 200 yds from the river. which is about 6 hundred yds long and 120 wide. it is composed of hard granite and is quite smooth, took a walk upon it   pretty hard to accend. I am now seated on top journalizing. There are thousands of names and some are verry nicely chiseled on, but mostly put on with tar, left ours with the rest Here I have a full view of devils gate where the sweet waters pass between or through the mountains. This is an independent rock standing aloof from the rest of the mountains. and has a singular appearance look like a great rock rooled down from the rest of the mountains. It has the apearance of a court house standing in the centre with a block all around. I never saw any thing more splendid   scc a great many names of whom I knew

Tuesday June 17   After leaving here and traveling 5¼ miles west of this rock you come to devils gate which is from 20 to 30 ft and 400 ft high and a quarter of a mile through   this is a great curiosity here are also an abundance of names   The current is swift through here like foam   here is a grave at the entrance and at the outlet, just by the side of the river there is also a grave of a lady at independence rock   her name Elizabeth Campbell, died 1850 aged 23 years and on the bank of the river oposite independence rock are the graves of 2 girls   I think these may well be termed rocky mountains for they are pure granite rock with no earth on them with now and then a shrub cedar springing out of a crevice   We are now in a beautiful valley between the mountains which is delightful, considerably alkali grass good in spots   have verry good road by traveling up the river. passed 3 graves this afternoon died in 51   travelled 23 miles to day camped on sweet water road hard this after noon, on account of crossing the river so many times and so many rocks in the river.

Wednesday June 18   travelled 22 miles   heavy sand tolerable level, crossed the sweet water in all 5 time came through at the last crossing a narrow Kanyon between the mountains just like a narrow street about as wide as a narrow road   is thousands of names written in here which looked like a street in town with their signs up   passed 2 graves to day   saw a name on the rock W. T. Shinn   thought perhaps that it was W. S. of Newark, Ohio, camp to night on the S. W. river where there is as you may say no grass at all and hardly any roots left   here are 5, or 6 trains, also but will soon have to share or starve there has been good feed here, but a number have stoped here to recruit, and eat it all out, Some of our Company killed a mountain sheep or more properly a mountain goat for they look about the head like a goat, while the body is covered with hair and short fine wool which looks some like fur   had some to eat. I merely tasted it so as to say I had eat some, but do not like it   the rest said it was good but

I know they think better all the time for they taste of every thing they get even to black birds and call them good. We have 3 English men in our train who eat everything have a kettle of soup every day. One day they had a black bird soup.

Thursday June 19   Travelled 21 miles   passed 2 graves to day one by the name of Stantlif   here we have a grand view of the wind river mountains which are always covered with snow   they have a verry white appearance   passed ice spring to day   about 2 yds to the right up the road is where the spring breaks out and leads of[f] down the road in a marshy swale, which is mirey   here you obtain pure ice by diging down to the depth of 4 to 6 inches   dug down and got some there is a solid cake of ice as clear as any I ever saw and more so   cut a piece as large as a pail and took and rapt it in a blanket, to take along camp to night on the river   not verry good grass.

Fryday June 20   Passed to day a company of packers comeing home from California   were with mules which were seal fat   they were well fixed   one woman packing with them. Travelled 21 miles camped on Willow creek   tolerable good grass, and Willows for fuel. crossed Strawberry creek so named from the quantity of vines up and [down] the creek   they are just in bloom   found plenty of snow in some ravines side of the road   some of the boys had quite a snow balling   The air has been verry cold to day. passed 5 graves to day all in a row   the wolves had made holes in all of them

Saturday June 21   Travelled 17½ miles   camp on Pacific Spring which is the first camp after you get through south pass. There we saw the far famed south pass, but did not see it until we had passed it for I was all the time looking for some narrow place that would almost take your breath away to get through but was disappointed. It is a body of table land rooling but not mountainous and is 15 miles wide being the pleasantest place I have yet seen. The altitude here is 5 thousand & 30 ft. We have been on a gradual accend since we left Larimi and now we shall decend the same to the pacific   at Pacific Spring the water begins to run to the pacific   verry cold to day Water standing the night of the 20 froze a quarter of inch thick on a pail   in sight of snow all the time from 5 to 8 ft deep side the road in some places north side mountain.

Sunday June 22   travelled 20 miles   camped on little sandy,   road tolerable level and I never saw nicer in the states. No grass in the distance and no water except a small spring which is verry brackish and fit for man or brute. From Sweet Water to south Pass is 10 miles. To Pacific Springs 3 miles   ditto creek crossing 1½ dry sandy and brackish water 9 m   To forks of road Sublet cut off 6 m   To Little Sandy 2 ft wide 2 ft deep 4 m   To Big Sandy 4 wide 2 deep 5 m   To Green river 45m. This entire road from Pacific Spring is a verry level sandy and Ashy desert, no green of any account on the stream. The sand and ashes drift like snow, altitude 8080 ft here.

Monday June 23   Camped on little sandy   here we lost one of our carriage horses from a kick in the side   good grass along the bank of the stream though high banks to get to it.

Tuesday June 24   Traveled 6 miles to big Sandy   here we stop until about 4 o'clock and then travel all night. We here shall take Sublets cut off which is a barren desert of 45 miles   no water   we think our teams will stand it better to travel it in the night. This shortens our distance about 75 miles.

Wednesday June 25   arived about noon at green river after such a jant for our teams they were pretty well go drayed[7] after traveling all night and till noon the next day. There are 3 deep ravines near the river   they are 4, 6, 8 miles from the river   steep hill at river   this is the place to try men and teams   here are 3 or 4 good ferryes, the best we have seen   about 30 or 40 white men live here among the indians   4 white familys white women also a small Grocery, and plenty of indians for the Snake tribe and some Flat heads   The most of these men have squaw wives and some 3 or 4 and a great many children   as funy sight as I saw was a little pappoose about 2 years old run along the fery almost naked and Its white dady took it up and carried to the wigwam and gave it to its mama   Had to pay the enormous sum of 10 dollars a waggon and 1 dollar a horse to cross, swam our horses rather than pay so much   river 100 yds wide swift & deep   dangerous too   traveled 9 miles from river and camped on Salmon Trout branch 7 or 8 miles above its union with green river.

[7]Dragged out.

Thursday June 26   remain in camp to day to rest our teams   caught some beautiful fish of 3 kinds spotted and mountain trout and a kind of whitefish   there are here 4 graves and some Indian wigwam. There is a road leading from green river to salt lake, a great many go to Cal on this road, the road from Green river here is verry hilly and circuitus   this branch is 2 rods wide 2 ft deep

Fryday June 27   Travelled 20 miles   camped on Nettle creek which is a small run. Our road to day has been verry hilly   nooned at Fire wood grove which is Spruce Pine   here is a fine spring, gathered a quantity of beautiful green and some fine strawberryes.

Saturday June 28   Travelled 18 miles   verry hilly road,   some accents looked almost impasible   plenty of indians Snake tribe scattered all along the road   snow all around us and above us and cold enough to freeze. good grass and It seems singular how it can grow when it is so cold   camp to night in a nice little grove of pople and birch between the hills or in a ravine   plenty of currents but not large enough to eat. looks rather singular to see currents here   the bushes the same as our tame ones   plenty of Strawberrys vines in abundance. Nooned to day on Hams Fork of Green River. Here is an Indian Camp

Sunday June 29   Travelled 18 miles   had awful hills and verry steep   camp to night on a fork of bear river. good grass, good water plenty of strawberryes and current but the currents are not large enough to cook went out and gathered 4 or 5 quarts which was a great rarity and served fine with bread butter, & tea, stop here the remainder of the day.

Monday June 30   Lay by to day which gives our horses as well as ourselves rest, here is a small grove of timber where we are camped. weather cold, no rain since we left the Platt not a sprinkle.

Tuesday July 1   Traveled 20 miles   had verry hilly and slik road traveled 10 miles to Thomas Fork of bear river   There is an Indian vilage also a bridge across the river which has been constructed by some white men who stay here to receive toll. They also have a small grocery and horses to trade. bought a coupple of poneys camped on bear river about 10 miles from the fork.

Wednesday July 2   Traveled 25 miles   had verry good road, quite level and few hard pitches. Stoped to noon at a small stream   good water   some small willows and a few strawberrys. camp to night on bear river about 2 miles from the river to the road. this is the main river and quite a large stream   large fish in it salmon and speckled trout but the salmon are small here, good grass   awful high mountains all around us.

Thursday July 3   Travelled 20 miles   had tolerable level road. after travelling some 10 miles we came to soda springs which are along the bank of the river. The water boils up from the bottom sparkles and tastes just as a glass of soda will, pure and cold. There is one called steamboat spring which boils up from an opening in a high rock about a foot across and boils up about 18 inches high. I never saw anything so splendid in all my life. This water is merely warm, it is thrown up by means of gass, or something of the kind in the earth. There is a tradeing establishment here, a number of whites spaniards and Mexicans. They have droves of horses and fine looking ones. At Thomases Fork was a chance to send letters to Fort Leavenworth on the Mo. and one of the whites who registered the names of the emigrants. we had ours put down   bought some horses of the Mexicans. We have now 18 head which look well   we are pretty well in the mountains and among the shoeshone or Snake indians. They at present appear friendly

Fryday July 4,   Travelled 23 miles   had good road except a few stoney hills. stoped to noon on a small stream   tasted a verry little of soda   The air is verry warm to day and we can see any amount of snow all the time. camp to night on a fine stream of water   had to cross   some few willows on it and excelent grass. To day has been the 4, Our company and another joing fired guns and drank toasts and had a merry time.

Saturday July 5   Traveled 25 miles to day   In the fore part of the day had some verry hilly road. excellent spring of water by the road side ozeing from the mountains. There is an insect which I shall call a cricket but some resembles a grass hopper   they are as large as your thumb, and everry hush & shrub is covered as full as it will hold, the coller of a black cricket   The indians gather them and dry them and pulverize them to put in soups. They wanted us to buy some. camp to night 11 miles east of fort hall, on a fine stream called Port neuf made up from fine springs, good water, willows for fuel, poor grass, being very dry.

Sunday July 6   Traveled 20 miles   found verry level road. The fore part of the day being very heavy sand. Struck a beautiful plain which is called snake river valley. skirted along the banks of the river with better cotton wood and popple, arived at fort hall, about 2 o'clock, passed old fort Lorim an American post about 5 miles above, fort hall.[8] This is where the soldiers were stationed,   fort hall is about 50 yds from the river and is built of doby brick, only one large building 2 story high and looks verry pretty. this is the Hudson Bays fort as the brittish   Although they never had soldiers stationed there it has been used as a fur traders establishment   about there they can get any quantity of fur, plenty of otter and beaver, bear buffalo, and many other kinds   This old house is now filled up with low dirty French, that have squaw wifes any quantity of Indians and half breeds. There are left 60 old United States waggons, and a great quantity of plunder, belonging to the soldiers, they left Fort Loraim last fall and were deposited at fort hall. There will have to be a station as another It will not be safe for emigrants to travel, camp about 2 miles from the fort, on a fine stream delightful grass and a large feild "or as you may say foild although it is not enclosed) of wild wheat which at a distance looks like a beautiful feild of wheat. There are any quantity of wild currents of which are yellow, red, & black. the red ones are like our currents in the states, are quite a luxury, could gather a bushel in a short time.

Monday July 7   Lay by to day at camp. Plenty of Indians about us and some not verry well disposed look rather suspicious.

Tuesday July 8   Travelled 21 miles   had some verry rough road, and some sand, nooned on an old camp ground, where is a nice spring an excelent water, good grass   Camp to night on Snake river at the great American Falls Which for the most part of them are more cascades than falls   They extend to the length of 300 ft and,

---

[8]Fort Loring was a U.S. Government Cantonment adjacent to Fort Hall, Idaho, from 1849–64.

in that distance their fall is 60 ft, being 150 yds wide. This is in Snake river or Clarks, & Lewis river. The bank or basaltic rock all together presents a beautiful prospect. We now have to travel about 2 hundred miles on this river.

Wednesday, July 9   Traveled 25 miles, had some verry hilly road, several small streams to cross any one of them large enough for a mill stream. Camp to night on Cassia creek, which is quite a stream here. Stay to night with a company of packers from Oregon returning to the States   sent some letters back by them. they gave us a great account of Oregon, and California

Thursday July 10   Travelled 22 miles   had verry rough road, verry rocky, hard traveling. travelled 16 miles without water Then struck a creek of verry poor water   any quantity of wild wheat up and down the creek   stock does not eat it if they can get any thing else. but in most places there is bunch grass which is good, and will grow on a mountain in the place of the low lands, were it not for that stock would suffer, In many places we have found plenty of red top grass, looks like the tame with the exception of the top which is not as red, our road to day has been over a sage barren and ashes which has the appearance of an old ashery. The soil all looks more like ashes than dirt. It puts me in mind of the white bean story. An old Indian came verry near stealing a horse from our company last night   when he was in the act of leading him of[f] the guard shot at him and he ran, without the horse. We had 2 stolen out of the train at fort hall, that belonged to Mr. Rose[9] of Michigan worth 100 dollars a piece. We have all the Denies[10] in our company. The old man & the surveyor, that surveyed Ontario, and whom you know. The indians are every day commiting some depredation or other, they steal and rob from every train and those dirty french put them up to it. I think if congress knew how bad they were they would protect the emigration as I have said it is cruel, for them to hold out inducements for people to settle Oregon and leave them unprotected and to fight theyr

---

[9] Aaron Rose, founder of Roseburg, Oregon. See introduction to this document, p. 118.

[10] John Denny was a War of 1812 veteran. With him on this journey was his wife, Sarah, a daughter, Loretta, and six sons and their families. They became Pacific Northwest settlers all the way from the central Willamette Valley to Puget Sound. Sarah H. Steeves, *Book of Remembrance* (Portland, Ore., 1927), pp. 211–13.

way as best they can,   passed 2 graves to day   camp to night on
Snake   good grass   no wood but sage, find plenty of currents so far
up the river.

Fryday July 11   Traveled 30 miles which we were obliged to do on
account of water & grass. traveled 22 miles before we stoped   here
we found a little grass baited[11] our horses and then traveled 8 miles
farther before we could find grass enough to camp. Had some of the
roughest stoney road you ever saw. Camp to night on a fine stream
plenty of grass and good dry willows for fuel.

Saturday July 12   Traveled 16 miles over verry rough road. It seems
the nearer we approach Oregon the worse roads we have, and a worse
more rough looking country   Camp to night on a stream of good
water   bank basaltine rocks.

Sunday July 13   Traveled 23 miles   had verry good road with the
exception of two or 3 hills   crossed warm spring creek to day which
at it head or at the spring it is boiling hot, and would boil a piece of
meat as quick as if over the fire, some of them tried it. It is about
blood warm at the crossing. Camp to night on Salmon fall creek in
which there are any quantity of fish   emptyes into snake river about
300 yds below us. This place is an especial resort for the Indians
thousands of their old camp, here they come in summer time to fish
and secure them for winter. Which with roots & what they steal is
their subsistance.

Monday July 14   remain in camp to day to rest our teams, good grass.

Tuesday July 15   Had last night a good horse stole from camp
which belonged to Mr. Strong[12] of Michigan. Mellville Hadley,[13]
Mr. Strong and 2 or 3 others went in pursuit of him   overtook it
about 12 miles from camp the indian riding him still off. The Indian
saw them jumped from his horse, and went to a ledge of rocks, wher
they said they could look of[f] some 300 ft and secreted himself
(knowing every crevice I suppose) and when they rode up on the
point of them to ascertain which way he went The Indian shot
Hadly, through the right side the ball passing in between his ribs and

---

[11]"Bait" was an old word for feeding horses during a pause on a journey.

[12]Mr. Strong of Michigan is so far unidentified.

[13]Melville Hadley, who was shot in this episode, was Samuel Hadley's younger brother.

out within an inch of his back bone   he is brought into camp alive Have a good Doctor[14] in our train, that went as soon as we got the news, which we heard from a young man by the name of Godfrey,[15] that was with him, he went out with 7 or 8 others and brought him in almost lifeless from loss of blood   was shot 12 o'clock in day time, brought in camp 11 o'clock at night.

Wednesday July 16   Lay by to day on H. account. He is some revived is verry sore and weak   can hardly be moved They did not get the horse. This is a wretched place to camp   all suffer from fear I am sure I can hardly lay down to sleep without It seems as though The Indians stood all around me ready to masacree me, shall be glad to go.

Thursday July 17   Are still in camp, Mell is better a little   are in hopes we can soon travel for we are in danger stoping here.

Fryday July 18   Traveled to day 12 miles which we were all day doing on account of Mel. he stood it better than we expected, we fixed a bed in our caraige and bolstered him up and drove slow with him, but after all every little jar he would hollar, and grown all the time but we were obliged to travel which seemed awful hard.

Saturday July 19   Traveled 15 miles   tolerable good road, some of our men went ahead and threw out all the stone so that Mel got along verry well, but was verry glad to get in camp. Camp on snake river   tolerable grass, heavy sand, killed several large rattle snakes in camp. There is some of the largest rattle snakes in this region I ever saw, being from 8 to 12 ft long, and about as large as a man's leg about the knee. This is no fiction at all. Traveled 20 miles   verry good road, plenty of Sage which has become a perfect nuisance   no grass of any account & poor water. Melville is quite smart to day am in hopes he will get well   he has every attention that is necessary, and a good phycian, to ride side of him.

Monday July 20   Traveled 14 miles and camped on a creek, not verry good water, nor grass, plenty of wild wheat, which our teams eat the head of. The sick still recovering. Do not feel verry well my self. am afraid I am going to be sick from constant fatigue, am not strong no why

---

[14]Presumably Dr. James C. Cole. See introduction to this document, p. 117.
[15]Godfrey is so far unidentified.

Tuesday July 21   Traveled 25 miles   had verry good road or M. could not have stood it to have rode so far, gets verry much fatigued before we stop to camp   still getting better   have to handle him verry careful. Am no better myself, feel as though I could not hold out much longer   I have the flux,[16] which is fast running me down am doctoring for it, but does me no good as yet.

Wednesday July 22   A beautiful fine day and Mell much better, so that it does not hurt him much to travel, or ride as he is comfortable in the caraige   I have the mountain fever[17]   the Doct. say with the flux, and am not able to set up, and hurts me verry bad to ride   yesterday camped on snake river, I am not hardly able to keep journal, to day we travel down the river, From where the road strikes river 6¼ rds to small creek   plenty of water   above and below crossing the road is level, but deep, dust, & some sand   no grass except on the margin of the river   do not know the exact distance we have travelled, to day, shall be brief in my descriptions.

Thursday July 23   From this creek to warm spring, 3 miles, These spring are to the left of the road 150 yds, the water to hot to bear your hand in. Heavy dust, from these spring, to a good camp on the road, distance 11 miles. There road leaves river, and takes up gradual, accend to left, The first 6 miles of the 11, from springs, road level then hills to accend & decend over bluff or river. This is a white clay bluff and you will find many small hills between this and camp, which is situated as described. Where road leaves river & on the oposite side from camp on the bottom some ¾ miles from the river is a round black mound of rock standing by itself, some distance from bluffs, I am no better and shall have to give up my journal for a few days, Mell is still improving, I will just give you the camps, and distances from here to Columbia river, in short, to sturgeon creek from this camp 11 miles, good camp, good camp on snake river 3½ miles, to the crossing of owyhe 12 miles, good camp   4 miles from there to fort Bossissee good camps all the way, From Fort Boissee to Malheur river 15 miles   good camp which is the first water from

---

[16]The "flux" was a term for bowel disorders.

[17]The best discussion of "mountain fever" is in John D. Unruh, Jr., *The Plains Across* (Urbana, Ill., 1979), p. 409. Unruh designated it either as Rocky Mountain spotted fever or as Colorado tick fever, saying it was "less virulent than cholera but deadly enough."

fort. To Sulpher springs 12 miles   poor camp, little water good to drink but verry sulphury   10 miles to birch creek, good camp, 3½ miles roads strikes snake river, good camp. There is the last you see of Snake river. 4½ miles to (burnt river) good camp, Travel up burnt river 34½ miles, good camp, all the way. From head of burnt river to Powder river slough 17 miles, 15 without water of that, good camp at slough, 9¼ miles to crossing of Powder river, good camp, 9 miles to fork of powder river, good camp, 3 miles to Sechend [second?] fork of powder river, ½ miles good spring, 14½ miles to grand round, plenty of water and grass in that distance. Then you have a splendid country of fine grass. 7¼ to a branch north side grand round, here you enter the blue montains   7½ miles verry rough road to crossing of grand round river, poor camp, no grass, plenty of water, Next water is a spring to left of road, 13 miles, poor camp   spring hard to find. not many emigrants find it and suffer for water before they get any. 7½ miles fa[r]ther is Lees old encampment   good camp, 19½ miles to Umatila spring, good camp, 14 miles to crossing of Umatila where road strikes bottom. From here to Columbia 13 miles ½

Saturday August 9   After strikeing the Columbia I again resume my journal. I have been very sick for the past 2 weeks and not able to wait on my self and of course my book neglected   I am now able to be about and Mellville able to ride on Horse back, Travelled 20 miles and verry sandy road, and but verry little grass and that is dry as hay. Camp to night on Columbia, bank verry sandy, no timber but plenty of Indians all along the shore fishing   catch a great many salmon Columbia is a pleasant river but is not as large here as I had supposed. We are in the Walla, Walla, nation and among that was a horrid murder, but the catholicks were the cause, they put the indians up to perpetrate the deed,[18] they are civil to us, and we have no trouble to watch our horse among them.

Sunday August 10   Traveled 16 miles heavy sand, folowed the banks of the columbia, down not much grass, barely enough to sustain life

---

[18]The work of Clifford M. Drury has proved that the Roman Catholics did not provoke the killing of the Protestant missionaries at the Whitman Mission. See especially his *Narcissa and Marcus Whitman and the Opening of Old Oregon*, 2 vols. (Glendale, Calif., 1973). He discusses this issue on pages 205–265 in volume 2. He even shows that Father J. B. A. Brouillet risked his own life in order to be helpful and helped to save Henry Spalding's life (v. 2, p. 287).

every thing is so dry that you cannot decern any thing green except a clump of willows, But the dry season is almost over, camp to night again on the river, I am getting considerable smart, no other sickness in the train.

Monday August 11   Traveled 14 miles   had very sandy road and enormous stony   still traveling down the river   Camp on willow creek a little stream which emptyes in Columbia   not much grass, but plenty of Grouse which is a kind of prarie chicken and you could not tell them from tame chicken   they are blacker than a prarie chicken, but the meat is as white and sweet as tame chicken.

Tuesday August 12   Traveled 17 miles   roads verry sandy, and rough plenty of salmon weighing from 20 to 30 lbs, 3 or 4 of our company and an ox train bought a canoe, and went down the river, camp to night on river. Had a fine sprinkle of rain which was something new

Wednesday August 13   Traveled 12 miles over verry hilly road, accended a mountain which we had to double teams, and could hardly get up at that, Camp to night on John Days river a pleasant stream, upon the mountain just before we crossed the river we saw Mt Hood towering high above the Cascades, A beautiful snow capt Mt.

Thursday August 14   After leaveing camp and river we accended a mountain which seemed almost insurmountable but by perseverance we accended the top, road to day over a mountainous country   have traveled 19 miles to day   camp to night on the Columbia. There is a small tradeing establishment here and also a place where people can take boats and go down the river   this is 6 miles from what is called the dalles, the price is 10 dollars a person, and 50 dollars pr waggon or one waggon for another, We shall cross the mountains ourselves, cant afford to give all we have to get through.

Fryday August 15   Traveled 14 miles over a very hilly road where the hills are dificult to get up without doubling teams   crossed the Deschutes river a little above where it emptyes in Columbia   had to ferry   paid 5 dollars per waggon   here we learned the sad intelligence that those that went down in a canoe were drowned. It is dangerous going down especialy when heavely loaded as they were, there being so many rapids in the river, their canoe was found bottom side up, with a pair of boots tied in the captern[19]   nothing has been seen of them. camp to night on an arm of the deshutes or fall river, Bought some potatoes at a little grocery here, for which we paid a bit pr pound   seemed like old times but rather dear eating to what we had been used to.

Saturday August 16   traveled 25 miles   had verry hilly and stony road, have seen several peaks of the cascades peering above the rest with their white mantles on   These mountains are heavy timbered with pine, hemlock cedar and shrub oaks with a little popple alder Hawthorn and birch and the largest elders I ever saw, from the size of the arm to some 10, or 12 inches through and many larger, Camp to night on the arm of the deshutes   good water   plenty of wood and the best kind, several indians here the Canakees,[20] the most filthy set I ever saw.

Sunday August 17   Traveled 12 miles over the most hilly rough road I ever saw   after we left camp we accended a mountain where we had eight horses to a wagon   camp to night at the foot of cascades called barlow gate, have only to travel 4 days before reaching Oregon Citty   what a joyful time will that be.

Monday August 18   Travelled 15   road awful hilly and mountainous, exceding anything yet   one hill was 1 miles ½ long, and verry steep, plenty of water isueing from the mountains, any quantity of plunder and waggons on the road.

Tuesday August 19   Traveled 12 miles over the worst road and mudy, it is indescribable   camp to night on a small opening, good grass to night but last night had none, there is little or no grass in these mountains except in spots, and hard to be found.

---

[19]She evidently means the "capstan" of the boat. The Oxford English Dictionary indicates nine variations of spelling in connection with the use of the word. It could mean something to wrap a rope around to secure the anchor or the boat. Amelia Hadley adds another spelling, "captern."

[20]By "Canakees" she may have meant the "Kanakas," or Hawaiians who present in old Oregon as a result of the maritime trade between Hawaii and the Northwest Pacific Coast.

[21]Philip Foster, a native of Maine, traveled to Oregon in 1843 by sea. His farm of Eagle Creek was a first stop for many travelers over the Oregon Trail, those who came the Barlow Road route south of Mount Hood. There is still a Foster Road leading in a southeasterly direction out of Portland.

Wednesday August 20   Traveled 20 miles over a much worse road than yesterday, accended a hill called Latrel hill steep & dangerous, enormous rock in the road so that waggons precipitate from 1, to 2 ft, perpendicular   cut a small tree and tied it to the back end of our waggons to keep them right side up.

Thursday August 21   Traveled 15 miles over a mud stony road over dividing ridge   all the team can do to strugle along.

Fryday August 22   traveled 18 miles   some of the day had verry good road   have had verry good luck in finding grass, cross the big and little Sandy, came to night within 10 miles of settlements.

Saturday August 23   traveled 10 miles   camp to night a farm, the mans name is Foster[21] from state of Maine   was kind and entertained us verry fine   could not walk strait after not being in a house for so long   when I got up to go across the floor I was like an old sailor that had not been on land for a long time, They had about 2 hundred bushels of peaches which looked delightful   And now you have seen me through this great Western thorough fare and you wonder where I have settled   I came from thence to O, citty and from there to Portland where I now remain, This is the end of a long and tedious journey

E. A. Hadley
Oregon

This is all I can tell you by pen and paper   my love to you all and should providence again call us together I can tell you more in an hour than I can write in a week.   E. A. Hadley

Twin Sisters on the Oregon Trail
Cecelia Adams & Parthenia Blank
1852

INTRODUCTION

The 1904 *Transactions* of the Oregon Pioneer Association printed a diary entitled "Crossing the Plains in 1852."[1] The author's name was "Mrs. Cecelia Emily McMillen Adams." Since its publication this journal has been quoted in many standard works on the overland trails.

Originally it was our assumption that on the face of it this was a correct rendering of Cecelia Adams' diary, and that no major changes would be necessary in its publication in our series. Never were we more wrong.

Upon studying the original manuscript in the library of the Oregon Historical Society in Portland,[2] we found a typewritten copy accompanying the handwritten original, transcribed by some unnamed volunteer who pointed out that there were two persons' handwriting alternating through the diary. After studying the manuscript we found this was true. As we studied it, it became clear that the diary was alternately kept by two women, but who was the other one? Then it became clear: There were twin sisters, Cecelia and Parthenia,[3] daughters of Joseph and Ruth McMillen. At the time of the overland journey the young women were 23 years old, having been born on February 16, 1829, at Lodi, New York.[4] Cecelia was married to a medical doctor, William Adams,[5] in Elgin, Illinois, on June 30, 1849.[6] Parthenia was married to Stephen Blank, a carpenter, in St. Charles, Illinois, on November 9, 1850.[7]

---

[1]Thirty-Second Annual Reunion, pp. 288–329.   [2]Ms, 1508.

[3]Occasionally there appear variations in the spelling of both names. Cecelia's name was often spelled "Cecilia"; Parthenia's name appears as "Perthenia." The name Parthenia derives from the same roots as the Parthenon. It means "maidenhood" or "maidenness."

[4]*Transactions* of the Oregon Pioneer Association, op. cit., p. 288.

[5]Manuscript letter of William Adams to George Himes, Hillsboro, Oregon, June 1, 1905 (Ms. 1508). Adams was a new graduate of Oberlin College, Oberlin, Ohio.

[6]*Genealogical Material in Oregon Donation Land Claims*, 1, (Portland, 1957), Claim No. 1617.

[7]This information is from Parthenia Blank's obituary, Forest Grove, Oregon, *Washington County News-Times*, Dec. 30, 1915. Stephen Blank is usually designated either a "carpenter" or a "cabinet-maker." Beulah Hurst and Beatrice M. Carstairs, *Early Oregon Cabinet Makers and Furniture Manufacturers, 1826–1897* (N.p., 1935), mimeographed, p. 65.

Many years after the 1852 overland journey William Adams reminisced about the twins in a letter to George Himes, Curator of the Oregon Historical Museum, Portland:[8]

The twins were always together when circumstances would permit and if they ever disagreed or doubted each other I do not know it. In all the long journey thro the wilderness they, with their husbands, slept at night in the same wagon, Mr. Blank's, walking much of the day, and as the oxen began to weaken they would walk together all day, sometimes over 20 miles. They were rather short, and in short dresses, looked shorter, and when we took the short steamboat ride from the Cascades to Portland, a lady asked my brothers wife if those little girls mother was with them.

William Adams, in the same letter, said of his former wife that Cecelia "was a born musician, Artist and teacher, and worker too." Of Parthenia he wrote, "Her twin sister was just like her but very different—taciturn, but never gloomy, never sang nor played on instruments—had good taste but no ambition in art—never taught nor wanted to—steady, earnest, cheerful work."

Neither of the couples had any children; however, Parthenia and Stephen Blank adopted and raised ten orphans.[9]

Cecelia died on August 12, 1867,[10] at age 38, in her sister's home in Forest Grove. Parthenia lived on many years. Her death took place on December 25, 1915, at age 86.[11]

The Blanks lived out their lives in Forest Grove, and the Adamses resided in neighboring Hillsboro.

Another member of the 1852 party was Joseph McMillen, father of the twins. He had left his wife, Ruth, and three other younger children in Illinois. Joseph was a millwright. He would return from Oregon in 1856 by way of Panama. Once more he crossed over the Oregon Trail with the family. They settled and lived out their lives in Forest Grove. Joseph died at age 93 in 1890; Ruth also lived into her nineties.[12]

James H. McMillen, older brother of the twins, had emigrated to Oregon in 1845, was already well-known in the Oregon Country. He,

---

[8]This letter is in the same folder as the twins' journal in the Oregon Historical Society collection. It has the same number also, ms. 1508.

[9]William Adams, Letter, op. cit.

[10]Portland *Oregonian*, Aug. 19, 1867. See also William Adams, Letter, op cit.

[11]Forest Grove *Washington County News-Times*, Dec. 30. 1915.

[12]*Portrait and Biographical Record of the Willamette Valley, Oregon* (Chicago, 1903), pp. 107–08.

too, was a millwright.[13] The overland party arrived just in time for the marriage of James to Tirzah Barton in the autumn of 1852.[14]

Also taking the overland trail with the 1852 party was Calvin H. Adams (brother of William) and his wife, Catherine. In writing his memorandum in 1905 William Adams told George Himes that he lived with his brother and "his invalid, aged wife" in Hillsboro. He added that Calvin, "now 85, often walks two miles to his work and back. . ."

It is with the permission of the Oregon Historical Society, Portland, that this record of two young women crossing the plains is printed. The society has also given permission to quote from the William Adams memo to George Himes.

The McMillens, Adams and Blank families were all active supporters of the Congregational educational institution in Forest Grove, now Pacific University. Then it was called "Pacific University and Tualatin Academy." Parthenia Blank took great delight in entertaining students in their home. William Adams even served as principal of the academy.[15]

THE DIARY

[Parthenia] . . . behind us. Staid where we were for 3 hours. Started on. Had a hard rain & hail storm. made the roads bad and we soon camped. Made 14 miles

Wednesday 19th [May]. Found we were on the road to St. Joseph instead of the Mormon trace.[16] Passed through Gentryville about noon. Here we had a prairie to cross 15 miles without water, staid till sunset and went on about four miles and encamped on the Prairie carrying our wood with us   made 18 miles

Thursday 20th.   Traveled about six miles on the road to St. Jo. then

---

[13]Captain J. H. McMillen," in *History of the Pacific Northwest*, II (Portland, 1888), pp. 464–65.

[14]"Mrs. Tirzah Barton MacMillan," (sic), Joseph Gaston, *Portland, Oregon, Its History and Builders*, II (Chicago, 1911), p. 792.

[15]James R. Robertson, "Origin of Pacific University," *Oregon Historical Quarterly*, VI (June, 1905), pp. 109–46, especially p. 127.

[16]The Mormon trace or trail was from St. Joseph westward along the Santa Fe Trail in Kansas to 110-Mile Creek [now Dragon Creek], thence to Fort Riley, on to Fort Kearny, Nebraska, and finally to Salt Lake City. Louise Barry, *The Beginning of the West* (Topeka, Kan., 1972), p. 1222.

took the Savannah state road and had rare fun in crossing some of the state mud holes for they beat anything we had before seen. Encamped on the bank of the Platte[17] forded near Hunts mill. Made 20 m

Friday 21st [May]   Commenced raining soon after we started and continued to rain all day mostly. Went on to Ogle's mill on the river 102[?] which we forded and encamped. Bought 200 lbs. flour and 4 bushels meal. made 5 miles

Saturday 22d   started to day and it soon began to rain but did not continue more than 2 hours. After traveling about 7 miles we came upon the road leading from Savanna [Missouri] to the [Council] Bluffs. Passed through Newark and crossed the Nottaway [Nodaway] River by ferry. Made 12 miles. Could find no grass for our cattle and as it was near dark we tied them up and staid till morning

Sunday 23d   started for good feed and encamped about 3 miles from the river on a Prairie and had first rate grass. Here we staid all day. Made 3 miles

Monday 24.   Started early. Had rough roads bad dry and very Hilly. Found some gooseberries and had them at supper. Calvin discovered a litter of young skunks but afterwards found they were calves— Reached the Missouri bottom about noon and traveled under the bluff the rest of the day. Made 18 miles

Tuesday 25th   Crossed the Little Tarkio and then left the bottom and traveled over hills till we came to the Big Tarkio then took the mud for it. O dear! for about ½ mile—Had some rain in the morning and roads not very good. Level ground is not known here. Made 20 miles

Wednesday 26th [May]   Had rain all last night and the roads bad in consequence. Traveled slowly till afternoon when we came to the town of Lynden. Here we found roads that had been traveled more and were very good and soon came again into the Missouri bottom and had good level roads for the rest of the day. Here we got our first sight of

---

[17]This was the "Little Platte River," so-called by Lewis and Clark. It flows in northwestern Missouri southward to join the Missouri River at Farley, some 15 miles northwest of Kansas City. The French called it *Petite Rivière Platte*, in contrast to the much larger Nebraska Platte River, which the overlanders would follow later. *Missouri, A Guide to the "Show Me State"* (New York, 1941), p. 388.

the Mo. river and encamped in sight of it on the banks of the Niskinabotany [Nishnabotna] which we crossed on a bridge. Made 17

Thursday 27th   Started early and traveled up the bottom for about 6 miles. Paid 25 cents for traveling the length of a ferry boat across a slough and then up the bluff again. Today we left the state if Missoury and entered Iowa. From this time we found but little bad roads. Mostly prairie and timber scarce. Passed near the town of Sidney. Made 18

Friday 28th   Roads still good—Traveled 17 miles.

Saturday 29th   Passed through Coonville and crossed Keg creek. To day we came upon the Mormon trace and traveled about three miles on it and encamped on Pony creek about 5 miles from Kanesville. made 20 miles

Sunday 30th [May]   In the morning found Esquire Hewitt from Dundee [Illinois] informed us that our company were encamped about a mile ahead of us. Hitched up our team and started about 11 o'clock but when we got where they had left, but we passed on and soon found them encamped again in a field on the Missouri bottom about 2 miles from Kanesville. Of course we camped too—

Wednesday   the same   Thursday [June 3d]   started and went to the ferry—the old Traders Point—Council Bluffs P. O. 6 miles.

Friday 4th   This is a day long to be remembered for hard work. Paid $1.00 per wagon and 25 cts. pr yoke of oxen for the privalege of ferrying ourselves over the Missouri in a flat boat which took us all day and till after dark. Made one mile. Our company now consists of six wagons, one of which is bound for California. A great many Mormons are starting for the Salt Lake.

[*There follows a poem written in pencil signed by Cecelia:*]
Home
what so sweet!
So beautiful on Earth! Oh! so rare
As kindred love and family repose!
        The busy world
With all the tumult and the stir of life
Pursues its wonted course; on pleasures some

And some on commerce and ambition bent
And all on happiness, while each one loves
With natures holiest feelings. One sweet spot
And calls it *Home*. If sorrow is felt there
It seems through many bosoms and a smile
And if disease intrudes the sufferer finds
Rest on the breast beloved

[*Parthenia*] Saturday 5th [June]   proceeded up a pretty hilly road
and but little of interest occurred. Made 15 miles [*Interlined by
Cecelia:*] Just commenced keeping guard   Found some strawberries
today.

[*Parthenia*] *Sunday* 6   proceeded on. At noon when we stopped for
dinner the cattle took a stampede for about a mile, cause unknown.
At night as we were about to encamp they took another with the
wagons but did not do much damage and were soon stopped Made
18 miles   [*Added by Cecelia:*] Last night my clothes got out of the
wagon & the oxen eat them up & I consider I have met with a great
loss as it was my woolen dress

[*Parthenia*] *Monday* 7th   Nothing of much interest occurred to day
except a cold night last night—Ferried across the Elkhorn and
forded Rawhide and reached the bank of the Platt—Made 24 miles
[*Written in margin*] While we were crossing the Elkhorn it rained
and hailed very hard   [*Cecelia*]   To day we saw four Indian's graves
They were quite open I could see two buffalo robes within which had
probably been wraped around the body   They were buried on the
surface of the earth and mounds erected over them and an opening
had been made in the side probably by the emigrants   As we were
looking at them we saw four Indians comeing towards us on horseback which caused us to be leaveing   they had been stealing sheep
from the Emigrants.

[*Parthenia*] *Tuesday [June] 8th*   Proceeded on up the Platte   caught
a few small fish. Roads fine and boundless level prairie   made 17
miles

[*Cecelia*] [June] 9th Wednesday. We are all very glad to get on our
clocks [cloaks] and overcoats and mittens this morning   it is so very

cold   North wind blows very hard—noon here we find a new made grave   on the headboard is inscribed "D Hherer [*sic*] died May 28th 1852   Aged 5 years"   To day we met Several teams on their way back   We made no enquires as they had the small pox   We also saw some mormons on their way back   they said the road was good and no Indians on our way as far up as *Ft Larimie*   Made 19 miles

10 Thursday   hard South wind for several days followed up the Loup fork   This is a branch of the Platte a very rapped stream filled with sand bars   Find a few wild roses and yellow daisys   To night we encamped on a beautiful spot with plenty of wood and grass   One of our oxen has become very lame   Timber is generaly very scarce. to day we saw two new graves   On the head board was writen with a pencil "Mary Morris aged 19 and M C Morris aged 9 yrs we saw good clothing scatter around which caused us to think they had died with some contagious disease here we done some washing   made 18 miles

[June] 11th Friday   S. W.   Took an early start this morning   P and myself walked on several miles   We have very cold nights and not very warm days which makes it fine for our cattle   12 o'clock stoped for dinner this is all the time I get to write or read   The horse flies are very bad today. I never saw such large ones and so many of them before   The boys arc all laying under the wagons asleep   To day crossed looking glass creek beaver creek plumb creek and Ash creek   We find quite a number of dead oxen and horses Encampd on the Loup fork bottom to night   we could hear the Indians but did not see any   made 20 miles

12 *Sat*   W. W.   quite warm to day with a cool breeze   P and self walked on several miles   We came to an old deserted Indian village We think by the looks of the land that it has been cultivated   in a few places found some Cedar for the first time   The soil is very sandy   Grass is very good here   Cotton wood is the principal timber on these rivers   See no Buffalo yet. this is a beautiful part of the country very level   We have some good neighbors in our company encamped for the night on the Loup Fork   had to go two miles for wood   made 19 miles

[June]   13 Sunday   W. wind very hard   This is a lovely morning
has the appearance of rain which made us very anxious to ford the
river so we started on   found it rather dangerous crossing on
account of quicksand   Mr Millers waggon came very near going
down   P. and self waded through   took father for our pilot   we
had a grand time as we had to follow down the river half a mile so as
to keep out of the deepest water so that we traveled nearly a mile in
the water   We feel all the better for our ducking   It took us nearly
all day, but got across safe at last   Seams but little like the Sabbath
find a few strange flowers made 6½ miles   Think of Anne[18] as it is
her birth day

[June] 14 Mon   very hard W wind   took an early start this morning calculating to stop and rest our teams as soon as we come to good
grass which our (*guide book*) says will be two or three days travel. here
we we find toads with horns and long tails   they are about three
inches long and very slender and tails as long as the body   they are
spotted white yellow and brown can run as fast as a man and very
wild   Musketoes annoy us very much and sometimes the air seams
to be filled with large bugs   Dust is very troublesome roads good.
water scarce. grass poor. no timber   This afternoon we passed seven
new made graves   one had four bodys in it and to all appearances
they were laid on the top of the ground and the dirt thrown over
them. most of them were aged people   it was writen on some of the
head boards that they died with the cholera We find good bed
clothes and clothing of all kinds but do not pretend to touch one of
them   Encamped for the night on the wide prairie creek   find
good grass & water but no wood but we brought wood with us as our
(Guide) directed us to do   Made 23 miles

15th *Tues* N. wind   quite cool, rained very hard last night which was
acceptable to us   Did not take an early start this morn as we do not
calculate to drive any great distance to day as our teams are getting
very tired and our lame ox is no better   I had the sick head ache last
night and do not feel able to sit up much to day   have a good bed in
the waggon   *Our folks had a new milk's cow to day.* Encamped on the

---

[18]"Ann E. (age 12) is listed along with "Perthena" (age 21) in the 1850 census of Illinois as
daughters of Joseph and Ruth "McMellen."

Platte poor wood and grass. rained all day which makes it very disagreeable getting supper to night   Made 11½ miles

[June] 16th   *Wednes*   Wind N. E   Rainy this morning very disagreeable getting breakfast   we concluded to go on slowly untill we find a better camping place   A man died this morning with the Cholera in a company ahead of us   find prickly pear. all the wood we find to day is quakeing Asp which is miserable for fuel   Have no wild game yet altho our boys arc on the chase most of the time   Passed 11 new graves Crossed weed creek   encamped one mile from the Platte   poor wood and miserable water   good grass Made 13 miles   Elected officers to night

17 Thursday   very warm and sultry concluded to stay and do our washing   by takeing our clothes down to the river we can wash very well   Another man died near us this morning   The Doct gets some practice Henry is quite unwell to day but as a general thing we are blessed with excelent health and good spirets 3 O'clock concluded to pick up and go a little ways as we shall have a long drive tomorrow Done a large washing had the hardest water I ever saw   Oxen getting better   Passed six new graves   Encamped on the prairie brought our wood and water with us found water enough for our cattle   Made 4 miles Had a new milks cow to day

18 Friday   Warm and sultry   took an early start this morning Our company at the present consists of eight waggons 16 men and 10 ladies besides children   A large company passed us to day from Kane *Co* Ill Elgin Dundee and St Charles   all horse teams   They seemed like our own folks   Another man died near us to day and an old lady 56 *yrs* old   The Doctors think that they drank poison water out of a spring near by

[*Parthenia*] here we find Lockspir and also a very prety dark flower strangers to us   they resemble the moss rose, this afternoon we had a very heavy shower accompanyed with hail and hard wind   we have passed 21 new made graves to day   it makes it seem very gloomy to us to see so many of the emegrants burried on the plains   made 18 miles

[June] 19 Saturday   very warm   took an early start crossed a very

deep ravene with steep banks which was entirely dry   Our boys have
been hunting all the forenoon   just returned with a buffalo covered
with feathers about the size of a prairie hen   is all the game we have
yet. Passed thirteen graves today   We just met a train from Ft
Larime going to St Joseph with the mail but would not wait for us
to write any letters so mother missed of one this time   encamped on
Elm creek a very beautiful spot   It seems too bad to see such pretty
places uninhabited   We see snipes turkey buzzards and a few blackbirds   We seen no Indians yet   The express men tell us we shall
find none untill we get to Frt L—   made 16 miles   At noon father
made us a good cup of tea

[June] 20 Sunday   This is a beautiful morning   very warm   did not
expect to travel any to day   a few sweet birds are singing and all nature
seems to be praising their Maker   I cannot help thinking of our dear
home to day   I think I see them going to the house of God to worship
there   O! what a blessed privelege Here I [am] on these wide prairie
we seldom here the voice of prayer   But I trust a spirit of prayer and
praise is felt in all most every heart   We have great reason to be
thankful for the many blessings and mercies that daily attend us
Through dangers both seen and unseen the hand of God has directed
us and while we see so many continualy falling around us We still live
in the enjoyment of good health and spirits "Bless the Lord oh my soul
let all that is within me bless his holy name"   It seems best for us to
travel to day as we shall be obliged to stop again in a day or two   We
have more time for reading and meditation when we are traveling than
we do when we stop and spend a day   we have so much to do when
we stop it keeps us busy all day   Passed 10 graves   We lost our Guide
Book on *Sat* which caused us to go much farther to day than we
expected   We find a great many sink holes   they are round hollow
places in the ground filled with Alkaly water   if they dry up it leaves
the earth covered with Saleratus   We have to guard our cattle from
them all the time   We saw some buffalo to day for the first time   Our
hunting boys ran after them with their guns prepared but they ran
towards them so fast it frightened them away   They were most to anxious   We encamped on the prairie   carried our wood with us besides
picking up buffalo chips for the fire   Made 16 miles

[June] 21st *Mon*   Wind N. E.   very pleasant   took an early start Mr Stoel [Stowell][19] came back to us last night   has not been with us before for five weeks or more   are glad to have our friend come back with us again   very high wind this afternoon which makes it very bad traveling   to day we can see teams on the other side of the Platte   that is the road that James[20] traveled   the bluffs are very high on that side   to day five men direct from oregon   they gave us the privelage of writing home   last night we had music and dancing it makes it seem quite like home to hear the Accordian which Cecelia plays most every evening   Not very good roads   Made 20 miles

[*Cecelia*] Tuesday [June] 22   cool and pleasant   Stephen [Blank] is quite unwell to day   Some of our boys are hunting to day   some men from Oregon came along to day on their way back to the states tell us we shall find plenty of grass ahead and no Indians   We sent two letters home by them   One of them said he was acquainted with James [McMillen]   Passed 7 graves   if we should go by all the camping grounds we should see five times as many graves as we now do   At noon it rained very hard and continued so all after noon very hard wind   Had rather a disagreeable time getting supper   Our chips burn rather poor as they are so wet   It seems like a winter night it is so very cold   Made 14 miles

23 Wednesday   this is a gloomy morning, it rained so much last night. To day we come to some bluffs for the first time   sandy roads and hard drawing good grass   find some wood very poor   take some with us   poor water   crossed Skunk creek   encamped for the night with no wood or water excepting what we had with us Passed 21 graves   Here we find a white poppy but they are so cov- ered with thorns that we cannot pick them   Made 18 miles

June 24   Wind N. E.   very cold indeed this morning   took an early start   Found some good looking springs but dare not use any of the water, roads good very sandy   We can see teams on the other side of

<hr>

[19] This was John Stowell, a Tennessean, who, with his wife, Margaret, and their family, later settled near Eugene, Oregon. Addie Dyal, *1860 Federal Census of Lane County, Oregon* (Eugene, n.d.), p. 13.

[20]James H. McMillen, older brother of the twins, was already settled in Oregon, having trav- eled over the trail in 1845. *History of Pacific Northwest—Oregon and Washington* (Portland, 1889), 11, pp. 464–65.

the Platte   the road that brother James traveled on   But our road is much the best as there are so many bluffs on the other road   Passed 18 graves   We met another Oregon train to day on their way back to Iowa   It consisted of men women and children   they were packed on horses   had but one wagon   We inquired if they were sick of Oregon They said no expected to go back next spring   They were in such a hurry they would not stop to talk   To day we see the last timber for 200 miles   *So our Guide* sayes   Made 18 miles

25 Friday   Wind E this morning   woke up and found it raining very hard   We expected to do our washing here to day but it rains so that we concluded to travel The roads rather bad   use Platte water   it is a very mudy stream   We can settle it with alum so that it is very good. generally get a pint of mud out of every pail of water To day we passed a grave that had been dug open by the wolves   all we could see of the remains were the clothes that it had been wraped up in   We found the head board some distance from the grave   on it was inscribed Henry Verdant Aged 52 from Edgar *Co* Ill Crossed the North bluff fork Passed 8 graves   traveled 4 miles on the bluffs   so much sand that it is almost impossible to get over them   Did not find a camping ground till very late Muskuetoes very troublesom   Made 18 miles

[June] 26   Saturday   Wind E.   Did not Start very early as we oversleept ourselves   Have a hard time getting a fire to cook our breakfast as everything is so wet   Some of our company had a regular fight to day but all of our folks kept out of the muss   One or two was knocked down but no injury done only they are obliged to leave our company   Find prickly pairs in great abundance   the flowers of one kind resemble the pink China Aster   The pink ones are very beautiful   Passed through another dogtown to day   they resemble the fox Squarrel in shape and color   it is almost impossible to kill one of them   they are so very shy   Passed some deep ravenes   Passed 9 graves   very sandy roads   find some beautiful looking springs but dare not use the water   Keep near the Platt good grass   no wood   Made 18 miles

27 Sunday   This is a lovely mornig   conclude to stay here to day and recruit our team   they have stood the journey very well but

want some rest   But we find a great deal to do   P done some washing and I baked bread and pumpkin and apple pies   cooked beans and meat   stewed apples and baked suckeyes in quantitys sufficient to last some time   Besides making dutch cheese and took every thing out of the waggons to air   A birth took place to day in one of the companies near us   It threatened a hard storm this afternoon but only gave us a few drops and passed on   Buffalo bones are scattered all over the plains   We can see emigrants as far as the eye can reach   I do not see any company that can get along better than we do   We all take a great deal of comfort especially sister P and myself we have some jolly times if we are in the wilderness

[June] 28   Monday   South W. cool and pleasant started early roads sandy   crossed two small creeks Stoped for dinner opposit Cedar Bluffs on the other side of the Platte   some of the boys are out on a hunting excursion   Passed 11 graves   Encamped for the night on the banks of the platte   Some little sickness in some of the companys but we all enjoy good health which we consider a great blessing   Made 19 miles

[June] 29   Tuesday   Wind E   last night about 12 o'clock the wind blew a perfect hurricane which made a scattering among the tents   We slept in our waggon and it rocked like a cradle   expected it to go over every moment altho they were chained down   but it is very calm this morning   After traveling some 4 miles of good road we came to some very high bluffs the highest we have seen yet   P and myself forded a little stream barefoot and walked over the bluffs which are a mile in length   sand very deep   Passed 10 graves Passed the lone tree the only stick of timber within 200 miles   this is about half way between   The tops have all been cut off   it is cedar   We took a few splinters in memory of it   Encamped on Cassel [Castle] creek   Passed another dog town   Made 20 miles Passed Ash Holler Station Where one man stays alone

30 Wed   W.N.   very pleasant   Last night had another hard wind and some little rain   The Bluffs look very beautiful on the other side of the Platte but should not like to travel over them   Good grass Passed 10 graves   find considerable drift wood   Made 22 miles

July 1st *Thurs*   Wind S. E.   has the appearance of a storm   We see Antilope very often but our hunters have not caught any thing worth speaking of yet have killed two or three yellow rattle snakes Large gray wolves are very plenty they will kill buffalo and the emigrants sometimes loose their cattle Passed 8 graves One of the men that left our *camp* is very sick one that had a quarrel with his son in law Made 21 miles

2 Friday Had a very hard wind last night The sick man is dead this morning We stop to see him burried They wraped him in bed clothes and layed him in the ground without any coffin We sung a hymn a had prayer O! it is so hard to leave friends in this wilderness Some of the bluffs look like old castles. Are in sight of chimney rock, can see it fifty miles off. Passed 8 graves. Follow on the Platte, very poor grass, quite warm, travel slowly. Made 16 miles.

3 Sat W.W very pleasant To day we come to the river opposite Chimney Rock which has been visible most of the way for the last 35 miles It is said to be 3 miles from the opposite side of the river but on these level prairies we cannot judge much of distances by the eye It does not appear more than half a mile It consists of a large square column of clay and sand mixed together with a base of conical form apperantly composed of sand, round base cone. and appears as if the column had been set up and the sand heaped around it to sustain it It is said to be 500 feet high but doubt it some Just back of it to the South is another structure of the same material which has the appearance of an Illinois Straw Stable[21] and a little to the west is a cluster which the imagination can easily make a barn and stacks and which bears this name We very much regret that we could not cross the river and get a closer view of it but we can see it very distinctly through our spyglass I love to look at it because I know that Brother James [McMillen] been on it We see a great many strange looking rock that look like old ruins but I could not discribe them accurately had I time *16*

[July] 4th *Sun* W. W. This is a delightful morning a few sweet birds are trying to sing their makers praise Our thoughts are continually turning homeward I suppose your all haveing a sabbath school celebration

---

[21]A "straw stable" or "straw shed" was a winter shelter for farm animals made of posts and covered with straw. Ramon F. Adams, *Western Words* (Norman, Oklahoma, 1968 rev.), p. 309.

to day   We would like to take a sly squint and see what you are doing This morning met a train from Call [California] on their way to the States they tell us we shall be rather late   but little trouble if any with the Indians   Seemed much pleased with our new stile of dress   To day Henry found an ox that had been left because he was a little lame they put some shoes on him and think he will do us a great deal of good Passed 2 graves   Encamped on the Platt   Made 15 miles

5 Mon   W. W.   The wind blows hard every night To day we see *Larime Peak*   It looks like a cloud   It is over 100 miles from here roads good   Passed graves   Made 18 miles

6 Tues   W South   pleasant and cool   To day we come to timber mostly cotten wood   a Mrs Wilson in our company is quite sick so that we cannot go very fast roads very good   Passed 6 graves   grass rather poor Has the appearance of a hard storm   Made 9 miles

[July] 7   Wed   W. W. Last night we had a very hard rain and O! how hard the wind blew   Our sick woman much better   Started on and commenced raining but it soon passed off and has the appearance of a pleasant day   Passed a tent where we found one keeping a grocery store   Kept a little of every thing but a person must want very bad before paying high prices

[*Parthenia*] Roads good most of the day but toward night sandy. camped 3 miles below Fort Larimie Plenty of wood a great luxury for it is the first time we have had it for more than 200 miles

Thurs 8th   To day we do not travel for we want to do some business at the fort and the women want to wash   Idy [?] is quite sick to day but hope she will be better soon

[*Cecelia*]   [July] 9   Fri   W. W. Started on very pleasant roads very sandy   Passed by the *Ft*   left 4 letters at the P.O   Saw some Indians   Find some wild currents two kind black and yellow ones Encamped on the bottom of the Platte   Made *14*

10 Sat   S.W.   very cold this morning to day we come into the Black hills   They seem to be solid rock and very high and Steep covered with Pitch pine and cedar   P and I climbed one of them and had as much as we wanted to do to get down, it requires long toe nails to go up and down them   Stoped for dinner but could find

nothing for our poor cattle neither grass nor water   Passed 8 graves
Encamped on the Platte poor grass   plenty of wood & water
made 14 miles

[July] 11   *Sun*   very cool north wind   Started very late [h]our
go up hill and down again   Find some beautiful yellow flowers that
resemble the evening beauties and some little blue bells and a white
flower resembling the lily and blue lark spur and the yellow
Suflowers   Find wild sage for the first time   no water   poor grass
Passed 15 graves   Encamped near the Platte   made 13 miles

12 *Mon*   W.N   Cool and cloudy   Started early find neither grass
or water till 5 o'clock   To day we left an ox   it was so lame but
Henry's ox takes it place   is cloudy every afternoon   Passed 5
graves   Poor grass   Made 15 miles

13 Tues   W S   very pleasant   Henry killed a mountain hen   it
resembled a prairie hen but I think superior in flaver   is some larger
P. and I walked on ahead of the rest of the *com*[pany] some distance
went down a steep hill   some Indians on horse back came along
We were somewhat frightened we turned back for our teams   found
they were nearer than we had expected and so we stood still and
looked at them   They looked at us very smileing painted faces and
long hair hanging down on the back   We passed on and left them
Standing gazeing at us   Our boys are on a buffalo hunt hope they
will get one   Well here they come each one loaded with buffalo
meat   have at last had the chance of tasting the long wished for
meat   We do not relish it as well as we had expected to, is very much
like beef, good roads   made 20 miles

[July] 14, 15 and 16   spent in resting our teams   by swimming
them across the Platte we found excellent grass   Spent our time
washing, repairing wagons and makeing a new tent   Our boys killed
an antilope which we all relish very much   also caught some nice
fish. it is very warm—

17   Sat   W S   very pleasant this morning   did not get started
very early it took so long to get our cattle over the river   find the
roads very sandy and hilly   no grass   Passed 3 graves   Encamped
on the Platte   Made 14 miles

18   Sun   W W   very pleasant with a good breeze   Think of home a great deal to day   now and then see a buffalo   no grass on this side of the river   we swim our cattle over every night and back in the morning 4 graves   keep a constant guard by them   roads very sandy   Encamped for the night on the Platte   Made 16 miles

19   Mon   W.W. cool and pleasant   roads very sandy and dust very troublesome   We walked most of the day   Passed but 2 graves The ground is covered with little purple, pink and white daisys Misquetoes very annoying   Made 14 m

[July] 20   Tues   W E   cool breeze   To day met some men from *Call* [California] on the way back to the States gave us much encouragement   We have nothing but sand to travel to day   We encamped to night on the Platte for the last time   see plenty of buffalo but can kill none of them   made 10 miles

July 21st   Wed   W.W.   concluded to spend the day here and repair their wagons and rest the teams   We do our washing   Find plenty of wild currents   they are very good but not equal to the tame Find good grass and water

22 Thurs   W N   To day passed the ferry where James came over in our road   I have the sick head ache to day so that I am not able to sit up   met another train of Oregon men   would not stop to talk with us   The Indians are gathered around us to day they look very savage but we are well prepared for them   we go in large companies very good roads To day we leave the Platte for good   Made 14 m

23 Fri   W.W.   This morning we started at three O'clock as we had 15 miles to go without water and wanted to travel in the cool of the day   did not stop to get any breakfast for our cattle or ourselves Passed 7 graves   We encamped to night on willows spring find good grass by driving our cattle two miles off the road and keep a strict guard   Good water   all keep well   Made 15 miles

[July]   24   Sat   W. W.   very pleasant and warm   Did not start very early as we do not expect to go far   Stoped at noon on greece wood creek   here we will stay till morning   Passed 3 graves   Poor grass   no wood, good water   Made 10 miles

25 Sun   W.W.   this morning we started at 3 o'clock to feed and get breakfast   Sand very deep and dust very troublesome   Stoped for dinner opposit Independance Rock   It is a great curiosity but we were all so tired that we could not go to the top of it   It is almost entirely covered with names of emigrants   Went on to the Devil's Gate and encamped   this is is a great curiosity but we have not time to visit it and regret it very much   Passed 3 graves   Forded the Sweet water. *M 16*

26 Mon   W.W. cool mornings and evenings but warm and sultry through the day   Find a great many dead cattle   to day passed a Station   here we traided off a yoke of oxen for a yoke of cows   our oxen were sore footed   Made 14 m

27 Tues   W N   very warm   we can see nothing on eather side but mountains   roads very sandy and dust troublesome   keep on the sweet water River   Find goose berys   they are very sour indeed   Passed 3 graves   Encamped on the river   made 14 m

28 Wed   W.W.   warm and pleasant   Perthenia and I climbed a very steep rock some 4 or 5 hundred feet high   got very tired indeed, found a great many names   To day we can see the snow cap mountains for the first time   roads in some places very bad   keep on the sweet water   Very poor grass   Made 17

[July] 29   *Thur*   This morning was obliged to start at One o'clock and go 10 miles before we could find any grass for our cattle   they had no supper last night or water   We stoped at Sun rise and find every good feed by driving our cattle 2 or 3 miles off   Mr Miller is quite sick to day   fear he has the mountain fever We shall stay here till noon   we do some washing and bakeing   Started on at noon went 6 miles   Encamped on the river near some willow springs, one of Jame's camping grounds [interlined: "here the river forks"] He is nine days in advance of us   very poor grass   Passed 8 graves within two days   made 16

30 Fri   W.N. Took an early start this morning. have some very bad hills to climb to day   Passed some very good springs and several Saluratus lakes   Last night One of the Doct's cows died   To day I have kept an account of the dead cattle we passed   the number to

day is 35   We passed a Station to day   here we saw plenty of
Indians   they seem very friendly they were engaged in dressing
some prairie dogs   They had several little Pappoos's   they look very
cunning   Some were makeing moccasins for sale they trim them
very nicely with beads   Went on a little farther and came to another
here is a black smith shop   We saw one white lady here   The men
engaged in gambling and playing cards   Passed five graves
Encamped on a branch of the Sweet water   every afternoon it
clouds up and threatens a hard storm but generaly passes of without
raining but gave us a little last night   Mr Miller is better   Poor
grass to night   We use wild sage for fuel   it grows very thrifty   I
have seen some 8 ft high   it is very dry   Made *15*

[July] 31   Sat   W.W. cool and pleasant   Did not Start very early
as we do not expect to go far to day roads very good   The snow cap
mountains lie directly north of us to day   here we find Strawberys
and huckelberies   the latter not ripe yet   Encamped at noon drive
our cattle off three miles and get excellent feed do some washing
clouds up and rains this after noon   made 12 miles

[*Parthenia*] August 1st Sunday   To day we left the waters that flow
into the Atlantic and proceed to those of the Pacific   We let our cattle feed till about noon and then started on, for the South pass 10
miles distant—It ill comports with the ideas we had formed of a pass
through the rocky Mountains, being merely a vast level sandy plain
sloping a little each way from the summit and a few hills for we could
not call them mountains on each side. Some few snowy peaks in the
distance, and this is the South pass through the Rocky mountains
From the summit we proceeded down a gentle slope to the Pacific
spring and creek 3 miles and encamped for the night. Here we could
find no grass except on a deep slough formed by the springs covered
with turf and grass on which a man can stand and shake the ground
for several feet around him it is so soft underneath. Upon this we put
our cattle to feed for it was the only chance and the sod was so tough
they did not break through a great deal   the Pacific spring rises in
the middle of this boiling up through the sod as cold as ice itself—
made 13 miles

2 Monday—To day left the spring for a long pull of 24 miles to

little sandy creek. Crossed dry Sandy creek, but it contained no good water and we made the whole distance without any—soon after we started we met a pack train from California on their way home. Came about noon to the forks of the old Oregon and Salt Lake road. Took the road to salt Lake with the intention of going by Kinneys Cutoff[22] to avoid the desert. Reached Little Sandy a little before sunset. Found plenty of good water though somewhat muddy like the Platte, but no grass for the cattle it having been all eaten off. We let our cattle feed as well as they could till dark and then tied them up to keep them from wandering off for feed. Hardest time yet. the road to day has been as level as you often find even in Illinois slightly inclining to the south and west. You hardly believe yourself among the mountains. Old Cataraugus [Cattaraugus][23] beats it all hollow—21 m.

[August] 3 Tuesday we started for the Big Sandy in hopes of finding better grass, but did not find it much better

[*Cecelia*] Stoped here at noon and concluded to stay a day or more as Mr Miller is very sick Find good feed by going three miles off We have very heavy dews this side of the Pass made 11

4 Wed Pleasant we shall stay here to as Mr M is not able to ride it rains some to day We meet a great many mormons Want us to go to Salt L

5 *Thurs* Our sick man is better and we make a move this morning in good spirits roads rather sandy but level Encamp on big sandy Made 17 mil

---

[22]"Kinney" Cutoff solved the problem of the desert crossing on Sublette's Cutoff, which had been troublesome since 1844. To take the new cutoff one followed the trail toward Fort Bridger down along the Big Sandy to within a few miles of where that stream joined the Green. One then cut across the angle between the two streams, a distance of about ten miles, and came to the Green at a spot where a ferry was operated at times of high water. At low water it could be forded. Then the traveler went on west along Slate Creek until he rejoined the main cutoff. George R. Stewart, *The California Trail* (New York, 1962), p. 304.

[23]The Cattaraugus hills are part of the Appalachian highland forty or more miles directly south of Buffalo. They constitute a "relatively flat-topped upland with deep intervening valleys." J. H. Thompson, ed., *Geography of New York State* (Syracuse, 1966), p. 33. The Federal Government's *Comprehensive Management and Use Plan* for selecting historic sites along the Oregon Trail indicates that "South Pass is perhaps the most important landmark on the entire Oregon Trail," and then goes on to say, "As a physical landmark, there is nothing dramatic about South Pass." *Oregon Trail: National Historic Trail*, Appendix III (Washington, D.C., Aug., 1981), p. 202.

[August] 6   *Fri*   This morning we leave big sandy for good   Have very sandy roads   met three men from Oregon on their way to the states   We see no water from morning till night   Encamped to night on the long looked for Green river a very mudy Stream   the water looks red. had a very heavy wind in the after noon but very warm through the day   See no flowers to day   Made *17*

7 Sat   very warm this morning   we ferry over green river   have to pay three dollars per waggon. Here is a station 3 or 4 white men and a few Indians   Passed but 8 graves within a week   traveled over rough roads   Made 16 miles

8 *Sun*   very cold this morning need over coats and mittens Father was very sick all night   is some better this *morn*   We take a late start on his account   This afternoon we climb some mountains worse than any we have seen since we left the Black Hills When we got to the top it rained and hailed very hard and turned very cold sudenly   *Doct* and I were out in most of the storm as we had staid so far from the wagons   Encamp on a little stream   do not know the name, see a few Indians of the Snake tribe. See few strange flowers very pretty, very poor grass very cold at night Made 18 miles

9   Mon   freezing cold this morning but as soon as the sun rises it is very warm   Father is much better to day   Our road to day is very hilly and sandy but the earth begins to look more furtile   Encamp to night on Ham's Fork   here is an Indian village   it consists of some 40 or 50 tents covered with buffalo skins   We have plenty of visitors to night. They are very friendly   Passed 4 graves   Find good grass and a beautiful camp ground   *16 m*

[August] 10 *Tues*   W S   Pleasant, conclud to stay here till noon to rest our cattle   find plenty of gooseburys   they are very sour and smooth   We do a little washing here   we caught some speckled trout. had a very high mountain to climb   Encamped in a beautiful grove of poplar   Good grass   Made 8 *mi*

11   *Wed*   W.W.   cool and pleasant   get an early start this morning   I have the teeth ache to day roads very mountainous   Passed 10 graves in two days   Encamped on Bear river   Good grass

Willow for fuel   made 18 mil   Passed through a beautiful grove of
Fir   find some pretty flowers

12   Thurs   traveled on till noon and then stoped to repare our
wagon   have some very hyh hills to climb, good grass   Passed a station   Met some packers from Oregon   find wild flax   red yellow
and black currnts   Narrow dock and cranesbill and wild pie plant
made 8 *mil*

13   Friday   W.W. very sultry in the vallyes but cool on the mountains   Come to another Station   here is two bridges and by going
over them we can take a *cut off* Saving 7 miles of very bad mountains
have to pay one dollar per wagon   see some Indians   Have plenty
of good water   some beautiful springs   Took a new road leading on
the banks of the river   it is two miles farther but saves some very
high mountains   Passed two graves   Encamped on the river
made *20m*

[August] 14   *Sat*   very pleasant this morning   Find a bury resembling the whortlebury rather larger. here we met a man that had groceries and potatoes to sell at 1½ *cts* per pound   Of course we bought
some the first we have seen since we left the states. The grasshoppers
are so thick that they look like snow in the air coming very fast   We
can get a good pair of mockersons for a dollar   Travel on the river
bottom most of the day   Made *16*

15   Sun   very pleasant   can see snow on the mountains   Find
good grass   Passed 2 graves   Encamp to night at Soda springs
[*Parthenia*] These consist of springs of water of an alkaline taste bubbling up through the rock and forming mounds of the mineral from
2 to 20 feet high and with bases of proportional size and gas sufficient coming up to keep them constantly boiling like a pot and the
opening at the top resembles a large kettle   Some are very cold and
others less so. The water sweetend and mixed with acid makes a
beautiful efervesceing draught. We saw some ten or 12 scattered over
a surface of less than ½ mile square. in some places it boils up in the
bed of the river.   18

16   Monday. This morning passed one of these springs about a mile

from the camp which has received the name of the Steam Boat spring. Here the gas rises with such force as to throw the water some 18 inches above the ground. Here we find a great many mounds which have evidently been thrown up by the water but have been cracked open and are now dry We left the track of the Californians to day for good about 6 miles from the springs. Crossed a chasm in the rocky road how long we could not tell and in places so deep we could not see the bottom. Must have been caused by an earthquake. About a mile from the road saw the crater of an old volcano. Stopped at noon near another Soda Springs—Found a trading station at the Steam Boat spring. Had a beautiful level road all day. Crossed some beautiful mountain streams and fine springs. Encamped for the night on a small stream 20

[August] 17 Tuesday. Found good level road for about half the day. Crossed two small streams and found trading stations at each. Then came to the dividing ridge between Snake and Bear rivers and had some pretty hard hills to climb up and down. Upon these hills we found a great many Sarvice berries very good to eat. Found two of the finest springs we ever saw. Encamped for the night in a valley among the mountains upon a very rapid little stream. Grass good. Made 21 m.

18 Wednesday started again down the mountains. A good many steep pitches but on the whole road very good. Followed down the stream on which we were last night toward Snake River. Found some fine choke cherries to day very large—Encamped at night on the same stream Grass not very good. Here we fell in with another company of 6 wagons mostly from Illinois with Mr. Hyland[24] of Plainfield for Captain and as we were now just on the borders of the Digger Indians Territory both companies thought best to increase

---

[24]Benjamin S. Hyland, b. 1804, emigrated to Oregon from Plainfield, Illinois, in 1852, with two sons, Amos D., b. 1837, and Burnham S., b. 1834. He settled on a claim in Lane County, Oregon, on July 19, 1853. There is an interesting note in the Oregon donation land records that reads, "1 Nov 1854, Salem, O. T., Hyland gave off that Abigail Hyland did not emigrate to Oregon & they were legally divorced at Nov term U. S. Dist Court for 2nd Judicial Dist of Ore. He further stated he had one minor heir in Ore." Genealogical Forum of Portland, Oregon, *Oregon Donation Land Claims*, IV (Portland, 1967), p. 90. See also A. G. Walling, *Illustrated History of Lane County, Oregon* (Portland, 1884), pp. 484, 490.

our strength by combining our forces. We now have 14 wagons in company and 32 effective men and keep a guard of four men at night. We are now in the valley of the Snake River   Made 20.

[August]   19   Thursday   To day came to Fort Hall on snake River and passed it at one in the P.M. It is made of unburnt bricks and is little larger than a good sized barn. It is not now occupied by the soldiers but is used for a trading station. Some 50 or 100 wagons, markd U.S. in large letters stand there rotting. Encamped about 2 miles from the fort on Pannock creek and had very good feed— Made 14m

20   Friday—To day crossed the creek and came to the Port Neuf river two miles. This is a stream of considerable size and we had to raise our wag[on] boxes to cross it. All the streams we have seen since we crossed the Mo. River have been rapid and indeed all since we crossed the Mis but those on this side of the mountains are more so but the Snake River is the most rapid one I ever saw for so large a one. running over a rock bottom and every now and then taking an offset of some 3 to 10 feet in the course of a few rods. Traveled down the river all day and could see plenty of good feed nearly all the way but were afraid to put our cattle upon it for the alkali water in the bottom—25 m   Did not camp till near sunset when we found a good spring and plenty of grass

21st   Sat. Did not exactly like our camping place and concluded to go on a few miles and find a place better and stay over sunday— Passed to day the American Falls where the river falls about 50 feet in 15 rods it is about 20 rods across at this place. Capt Hyland went before to find grass and a good place for the Sunday camp—After traveling about 15 miles on the road without feed for our cattle we started out ourselves for grass and found very good about ½ mile from the road and stopped for the night while his company followed on about 5 miles and encamped without grass—In the morn

[August]   22   Sun   started on and traveled about 10 miles and found them encamped for Sunday on Fall River a very rapid little stream full of little falls of from 2 to 10 feet   Found good bunch grass on the hills. Here we staid the rest of the day. From the time we crossed the dividing ridge between Bear and Snake rivers the soil or surface has changed   Hitherto it has been composed mostly of coarse sand but now it has a mixture of clay with it and when tramped up by the numerous teams and wagons, makes the most beautiful cloud of dust you ever saw. Many times it is so thick you cannot see ten feet and you have to shut your eyes and go it blind—12

23   Monday. To day got rather a late start and traveled over to Raft Creek a distance of 9 miles   found rather poor feed   9

24   Tuesday—Got a pretty early start as we had to travel 15 miles without water or grass. Had a very rough road over rocks varying from the size of a piece of chalk up to a fence block and so thick that they kept the wagons constantly upon the jump   dust very trouble-some. Killed a black tailed rabit. His ears and tail about six inches long—a terrible howling of wolves last night. Encamped on Bulroush creek a very swampy place. Grass all fed off except in the slough. Cattle did very well   15

[August]   25   Wednesday—Traveled on over a middling smooth road down the creek to Snake river and thence to Goose creek where we expect to find grass but were disappointed for it was all bare except sage brush, but we found a notice left there by some emigrant that about 3 miles ahead ½ mile from the road on the river there was plenty of grass. Proceeded there and found it so. Did not arrive till after sunset, put our cattle out to feed and let them feed till about 9 oclock then brought them into the Correll. 21 m

26   Thursday—found it so good feed that we concluded to remain the whole day and recruit our teams—doctored some for the hollow horn[25]

27   Friday—To day started again—Had a very dusty and rough road till noon reached the river again and gave our cattle water but found no grass. then on to Cut Rock creek. found it dry or nearly so.

---

[25]John N. Winbourne, in *A Dictionary of Agriculture and Allied Terminology* (East Lansing, Mich., 1962), p. 382, describes "hollow horn" as "An imaginary disease arising from the erroneous belief that loss of appetite and listlessness in a cow was due to *hollow horns.*" A cure for the sus-pected ailment was accomplished by boring a hole in each horn just above the base, then filling the hole with salt, pepper and sugar and plugging it with a wooden peg.

proceeded up it about 2 miles and found a hole where there was some water. Took some in our cans and proceeded up about a mile farther and found good grass, considering, and camped for the night. Did not put our cattle in correll but let them feed and guarded them outside as it was long after dark when we camped   25 m

28, Sat.   Concluded to stay another day as we learn from our guide that we are to have very hard feed for the next 70 miles. proceeded up the creek for about 3 miles for the sake of water. Here we found it coming out from between the mountains quite a stream but soon sinks away in the sand. Killed 2 black tailed rabbits. Country generally very sterile and sandy and a great many rocky hills. For the last week we have found a great many dead cattle—and the irons of a great many many wagons. the woodwork having been used for fuel. Timber is very scarce, very little except willow, wild sage constitutes much of our fuel. The river runs over a rocky bed and in most places has a high steep rocky bank—Our 3 miles to day dont count—Found a company here partly from Chicago who had lain here 3 days for the sake of finding 4 horses they had lost, probably taken by the indians. they did not guard them and they came up missing in the morning— To day one of them returned alone and taking this back track the men found tracks of indians who had followed him as far as they dared—Two of their men went forward to Rock Creek in search of the horses and were threatened with an attack by 7 indians who came out of the willows some of them armed with rifles and made an attempt to separate them but did not succeed and no shots were fired—

[August]   29th Sun. Remain to day also. Have a sermon from Capt. Hyland who is a methodist Preacher   feed is not very good but fear we shall have worse before we have better. Had a good sing to day.

30, Mon. To day started for Rock Creek and had to retrace our three miles we traveled up stream and nine miles more. Last night we guarded our cattle out 3 miles from camp on account of feed— Had seven men out on guard with the cattle and two at camp. The guard at camp shot an indian dog and heard and saw other signs of indians—Supposed they came to steal the captains horses but he was not there   9 m

[August]   31st   Tuesday — Traveled down Rock Creek 12 miles— Found good feed and concluded to stay till near night tomorrow and then start out on the long pull of 35 miles at least without grass and 22 without water—which we intend to travel in part at least in the night—Road very dusty and some rock—mostly level for we follow the valley of the Snake—The grass we found on Cut Rock was a kind of coarse grass as high as your head nearly and has a head on like blasted wheat. What we have found on this so far has been bunch grass dried as thoroughly as any hay and our cattle eat it with a good relish and it is hearty food. For the last 3 days the weather has appeared like the closing days of autumn in Illinois—Have had very warm days generally and very cold nights. makes it hard times for the guard at night. Rock Creek has very high steep rocky banks and in the course of the 12 miles we have traveled we have found only two places where a wagon could cross it   12 m

Sept   1st   Wednesday—Our cattle are well filled and in as good order as possible for the trip across the desert. Crossed Rock creek about 4 O'clock and started on our way. passed down the creek about 5 miles where there was a poor chance to get water but we had supplied ourselves before leaving our camp—traveled on till after dark and then halted till the moon rose about 9 o'clock and then started on again. Road in many places very rough and rocky and all the way dusty but the dust not near as bad as in the day time—weather very cold so that a man could not keep warm in walking without an overcoat and my hands suffered with cold—Came near the river once in the night but it was down a dreadful hill and we did not go to it. Just at sunrise we again came to the river down a very steep hill but here we found no grass and our cattle had kept so cool they were not very dry   Rested here about two hours and got our breakfast and started on in search of grass. Passed down the bottom with high rocky banks on each side nearly perpendicular—came to Salmon creek in about three miles but found no grass   Here is a fall in the river about equal to the American Falls—passed on ½ mile over bluff to the river again. Here we found a company with whom we were some acquanted who had been here 2 days and put their cattle over the river and found good grass and said they had been on before 7 miles to the commencement of the next desert of 33 miles and found no grass which would make us 40 miles more and that is too much for our cattle—It is dangerous crossing the river and they had drowned one horse and one ox in putting theirs over, but it was the only chance and so we put them over. and made a boat of one of the wagon boxes to ferry ourselves over all safe   Arrived here about noon and concluded to remain the rest of the day and tomorrow and recruit   find very good bunch grass and some bottom grass. Two large springs break out from the side of the mountain within 1 mile of each other at least 100 feet above the river and contain water enough to turn any mill in Kane Co [Illinois]—and dash down with great velocity to the river   32 m

Sept. 3rd   Friday—To day staid at camp most of the day. tried fishing some but did not make out much, weather very warm. can see plenty of large salmon jumping out of the water but cant catch them

4 Sat. This morning brought our cattle over again without any accident and prepared for the long pull—in 3 miles passed some hot springs in river bank   came to Bannoc creek but found no grass but found a notice that five miles below was a ferry across the river and plenty of grass on the other side. Went to it about 1 mile out of our way and the ferrymen recommended the route as so much shorter and better supplied with grass and water that we concluded to try it. The ferry consists of 2 wagon boxes lashed together so as to make a boat and a rope stretched across the river to pull it across—and all they asked was three dollars a wagon for ferrying. The day was so windy that we could not cross so we had to stay on this side and swimm our cattle across the river. found good grass about 1½ miles back. We have had some heavy sandy roads today the first for some time   3 m   Here we find some indians with some very nice salmon for sale and we all got a good supply—they will trade them for powder, lead & caps bread, beads, brass nails, old shirts or almost anything you have and they seem to have a great many. just below the

ferry is another great fall, Just above on the opposite bank very large springs break out high up in the bank and fall into the river with great noise a fine sight

[September] 5th Sunday No wind this morning and we ferried over in good season and proceeded on our way—A few rods below the ferry is another salmon falls fall in the river of some 20 feet where the indians catch their salmon in traps—found very rough rocky road for the first mile then deep heavy sand for five more when we came to a good sized creek in a deep valley with plenty of grass and encamped. Here are some 5 or six large springs breaking out high up in the rocky bank and running down part of the time above ground and part of the time below till they reach the creek which is very rapid. The water of these spring brooks has a greenish tint but otherwise is perfectly clear and the finest looking water I ever saw and good tasting but not very cold. The scenery for the last 3 days has been truly delightful and only wants a soil and what grows on a soil to make it one of the most beautiful spots on the earth—Within these three days mill seats enough for the whole state of Illinois and finer than I ever saw there. About a mile from us is the river and another great fall—The indians bring us salmon again but find dull sale for we are all supplied and the market is glutted   6 m

[September] 6 Monday—Had a steep rocky hill to climb this morning to start with then came to sand again which lasted 8 miles to another creek. very heavy road—Here the water fall down into a very narrow chasm some 40 feet and runs along it for half a mile or more dashing and foaming as it goes—a fine sight—Here we watered our cattle and proceeded on about a couple of miles where we found grass and stopped for dinner then proceeded on and did not find water till long after dark—when we came to a small creek. watered our cattle and put them into carrel without any feed. Some indians camped on the same stream   24 m

7th   Tuesday. This morning found plenty of excellent bunch grass on the hills near camp and let our cattle feed then started and traveled down the stream about 7 miles and stopped for dinner—then passed over the hills about 10 miles without water when we came to the same creek again and encamped for the night. Have found plenty of bunch grass all the way to day—and sage of an enormous size and the general appearance of the country has been more like live then any we have seen for the last thousand miles—Have seen 14 graves in a week   17 m

[September]   8th   Wed. Traveled over hills again about 8 miles to a dry creek but some little water standing in puddles. Here we stopped and took dinner. Plenty of dry bunch grass all the way. Afternoon started again and passed up a very rocky hill 3½ miles and in a most of the way steep. when we came upon a level table land and went about 3 miles more over a very rough rocky road when we came to another dry creek in a ravine with steep rocky banks—Here we encamped for the night   Find no good water and but little of it. Plenty of dry willows for the fuel   15 m

9   Thursday—Proceeded over a very rough road to another dry creek about 6 miles. Here we came upon the road leading from the ferry. 3 miles further on came to a fine stream and cold spring and several places some 10 feet across where water and mud boil up among the sand—Stopped here for dinner and had pretty good grass—Here we found ten graves all in a row—all had died from the 28th of July to the 4th of August. Disease unknown—About 7 miles farther on came to another stream from springs and stopped for the night. found plenty of grass about one mile below on the stream   16 m

10   Friday—Traveled about 8 miles to a stream of very black water and high colored—were afraid of it and did not let our cattle drink. About a mile further on came to a number of large boiling hot springs which make a stream 2 ft wide and 3 or four inches deep— Water very clear and not bad tasted—Here we stopped and fed our cattle but did not let them drink—traveled along the foot of mount about 5 miles to another creek and stoped for the night—plenty of dry bunch grass—no timber but willows and sage—Found 8 graves here   15 m

[September]   11th   Sat. came to another small creek in about 2 miles   then found no more water for 8 miles more. when we came to Charlotte creek down in valley with steep rocky bank   The road for the last 3 days has been mostly very rough and rockey but generally level and the dust has been very troublesome. This dust differs from sand in being mostly clay and is mixed up by the teams to a depth of from 2 to 4 inches and light as flour and under is a hard bottom so that a wagon runs very well on it where there are no stone in the way—but there is such a perfect cloud of dust rising constantly that it almost suffocates our cattle and is disagreeable to us. and we cannot keep anything clean—We find plenty of dry bunch grass all the way but no green feed have we had for some time. Our present position must be high above the river for we have not come down much since we climbed the long hill. All the living creatures we see are a few ravens and black-tailed rabbits and flies and white gnats and at night hear some wolves. Here we found tolerably plenty of dry grass from 1 to 2 miles back on the hills. Concluded to stay over sunday. plenty of willow for fuel and some balm of Gilead.   10

13   Monday—Today started again. had rough. (rocky and dusty) road along foot of Mount on right for about 5 miles then came to light sand and gravel and road hard and smooth. About noon came to a deep broad valley covered with dry grass as well as the hills. Begins to look live but our cattle are beginning to be tired of dry grass—Here we found a dry creek, some poor water. Traveled on till we came to a small spring. Had very scanty supply of water and it soon got rily. Hard case—Land covered with dry grass. Looks like a large wheat field   14

September   14 Tues—Traveled over hilly road of sand and gravel— In about 2 miles came to a small stream in deep ravine   Water sinks away in the sand in a few rods—then in about 5 miles more came to White Horse creek. Here we watered our cattle and drove on about 2 miles and fed. Then traveled on about 10 miles to another small spring a rather worse case then the other and stopped for the night   We have no trouble for grass—such as it is. Roads smooth but hilly   16

15—Wed. To day traveled up a long hill some 4 miles road good— ascent very gradual   when we arived at the top a grand view of the Boise River valley. It is all filled or covered with dry grass and a few trees immediately along the bank the first we have seen for more than a month. We traveled for some 4 miles on a high level plain then came down a steep hill about 200 feet to another equally level on which we traveled about 3 miles then took another offset of about 100 feet and in about a mile and a half came to another off-set about the same. and we were nearly on a level with the river. This is a fine clear stream and there are plenty of indians scattered along its banks. They bring us a great many salmon trout but no salmon—We have seen no fish since day after we left the ferry till now and we are getting hungry for some—These Indians have a great many fine ponies and most of them have guns and ammunition and many of them have almost a complete suit of clothes which they have got of the emigrants. They will trade a very good pony for a good rifle or a coat. Our company traded 2 guns for 2 ponies—Last night we had a very heavy wind all night and it sprinkled slightly for about ½ minute the first rain we had since time immemorial. On the other side of the river are lofty rolling mountains—14 m

[September] 16 Thursday—Traveled down the river. in about 3 miles ascended to platform No. 2 and traveled on it, level road, nearly all day then came down to the river. These offsets are about as steep as sand and gravel can be laid without mortar—pretty dusty most of the day—Saw the most rabbits to day 5 [miles] that I ever saw in the same length of time. Frank shot 18 in about an hour   To night have pretty good green grass for our cattle. Indians bring fish and rabbits   15

17 Friday. Some traders who are camped about 2 miles above came down and bought some of our lame and worn out cattle. Traveled down the bottom, Road sandy in many places and begin to find some sage again—Camped on river   13

18. Sat. Proceeded down the river—Road sandy and very dusty in places. A great deal of Grease-wood and some sage. Country looks about as desolate as ever—About 4, 1, clock crossed Boise river— Very good ford—This river is skirted with timber all the way consisting of Cotton wood, Willow and Balm of Gilead. Large quantities of

balm might be procured here. Camped on the river. Had good feed and fuel 15

[September] 19 Sunday—Thought we would just drive down to the fort as we thought it could not be more than 5 miles. Drove all day but did not see it Camped about sunset on river—Saw the most fish to day in the river that I ever saw 16

20 Monday—To day drove down to the fort about 4 miles. Crosed the ferry, It is built of unburnt brick a large yard inclosed by a wall some 12 feet high and 2 buildings of the same about 14 feet square and one story high It is tenanted by a rough looking Scotchman[26] and a few indians and squaws—It is a station of the Hudson's Bay Co—A great many had depended on getting provisions here but failed entirely of getting anything except fish— There is a little sugar for sale here at ,75, cents pr pound— Prospects seem to darken around us a good deal for some families are already entirely out of bread and many more will be in the course of one or two weeks—We have enough to last us through but we shall have to divide if necessary

21st Tuesday—To day Mr. McMillen,[27] Mr. Stowell and Mr Raymond left us to pack their way through to the Dalls in company with eleven others from our company—They have 3 ponies among them which carry the most of their provisions. They expect to make the trip (300 miles) in ten days while it will probably take our teams in their present condition at least 20 days and perhaps more. Had some difficulty in finding our cattle this morning as we do not keep guard over them now for we are not much afraid of the indians stealing them. Found them about noon and started them on the way. Had first rate green feed for them last night Proceeded about five miles against an increasing west wind over a very dusty road till it

---

[26]This has been thought to have been James Craigie, longtime Hudson's Bay Company employee, who was stationed at Fort Boise for many years. The "Scotchman," however, was Archibald McIntyre, who had taken over from Craigie. They both had Indian wives. Annie L. Bird, *Boise, the Peace Valley* (Caldwell, Idaho, 1934), p. 74. The government donation land records indicate that Craigie filed an intention to become an American citizen on August 13, 1852, in Clackamas County, Oregon, and he settled on his claim (#3268) in western Oregon on Nov. 2, 1852. *Oregon Donation Land Claims*, op. cit., II, p. 40.

[27]This was Joseph McMillen, the twins' father.

became so bad that we could not see our teams or hardly breathe and were obliged to heave to for a season. After a while the wind shifted more into the north and blew the dust across the road and then we proceeded on—followed up a deep ravine about three miles more and encamped for the night with out water or grass. plenty of sage. Cold   8

[September]   22   Wed. Started early. Followed up same ravine to summit. then followed another down to Malkeurs [Malheur] River. the most sluggish stream I have seen for some time   Here we found but poor feed but thought best to stay the rest of the day as the next stopping place was too distant to reach to day   Find plenty of willow—water not very good   7 m

23   Thurs. To day traveled over a smooth level road for about 15 miles when we came to a sulphur spring. Here we watered our cattle but did not find much grass. Country very poor—Nothing but sage and grease wood—From the spring we began to ascend hills and the country began to improve. Hills mostly covered with dry grass. Traveled till after dark without finding water. Camped in valley among hills. Plenty of thrifty sage. Plenty dry grass. Tied our cattle to sage brush   Mr. Miller thought he saw a bear in the night. The last three nights have been very cold froze some   22

24   Friday—After giving our cattle time to feed we started. In about a mile came to Birch Creek. Water not very good. does not run more than half the way above the surface. Stands in pools. Tastes of sulphur—In about 4 miles more over hills came to Snake River for the last time. Here it runs between lofty and inaccessible mountains. so farewell Snake—Traveled over high mount to Burnt River 4 miles. Here we stopped and fed our cattle on dry grass—They are getting tired of it for it is too dry. This river is fine clear water about 20 feet wide on an average and flows between very lofty mounts with just room to pass—Traveled up its banks about 4 miles and encamped. Plenty dry grass   13

[September]   25   Sat. To day crossed the river three times in going 5 miles, and climbed over high bluffs the most of the rest of the way. Soon left the river banks and traveled over bluffs very hilly for about

6 miles to a small creek and stopt for the night. Find very little sage or grease wood. Dry grass   12

26   Sun—Traveled down the creek to the river 2 miles. Here the mountains are so high and so close that they leave no room for bluffs and when they close down upon us on one side of the river our only alternative is to flee to the other. Crossed the river 5 times in about 6 miles. These mounts are as near as I can judge about 1200 feet high on an average and as stccp as thcy know how to be Mostly covered with dry grass, except where it is burnt off—See a good many fine fish but cant catch them—To day found a place where there were a good many green rushes and a good many Birch trees. Here we stopped for the rest of the day   8   River bottom at this place some 6 rods wide   covered with timber as is the bottom most of the way—Birch, Cotton Wood and Willow and some Balm of Gilead[28] a few scattering pines and cedars on the mount high above us. Scenery fine.

[September]   27   Mon. To day crossed the river for the last time 9 times in all about ½ mile from camp and started up a small creek. very rapid. got up hill pretty fast by following it—crossed it 9 times in going 4 miles—then turned from it up steep long hill in ravine and descending came to another small stream and spring. Here watered our cattle and drove up another steep hill and stopt to feed on some bunch grass—The grass along here has been mostly burnt off and we have to get it where we can catch it—Drove down the hill, found a spring brook which we followed down for some 2 miles then crossed over ridge to another creek and soon came again near Burnt river and camped on it—Grass good—Some packers overtook us from behind hurrying on to procure provisions. They give a sad account of the destitution of those who are behind. Say there are but few who have more than 5 days provisions   14

28th   Tuesday   This morning met some traders from Oregon

---

[28]The "Balm of Gilead" she writes of was the black cottonwood, a poplar. Charles R. Ross in his *Trees to Know in Oregon* (Corvallis, 1967), p. 61, describes it as a "friend of the pioneers." He adds, "To pioneers on the Old Oregon Trail the cottonwood was the most important tree. For nearly 1000 miles of their journey it was the only shade tree to be found." It was called Balm of Gilead because when the spring buds burst it emits a refreshing balmy odor. See also diary entries for October 10 and 24.

buying lame cattle   River forks some little distance above camp and we take the right hand fork. Follow up it all day among hills and camp on it at night   10

29   Wed. Cross the stream twice then leave it and follow up small creek to a spring and water our cattle as we are to have 18 miles without water   Traveled over hills till afternoon then came to a pretty level piece of land covered with sage on which we traveled till nearly night and then descended to another beautiful smooth plain several miles in extent bounded by grass covered hills except on the west which is bounded by the Blue Mountains beautiful in the distance covered with Pine   looks as if we were coming somewhere—Camped among the sage without water   Plenty of grass for our cattle on hill near by   18 m

[September]   30   Thurs. After going about 4 miles found a kind of dry creek where was plenty of water standing in pools but poor stuff—Here we watered our cattle—Drove on about five miles and got badly fooled by the willows growing very abundantly about 2 miles to the left as we supposed it was Powder River—Stopped on some good feed for our cattle and [page torn] there for water to get our dinner but found none but dirty pools—The soil on this plain is much better than we have seen before—Grass in many places fresh and abundant. In about a mile's travel came to a small stream a branch of Powder river. very sluggish, water poor, bad ford—and in about 6 miles more came to one of the main branches of Powder River and stopped for the night. found good grass—and fine water   Found some more Oregon traders here—They say we must hurry if we get over the Blue Mountains—Rains some in the valley and snows on the mountains—very cold all day   15 m

Oct. 1. Friday. Let our cattle feed till after noon. One of the packers we had seen before came back—Had been to the Grand Ronde and bought 50 pounds of flour for $30.00 and was hurrying back to the relief of his friends. Traveled about 2 miles down the stream then crossed it and in about 5 miles crossed another branch of Powder River. fine stream, then crossed several small streams and ascended to a high table land and went about 6 miles upon it before finding water. Nearly dark when we camped on a small stream—Water not very good—Grass tolerable—No wood but green—willows. very cold. Rained some in fore part of the day—Plenty of snow to be seen on mountains. Roads good, no dust—the first time we have been free from it for a long time. Have seen 35 graves since leaving Ft. Boise   12 m

[October]   2d   Sat. Could not raise fire enough to cook breakfast. Powerful cold—Started early and in about 3 miles came to foot of mount—Climbed the mount. Ascent very gradual—about 3 miles—when we came to a fine little valley with some springs in it. and plenty of grass. followed up it about a mile then up mount 2 miles when we came in sight of the Grand Ronde a beautiful level valley nearly round   I should think some 15 miles in diameter—but O the getting down to it over a long steep and stony hill is equal to any getting down stairs I ever saw, and I have seen some on this road—Arrived at the bottom   found feed had been mostly burnt off but found enough for our cattle. Here we found another trading station from Oregon—They sell flour for 60 cts. pr lb. Salt at 50 cts. and first rate fat beef which they brought with them or drove at 20 to 25. Stopped and fed and then traveled on about 5 miles to a spring and camped Good water and grass. but no wood except a kind of green stuff that *wont burn no how*. Still cold and freezes considerably—Did not get very near any snow nor to timber—The traders say they drove their beef cattle from the Dalles in 8 days—The soil of this valley is fine   16m

3d   Sunday. Have not seen any of the clover spoken of by others but have found plenty of red top grass. both here and on Powder River and it grows very thrifty. The indians have all left for their winter quarters. Traders say they were very thick here about 2 weeks ago—are said to be very rich in ponies and trade a good many for cows. considerably civilized. Raise some cattle and some vegetables for sale—but they did not leave much marks of civilization on the road or near it to be seen. Traveled along the west side of the valley at foot of mount about 3 miles when we came to a small stream and then commenced ascending the mountain, very steep in many places and continues to ascend for about 6 miles. very hard drive but at the top found the grass burnt off and there was no water, so had to go on till we came to Grand Ronde, ten miles, worst hill to go down that we have found yet. long, steep and rocky. Our road to day has been mostly through lofty pines as fine as I ever saw and to night we have plenty of dry pine for fires. The feed here has been very thoroughly fed off but we found plenty on the mountain side among the pines. This river runs through the middle of the Grand Ronde, a fine little stream, rapid and shallow—15 m

[October]   4th   Mon. This morning got a late start and commenced climbing again—very steep hill to start with about a mile long. then had hills to ascend and descend all day, many of them steep. About night found a place where we could find some standing water about ½ mile from the road, down a very steep hill all the way—poor stuff but it was the best we could do. Camped and turned our cattle out to grass but did not drive them down to water as it was almost dark. Plenty of pine   Today saw two very small black squirrels   15 m

5th   Tues   Staid till near noon and let our cattle feed   The grass is very good and quite fresh in many places among the pines. We find Pine, Spruce, Tamarack and Fir here—Mr Millers co. from Iowa are here entirely out of flour. Have some loose cattle which they kill now and then for food. Traded them some flour for beef, sold them some and lent them some to be repaid at the Dalles. Hard times. many cattle are failing and all are very poor and a good many get lost among the thick timber. A good many wagons are left, some broken and some good and sound because the cattle are not able to take them along. So much good pine here they do not burn them. The general appearance of the country is altogether changed. The soil even on the mountains is quite good and in the valleys it is excellent. In many places the road has to twist round a good deal among the trees. Traveled on about 7 miles on a mountain ridge sometimes on one side sometimes on the other. pretty sideling in places—Do not have to rise and fall as many notes as common to day   begin to hope we are getting out of the mounts. Camped on mount. A good spring about ¼ mile off down at the foot of mount. Timber very thick to day. Good grass—7 m

[October] 6th Wed. Concluded to rest to day and recruit our cattle as we have good feed and they have had a hard pull of it for the last 4 days—Spent the day in cooking and hunting for cattle lost in the brush as a great many have been lost here.

7th Thurs. To day staid till about noon and then started on about 6 miles to another spring still in the thick timber very thick. Find plenty of good grass all the way 6

[October] 8th Friday—Started for the Umatilla river. Road slightly descending nearly all the way and in some places steep. At last came in sight of the valley covered entirely with dry grass except a small skirt of timber along the river—and literally dotted with indian ponies—and cattle. Commenced the descent into the valley very gradual. said to be five miles down hill. Dont think is was much overrated. The grass here is very poor having been fed off by the ponies and cattle. Soil excellent. This valley is the head quarters of the Cayuse Indians. They are more civilized than any we have seen before Bought a few potatoes of them. They are killing some very fat cattle and sell the beef at 15 to 20 cts. pr lb. No other provisions can be had here and that is a death blow to the hopes of many hungry people. Found a man here who had left our company some time ago and been on to the Dalles and returned with a pony load of provisions. Gives a very discouraging account of the prospect before us. Grass is very poor all the way. No provisions for sale between here and the Dalls. 15 m

9th Sat. Our friend from the Dalls advises us to stay and recruit our cattle as we shall have no more as good grass as we have here. but the prospect here is nothing but starvation for ourselves and teams. Started off after noon and went down the river 6 miles. put our cattle over bluffs but found poor feed. Find some prairie chickens 6

10th Sunday—Traveled down river, passed over bluffs, some sand, crossed river passed down some 3 miles and camped—Find a great many mice living in holes in the ground—Timber mostly Balm of Gilead—some willow. 9 m

[October] 11 Mon. Climbed the bluff, ascent very gradual but some 3 miles long. after passing some 7 miles found good feed, dry grass and stopped for noon. then passed on some 7 miles more and stopped for the night. No water. Road good, plenty dry grass. mice very plenty   14

12th   Tues. put our cattle down to the river about 2 miles for drink and got one of them stuck in the mud. Spent the forenoon in trying to get him out, but failing we killed him—Started on and came to the river in about 3 miles and traveled down it about 3 miles and camped on it. poor feed—6 m

13   Wednesday, Traveled down 3 miles to the Indian Agency, the first framed house we have seen since we left the Mo. River—and they have actually got a stoned up well. The agent was gone to the Dalles. but we left 2 of our wagons there and sold 3 cattle to some traders and put all the teams to Stephens wagon and proceeded. Our loads are light but our cattle are getting powerful weak and we think best to favor them as much as possible. An indian here has some flour for sale at 50. cts. pr. lb   A white man has some corn brought from Ft. Wallawalla which he sells at the rate of six pint cupfuls for a dollar and it sells fast. Traveled on about 5 miles after crossing the river and leaving it Road very sandy the heaviest I ever saw for so long a distance. Camped on the open prairie   no water. Burn grease wood of which we have seen a good deal to day— Looks familiar but old fashioned. We find it to our advantage to camp between the watering places on account of grass—70 graves since leaving Ft Boise   8

14th   Thursday—Started on again and traveled over the same heavy sand about 5 miles more to Alder creek. A sluggish dirty stream. some willow on banks

[*Cecelia*] Here we saw Mr. Torance[29] the Indian agent on his way back to the Station from Milwaukie [Oregon] loaded with provisions Seemed much pleased to see us told us a great deal about James as he is well acquainted with him   After dinner started on   carried water

---

[29]William S. Torrance had settled a claim in the Milwaukie, Oregon, area in 1849, *Oregon Donation Land Claims*, op. cit., I, p. 30, claim #725. The pioneer Oregon City newspaper, the *Oregon Spectator*, contains many reports of his traveling to The Dalles and even to Salt Lake City on mail contracts. He seemed to have a passion for giving aid to the overlanders approaching the Columbia River. (Oct. 28, 1847; July 13, 1848; May 22, 1851; Aug. 19, 1853.)

with us   very warm and sunny encamped on the prairie   no wood or water for our cattle   Warm nights   11 m

[October]   15   Friday   looks very much like rain, cool   Frank and Doct have concluded to start on a head as Stephen bought an Indian pony & they will take it & go to the dalls and there meet us Encamped at a spring of miserable water   Here we met Lot Whitcomb[30] direct from Oregon   told us a great deal about Oregon was well acquainted with James and spoke very highly of him   He had provisions but not to sell but gives to all he finds in want and are not able to buy. Took supper and breakfast with us   Traveled all day Made 15 miles over deep 16 sand and dust   had no water till night Encamped on Willow creek   the water stands in holes but found three good springs. Made 18 miles.

17   Sunday   warm and pleasant   Stay here to day to rest our teams   some cedar and willow   see no Indians   drive our cattle over the bluffs some three miles

[*Parthenia*] find very poor feed all along here—Here are 12 graves all together. We hope this is the last sabbath we shall spend on the road

[October]   18   Monday   Very cloudy. Started on and it soon began to rain. As we left the creek we had a very long steep hill to climb. The train we started with are all behind and we travel alone. At noon it rained very hard and we all got wet which was very reviving   Pleasant in the afternoon. Road very hilly all day and dusty. Camped without wood or water and with little grass. 13

19   Tuesday   Cool and pleasant. High W. wind. Road lay through a deep narrow valley, but very barren. At noon camped by a small spring coming out of a hill. No grass here. From here pass over high bluffs and descend a very steep hill to John Day's River a very rapid stream. No wood here except a few very small willows. All the country from the indian agency to this place is about as barren and desolate as any we have passed over and we have seen nothing that could be fairly called wood since we left the Umatilla   13

---

[30]Lot Whitcomb was a well-known old time riverman on the Columbia, everybody's favorite. He is reputed to have named the Oregon town of Milwaukie. His river boat was named the *Lot Whitcomb*. Howard M. Corning, *Dictionary of Oregon History* (Portland, 1956), p. 263.

20   Wednesday   Very pleasant this morning. Our first act was to pass up a very long rocky and sandy hill as bad as any we have had all things considered and when arrived at the top stopped for dinner. Here we have good grass. the first since we left Umatilla. Here the Doct. met us on his way back from the Dalls. Franklin had gone down by the boat. He brought some flour, pork, Salt, and saleratus. Prices are coming down at the dalls. flour can be had at 15 cts. Pork at 37½, Salt at 25, Saleratus 25, Sugar 25 to 30   Afternoon traveled on about 6 miles and encamped on the prairie Plenty of dry grass. but no wood or water. country quite changed land all covered with a fine growth of dry grass. Pretty hilly. Soil good   9 m

[October]   21st   Thurs. Travel on. Road good but rather hilly. Plenty of grass all the way. Came to a spring of poor water in about 9 miles, stopped and watered our cattle but did not feed. passed on about 3 miles more   12 and camped for the night. grass excellent for dry—but no water

22nd.   Friday. Rose early and drove down to the great Columbia River for wood and water for breakfast. Had a very long but not very steep hill to descend. At the foot found a trading station. Sell flour, pork, Sugar and tobacco at 40 cts. pr. lb. Stopped and got our breakfast—no wood but very poor willows and some grease wood. Drove on to DeChutes River 3 miles. No grass in the bottom, all eaten off. The Columbia here is a very rapid and shallow stream apparently about the size of Rock River Ills. flowing over a rocky bottom with frequent falls and not navigable for sap troughs[31] or canoes. Banks very high steep and rocky and bottom very narrow and in some places sandy. DeChutes river is to appearances nearly as large as the Columbia though it must be much smaller and comes dashing down over the rocks—as rapid as water can come on a plane inclined one foot in 20. Here is a ferry at $2.00 for those who have money and a ford for those who have not. The latter is the most numerous class—After crossing this river we climbed a very steep and long hill but good road and passed on about a mile on the level and camped for the night. Here is a good spring on the

---

[31]Sap troughs were hollowed out logs made to collect maple syrup. In an emergency they could be used as dug-out boats.

hill. Found rather poor grass but thought best to stop for fear we could not climb the other hill   7 m

[October] 23 Sat Traveled on about 2 miles and came to another hill as bad as the last. Hard pull our cattle are so much weakened, but it is the last we shall have. Then down steep hill to Olney's creek. Here is a house and a white man Mr Olney[32] living with a squaw. There are also 2 houses at DeChute river. and some tents belonging to the Walla Walla indians who do some ferrying and act as guides to those who ford. Pretty shrewd fellows for money—but very civil   From thence we went over bluffs ascent and descent very gradual to a creek 5 miles from the Dalles called 5 miles creek and encamped for the night. Stephen had gone before to the Dalls and returned bringing the intelligence that Mr. [Joseph] McMillen had returned there with some provisions for us from the valley. Staid all night and did some cooking for the journey down by the water. Have long been convinced that we are too late to cross the Cascade Mountains with safety so we concluded to leave our cattle and wagon at the Dalls and proceed down by water. Hire a man to take care of the cattle at $6.00 pr head and deliver them in the vally in the spring as soon as it is safe to travel over the mountains   9 m

24   Sun. Traveled to the Dalls, 5 miles, and found a boat ready for sail   Put our loading on board and got on ourselves and were ready to be off   Stephen staied to take care of the cattle and some other business and the rest of us went on—It was an open kiel boat rowed by three men and we went on at a pretty good rate. The appearance of the river here changes from being a rapid, shallow, and narrow stream   it becomes a wide deep and still on in places more than a mile wide and too deep to be sounded—The water is clear and fine and the banks are precipitous and rocky and several hundred feet high in most places. We had a very favorable run for the weather was calm. This is said to be a very windy stream and the channel being so deep it follows it up and often prevents boats from running for 3 or

---

[32]Nathan Olney was a friend of northwest Indians. His wife, Annette Hallicula, was a Wasco Indian. He traded all around the Deschutes—The Dalles area. Roscoe Sheller's book, *The Name was Olney*, is a somewhat romanticized story of the life of Nathan and his Indian "princess" wife and other Olneys. (Yakima, Wash.., 1965), pp. 55–66.

4 days. During the night it rained a good deal and we got pretty thoroughly wet. About 2 oclock hove to, to wait for daylight. Went on shore and got breakfast. Rained hard nearly all the time. Here is a narrow bottom and some balm of Gilead growing, some of the trees more than 4 feet in diameter. We are now only 6 miles from the Cascades. The mounts, are covered with a thick growth of lofty pines and fir and the pack trail which passes along here seems almost impassable the mounts are so very steep—Passed down to the cascades which consists of an emmense pile of loose rocks across the stream over which the water runs with great rapidity for 6 miles. The indians have a tradition that many years ago the Columbia ran above here the same as above the Dalls but the mountains got into a fight and threw large rocks at each other which falling into the river dammed it up and indeed the river appears like a vast millpond. The distance from the Dalls to the cascades is 45 miles. Here is a large warehouse and from it proceeds a rail road 3 miles long made of scantling and plank without iron. On this runs a small car propelled by a mule attached to by a long rope for an engine and a pair of thills[33] between which the engineer stations himself and walks and guides the car. on this the charge is 75 cts. per cwt. but takes no passengers. At the end of the railroad the goods have to be let down perpendicularly some 150 feet to the river from whence they are taken on a boat to the steam boat landing about 3 miles more. Charge 75 cts. in all. Rained hard most of the day. Women walked down on land and expected their goods that night but could not get them down. Had no tent, no beds, and no feed except what they bought. Mr. Miller staid with the goods and the rest of us went the tavern to stay. The steamer Multnomah came up about dark and staid till morning. Here we came across Mr. Stowell who had been detained by sickness. Early in the morning Mr Miller came down with the goods and we all got on board the steamer. Charge 6 pr. passenger. distance to Portland 65 miles—The appearance of the river below the Cascades is about the same as above. Rises and falls with the tide in the Pacific. Had a very pleasant ride. Much better than an ox team where you have to work your passage by running on foot. The banks soon began

---

[33]Thills were wagon or buggy shafts used one on each side of a single animal.

to grow less steep and high and soon we were in the valley but could see nothing except timber on shore. but that was fine. Passed some timber farms and good dwellings and one saw mill belonging to the Hudsons Bay Co Passed Ft. Vancouver pleasantly situated on the N.W. side of the river. About 2 O'clock came into the Willamette (pro. Will am´ et) River. Much like the Columbia wide, deep and slow. and soon were at Portland the largest town now in the Territory and a fine town it is and would compare favorably with many eastern cities. At the head of ship navigation it is bound to be the great commercial emporium of the North west   Here we remained 3 days nearly—when brother James came for us with his team and we started for his farm   10 miles distant

AMELIA KNIGHT
Used with the permission of the Oregon Historical Society.

Iowa to the Columbia River
Amelia Knight
1853

INTRODUCTION

Saturday, Sept. 17—In camp yet. Still raining. *Noon.* It has cleared off and we are all ready for a start again for some place we don't know where. *Evening.* Came 6 miles and have encamped in a fence corner by a Mr. Lambert's about 7 miles from Milwaukie. Turn our stock out to tolerably good feed.

A few days later my eighth child was born. After this we picked up and ferried across the Columbia River, utilizing a skiff, canoes and flatboat. It took 3 days. Here husband traded 2 yoke of oxen for a half section of land with ½ acre planted to potatoes, a small log cabin and lean-to with no windows. This is the journey's end.

This quotation from Amelia Knight's "diary" is illustrative of the fact that many women traveling overland were pregnant during their journey, and it has been one of the most quoted statements about the overland journey by others as well. We estimate that we have used it in 80-some speeches. It is magnificent! It is also incorrect.

The second paragraph above simply does not appear in the original manuscript; however it is to be found in all heretofore printed copies.[1] This means that some time between September 17, 1853, and 1928, when it was printed in the *Transactions* of the Oregon Pioneer Association, the extra paragraph was added.

The question arises, "Who wrote it?" Probably not Amelia Knight, because of all people she would know that the baby was born not "a few days later," but the very next day, on September 18, 1853.

This corrected rendering of the diary in no way denigrates Lillian Schlissel's statement: "What is not mentioned at all is the fact of another pregnancy. The diary must be read with this unstated fact in mind."[2]

[1]*Transactions* of the Oregon Pioneer Association, 56th Annual Reunion (Portland, 1928), pp. 38–54; Clark County Sun, Vancouver, Wash., Oct. 24, 31; Nov. 28; Dec. 5, 12, 19, 26, 1930; Fort Vancouver Hist. Soc., *Clark County History*, VI (1965), pp. 36–56.

[2]Lillian Schlissel, *Women's Diaries of the Westward Journey* (New York, 1982), pp. 199–200.

The lesson for all of us who do serious research in history is that one must always seek the original of any document. A copy, either in typescript or in print, cannot take the place of the actual primary document, whether diary or letter.

Amelia Stewart was a young lady from Boston, who, at age 17 met a young English-born medical student, age 26. They were married on September 18, 1834. Joel Knight had worked for some years as a traveling hatter when he decided to become a doctor.

Over the following years the family made two great moves westward: First they moved to the vicinity of Vernon, Van Buren County, Iowa, in March 1837. Their farm was on the south shore of the Des Moines River near the southeast corner of Iowa, which became a new state in 1846. They lived a short distance north of what became the Mormon Trail from Keokuk to Council Bluffs (Kanesville), that is, from the Mississippi to the Missouri rivers. They must have seen thousands of travelers with their wagons on the trail in the years that they lived in Van Buren County.

When Amelia wrote her first journal entry on Saturday, April 1, 1853, the family was just beginning the long journey from the south shore of the Des Moines River to the north shore of the Columbia in the newly named Territory of Washington. This new political entity was established by Act of Congress on February 10, 1853. The Knights began their journey west by following what was already called "The Old Mormon Trail."

When Joel and Amelia settled on their new claim in Iowa in 1837, they already had one child, Plutarch, who was born in Boston on October 21, 1836. Over the next sixteen years in their new midwestern home six more children were born. There were seven, therefore, who traveled over the Oregon Trail. When Amelia made her first diary entry on April 9, she was three months pregnant. One might say that she had her hands full.

We are grateful to the University of Washington Library for making a photocopy of Amelia Knight's original diary available to us. The firm, clear handwriting is so easy to read that we could copy it directly. There is a note with the photocopied diary from Dr. Edmond S. Meany, Professor of History, written to Chatfield Knight, telling him how careful the university would be with such an original manuscript. This note is dated October 13, 1934. There is another handwritten note appended which says "Chat Knight—aged 84, died 1934—requested that diary and desk be given to the University of Wash, in response to letter written by Prof. Meany in 1934."

We would also like to thank the Clark County Historical Museum, Vancouver, Washington, and particularly David Freece, museum director, and Lesla Scott, librarian, who have both been helpful.

Mrs. Mary Craine of Vancouver, a descendant of the Knights, has been encouraging and has gladly approved of our publishing of Amelia Knight's journal.

CHILDREN WHO WENT WEST
WITH AMELIA AND JOEL KNIGHT:

Plutarch Stewart Knight (Oct. 21, 1836–Jan. 29, 1915), was age 17 in 1853. He was a big help to his father with the work of the wagon train. He attended Willamette University in Salem and later became a well-known Congregational minister. He was pastor of the First Congregational Church in Salem from 1867 to 1883. Knight Memorial Church in Salem is named after him. He and Eleanor Smith were married on April 21, 1861. He served as editor of the *Oregon Statesman* newspaper for a period. He also was Director of the Oregon School for the Deaf. *Oregon Statesman Illustrated Annual* (Salem, 1893), p. 17; H.O. Lang, *History of the Willamette Valley* (Portland, 1885), p. 809.

Seneca Knight (1838–Jan. 8, 1873), was age 15 in 1853. Amelia characterizes him with the words, "Seneca, dont stand there, with your hands in your pockets, get your saddles and be ready." He became a farmer and stockman. He was evidently a single man and died at the home of his mother.

Frances Amelia Knight (1841–April 1, 1927), was 14 years old in 1853. She married a widower, Nathan Pearcy, a Virginian, in 1865. There were two small children by his first wife, Fanny. They were Fanny, age 7, and Nathan, Jr., age 5. Pearcy moved her into his beautiful home on Pearcy Island, at the confluence of the Willamette and Columbia rivers. They lived there until moving to Portland in "about 1879." They had famous peach orchards and livestock on their river-bottom with its rich alluvial soil. But the floods came, and the homestead went back to bulrushes. There was still enough of the house left in 1928 for the Portland *Oregonian* to run a story in its Mar. 25 edition, "Old, Forlorn Pearcy Home Once Scene of Happiness." Nathan died in Portland on May 30, 1903. Frances lived on for another 24 years, and died also in Portland.

Jefferson Knight (1842–Oct. 18, 1867), was 11 years old in 1853. He took up farming with his father on their donation land claim on the north bank of the Columbia, ten miles up the river from Vancouver, Wash. He died of drowning in the river near the homestead.

Lucy Jane Knight (1845–May 15, 1877), was age 8 in 1853. She started the long journey with the mumps (entry for April 11). Lucy and Almira were filled with fear when they saw the first Indians on Apr. 29 and ran to hide in the wagon. She was lost on Aug. 8, having wandered behind the wagon train. Emigrants in another train picked her up and returned the frightened little girl to her family. In 1865 Lucy married an energetic Swiss steamboatman and boat builder, John Jacob Wintler, who came to the Vancouver area via the Panama Canal route in 1857. She lived for only 12 years after her marriage. In that time she bore 6 children.

Almira L. Knight (1848–?), age 5 in 1853; grew up in Clark Co., Wash.; married W.B. Patterson.

Chatfield Knight (1851–Dec. 27, 1934), age 2. Received much attention from his mother on the westward journey. She mentions him being sick and how he "fell out of the wagon, but did not get hurt much," (July 17). He lived a long life in Washington State and donated the diary to the University of Washington, Library.

Wilson Carl Knight (Sept. 18, 1853–Sept. 6, 1886), was the baby born near the Lambert farm, just out of Milwaukie, Oreg., at the end of the westward journey. There is a handwritten note in the Clark County, Washington, Historical Museum saying that he had been of delicate health over much of his early life and went to New York for special treatment. It seemed to help as his health improved. In New York State he married Esther Nelson. He inherited the family homestead on the bank of the Columbia, ten miles upstream from Vancouver. He died of consumption on Sept. 6, 1886.

There was another son, Adam, who was born in 1855 and lived until 1928.

THE DIARY

Saturday April 9th 1853. Started from home about 11 oclock, and travel 8 miles and camp in an old house, night cold and frosty—

10, Sunday M, Cool and pleasant, roads hard and dusty, evening came 18½ miles and camp close to Mr Fulkersons house

11, M. morn, Cloudy and signs of rain, about 10 o'clock it begins to rain, at noon it rains so hard we turn out, and camp in a School house after traveling 11½ miles, rains all the afternoon, and all night   very unpleasant, Jefferson and Lucy have the mumps, poor cattle bawl all night

12, T, morn, Warm and sultry, still cloudy, road, very muddy, travel 10 miles and camp in Soap creek bottom creek bank full, have to wait till it falls—

13 W, Noon, Fair weather, have to overhaul all the wagons and dry things, Evening still in camp

14th   Quite cold   little one crying with cold feet, sixteen wagons all getting ready to cross the creek, hurry and bustle and get break-fast over, feed the cattle, and tumble things into the wagons, hurrah boys all ready, we will be the first to cross the creek this morning, gee up tip and tyler[3] and away we go the sun just rising   Evening we have traveled 24 miles to day, and are about to camp in a large prairie without wood, cold and chilly east wind, the men have pitched the tent, and are hunting something to make a fire, to get supper, I have the sick headache and must leave the boys to get it themselves the best they can—

15th   Cold and cloudy   wind still east   bad luck last night, three of our horses get away, supper   they have gone back, one of the boys have gone back after them, and we are going on slowly   Evening Henry has come back with the horses all right again, came 17 miles to day roads very bad and muddy   cold and cloudy all day   it is begining to rain, the boys have pitched the tent. and I must get sup-per—

16th   Campt last night 3 miles east of Chariton point in the prairie. made our beds down in the tent in the wet and mud, bed clothes nearly spoiled. Cold and cloudy this morning, and every body out of humour, Seneca is half sick, Plutarch has broke his saddle girth, Husband is scolding, and hurriing all hands (and the cook) and Almira says She wishes she was home, and I say ditto, Home sweet home—Evening we passed a small town this morning called

---

[3]Oxen were often given names. Here they were named for the battle cry of the 1840 election of President William Henry Harrison and Vice-President John Tyler: "Tippecanoe and Tyler Too."

Charitan point, the sun shone a little this affternoon   came 24 miles to day, and have pitched our tent in the prairie again, and have some hay to put under our beds, corn one dollar per bushel, feed for our stock cost 16 dol, to night—

17th Sunday   It is warm and pleasant, we are on our way again traveling over some very pretty rolling prairie, corn is up to 3 dollars a bushel, travel 20 miles to day, and have campt in the prarie, no wood to cook with, have to eat cold supper, have the good luck to find corn at 80 cts a bushel

18th,   Cold breakfast the first thing, very disagreeable weather, wind east, cold and rainy, no fire, we are on a very large prarie, no timber to be seen as far as the eye can reach,   Evening have crossed several very bad streams to day, and more than once have been stuck in the mud, we pass Pisga this afternoon, and have just crossed Grand river, and will camp in a little bottom, plenty of wood, and we will have some warm supper I guess   came 22 miles to day, my head aches, but the fire is kindled and I must make some tea, that will help it, if not cure it—

19th, Still damp and cloudy, corn very scarse and high travel 20 miles and camp.

20th   Cloudy,   We are creeping along slowly, one wagon after another, the same old gait, and the same thing over out of one mud hole and into another all day   crossed a branch where the water run into the wagons, no corn to be had within 75 miles, came 18 miles and camp

21st   Rained all night, is still raining   I have just counted 17 wagons traveling ahead of us in the mud and water, no feed for our poor stock to be got at any price, have to feed them flour and meal   travel 22 miles today—

22nd   Still bad weather, no sun, traveling on mile after mile in the mud, travel 21 miles and cross Nishnabotna and camp on the bank of it

23rd   Still in camp, it rained hard all night, and blew a hurrican almost, all the tents were blown down, and some wagons capsized,

Evening it has been raining hard all day, every thing is wet and muddy, One of the oxen missing, the boys have been hunting him all day. Dreary times, wet and muddy, and crowded in the tent, cold and wet and uncomfortable in the wagon   no place for the poor children, I have been busy cooking, roasting coffe &c to day, and have came into the wagon to write this and make our bed—

24th   Sunday, The rain has ceased, and the sun shines a little, must stay in camp and dry the bed clothes   no feed for the stock but what little grass they can pick, after noon found the ox, and lost our muley cow   must wait and find her

25th   Rather cold but the sun shines once more, still feeding the cattle and horses on flour, one of our horses badly foundered, On our way again at last, found our cow with a young calf, had to leave the calf behind then travel on a while, and came to a very bad sideling bridge to cross over a creek, came 18 miles—

26th   Cold and clear   found corn last night at 2 dollars a bushel, paid 12 dollars for about half a feed for our stock,   I can count 20 wagons winding up the hill ahead of us, travel 20 miles and camp—

27th   A nice spring morning, warm and pleasant   the road is covered with wagons and cattle, paid $2,40cts for crossing a bridge, travel 25 miles to day and camp on a creek (called keg) about 10 miles from the Bluffs—

28th   Still in camp, pleasant weather, we will stay here a few days to rest and recruit our cattle, wash cook ect.

29th   Cool and pleasant, saw the first indians to day Lucy and almira afraid and run into the wagon to hide, Done some washing and sewing to day—

30th   Fine weather   spent this day in washing, baking and overhauling the wagons,   several more wagons have campt around us

Sunday May 1st   Still fine weather, wash and scrub all the Children

2nd   Pleasant evening, have been cooking, and packing things away for an early start in the morning, threw away several jars, some wooden buckets, and all our pickels   too unhandy to carry, Indians came to our camp every day begging money and something to eat children are getting used to them

3rd   Fine weather, Leave Loudenback and his team this morning, and are on our way again, travel 6 or 7 miles and camp on pony creek, here Plutarch is taken sick

4th   Weather fair, travel 4 miles to day   passed through Kanesvill, and camp in a lane, not far from the Missouri river, and wait our turn to cross   no feed for the stock, have to buy flour at 3½ per hundred to feed them

5th   We crossed the river this morning on a large steamboat called the Hindoo,[4] after a great deal of hurrahing and trouble to get the cattle all aboard, one ox jumpt overboard, and swam across the river, and come out like a drowned rat   The river is even with its banks, and the timber in it, which is mostly cotton wood is quite green, Cost us 15 dollars to cross, after bidding Iowa a kind farewell, we travel 8 miles and camp about noon among the old ruins of the Mormon Town[5] we here join another company, which will make in all 24 men, 10 wagons, and a large drove of cattle   have appointed a Captain, and are now prepared to guard the stock, 4 men watch 2 hours, and then call up 4 more, to take their places, so by that means no person can sleep about the camp, such a wild noisy set was never heard.

6th   Pleasant, we have just passed the Mormon graveyard,[6] there is a great number of graves on it, the road is covered with wagons and cattle, here we passed a train of wagons on their way back, the head man had been drowned a few days before, in a river called Elk horn while getting some cattle across, and his wife was lying in the wagon quite sick, and children were mourning for a father gone and with sadness, and pitty, I passed those who perhaps a few days before had been well and happy as ourselves, came 20 miles to day,—

---

[4]According to the *Missouri Republican* of St. Louis in its edition of May 11, 1853, the *Hindoo* was "still engaged in ferrying emigrants across the river at Council Bluffs," but the "larger portion" had set out for the West. The *Hindoo* left for St. Louis on May 13. Louise Barry, *The Beginning of the West* (Topeka, 1972), p. 1146.

[5]In the fall of 1846 the great migration of Mormons had crossed the Missouri and spent the cold months at their "Winter Quarters," now part of greater Omaha, Nebr. Leonard J. Arrington and Davis Bitton, *The Mormon Experience* (New York, 1979), pp. 97–98.

[6]Ibid. Some 200 persons had died at the 1846–1847 Mormon Winter Quarters.

7th   Cold morning, thermometer down to 48 in the wagon   no wood, only enough to boil some coffee, good grass for the stock, we have just crossed a small creek, with a narrow indian bridge across it, paid the indians 75 cnts too, my hands are numb with cold— Evening travel 23 miles and camp on Elk horn bottom close to the river, it is very high and dangerous to cross—

8th   Sunday morning. Still in camp waiting to cross, there are three hundred or more wagons in sight, and as far as the eye can reach, the bottom is covered, on each side of the river, with cattle and horses, there is no ferry here, and the men will have to make one out of the tightest wagon bed, (every camp should have a water proof wagon bed for this purpose) every thing must now be hauled out of the way head over heels (and he that knows where to find any thing will be a smart fellow) then the wagons must be all taken to pieces, and then by means of a strong rope stretched across the river, with the tight wagon bed atached to the middle of it, the rope must be long enough to pull from one side to the other, with men on each side of the river to pull it, and in this way we have to cross every thing a little at a time, women and children last, and then swim the cattle and horses, there were three horses and some cattle drowned at this place yester-day while crossing, It is quite lively and merry here this morning, and the weather fine, we are campt on a large bottom, with the broad deep river on one side of us, and a high bluff on the other

9th   Morning cold within 4 degrees of freezing, we are all on the right side of the river this morning   it took the men all day yester-day to get every thing across which they did all safe by working hard, we are now on our way again   Evening we have driven a good ways out of the road to find grass and camp after traveling 22 miles

10th   Cold   thermometer down to 30 in the wagon ground froze last night, came 20 miles and camp.

11th   Evening, it has been very dusty, yesterday and to day   the men all have their false eyes[7] to keep the dust out, we are traveling up platte river bottom, the north side   we have been near the river several times, it is a beautiful river about a mile across, full of Islands

---

[7]Goggles.

and sand bars   as far as the eye can reach the road is covered with teams   Plutarch is well and able to drive, came 23 miles

12th   Thursday noon, beautiful weather, but very dusty, we are campt on the bank of Loop [Loup] fork waiting our turn to cross, there are 2 ferry boats running, and a number of wagons ahead of us, all waiting to cross, have to pay 3 dol a wagon, 3 wagons, and swim the stock, travel 12 miles to day, we hear there are seven hundred teams on the road ahead of us, evening wash, and cook this afternoon,—

13th   It is thundering and bids fair for rain, crossed the river very early this morning before breakfast, got breakfast over after a fashion, sand all around us ankle deep, wind blowing, no matter hurry it over, them that eat the most breakfast, eat the most sand, we are all moving again slowly—Evening came 24 miles to day, finding we can get along faster and more comfortable alone, we left all company this morning and have campt alone, our company passed us while at supper and said good evening, and campt a little ahead of us—

14th   Had a fine rain last night, laid the dust, cool, and the sun shines this morning, we see very few Indians, did not see more than a dozen Pawnees, we are now in the Souis country, passed the sand bluffs, travel 5 miles and obliged to stop and camp on the prairie near a large pond of watter, on acount of the high winds and some rain, wind so high that we dare not make a fire, impossible to pitch the tent, the wagons can hardly stand the wind, all that can find room are crowded into the wagons, those that cant have to stay out in the storm, some of the boys lost their hats

15th   Sunday morn, Cool and pleasant after such a storm, travel 18 miles and camp—

16th   Evening we have had all kinds of weather to day   this morning was dry dusty and sandy, this afternoon it rained hailed and the wind was very high, have been traveling all the afternoon in mud and water up to the hubs, broke chains, and stuck in the mud several times, the men and boys are all wet and muddy, hard times but they say misery loves company, we are not alone on the bare plaines, it is covered with cattle and wagons, we have come to another muddy branch, we will cross it and find a camping place, good grass for the stock and thats one good luck we have, travel about 20 miles, the wind is getting higher

17th   Tuesday morning. we had a dreadful storm of rain and hail last night, and very sharp lightning, it killed 2 oxen for one man, we had just encampt on a large flat prairie, when the storm commenced in all its fury, and in two minuets after the cattle were taken from the wagons, every brute was gone out of sight, cows, calves, horses all gone before the storm like so many wild beasts. I never saw such a storm the wind was so high, I thought is would tear the wagons to pieces, nothing but the stoutest covers could stand it, the rain beat into the wagons so that every thing was wet, and in less than two hours, the water was a foot deep all over our camping ground, as we could have no tent pitched, all hands had to crowd into the wagons and sleep in wet beds, with their wet clothes on, without supper, the wind blew hard all night, and this morning presents a dreary prospect, surrounded by water, and our saddles have been soaking in it all night and are almost spoiled, had little or nothing for breakfast our cow (rose) came up to be milked, the men took her track, and found the stock about 4 miles from camp, start on, and travel about two miles, and came to dry creek, so called because it is dry most of the year   I should call it water creek now, as it is out of its banks and we will have to wait till it falls, no wood within 8 miles,   raining by spells,—

18th   Wen [Wed.], Still in camp, very high winds again last night blew some of the tents over, Cold and windy this morning and not a stick of wood to make a fire, trying to dry the bed clothes between showers, the creek is falling—

19th   Thurs, morn, Clear, all getting ready to cross the creek afternoon   crossed dry creek this morning and have traveled 10 miles, and come to wood creek, and are up a stump again, it is also very high, and we will have to cross it as we did Elkhorn, in a wagon bed, and swim the stock, just got things packed away nice this morning, now they must all be tumbled out again, well, there is plenty of wood, and I will spend the afternoon in cooking—

20th   Friday morn, crossed wood creek last night, and got loaded up a little after dark, and drove out 3 or 4 miles where we found a good camping place, We are now traveling between Platte river and wood creek, plenty of water and grass, not much wood and that cotton wood   travel 21 miles.

21st   Sat, We have just crossed deep dry creek, it had a little muddy water in it, Very warm   it is the first day the cattle have lolled, thermometer up to 92 in the wagon, good grass, bad water, and no wood, came 20 miles

22nd, Sunday, fine weather, crossing branches, and mud holes all day, traveled about 18 miles—

23rd, Monday   the road is covered with droves of cattle, and wagons, no end to them, dry and dusty all day, travel 20 miles and camp on the bank of Platte river, plenty of wood, by wading across to the islands for it,

24th   Stay in camp to day, to wash and cook, as we have a good camping ground, plenty of wood, and water & good grass   weather pleasant, I had the sick headache all night, some better this morning, must do a days work, husband went back a piece this morning in search of our dog, which he found, with some rascles who were trying to keep him,—

25th   Wendsday, It is raining, we have got our washing, and some cooking done, and with a bunch of wood tied on each wagon (for the purpose of making coffee, as we will not see wood again soon) we are ready for a start as soon as the rain holds up—evening it has been cold and rainy all day, only travel 12 miles and camp,—

26th Thursday   Evening it rained all the fornoon, cleared off at noon, we started and traveled about 14 miles over marshy wet ground, while the team were creeping along I went up on a high bluff, and had a splendid view of platte and her beautiful timbered Islands

27th   Friday   Cloudy and wind cont. we are now traveling along the edge of platte, it is so wide here, we can just see timber the other side, it must be 2 miles across   travel 20 miles to day—

28th Saturday travel 18 miles to day, over very sandy ground passed a lot of men skining a buffalo, we got a mess and cooked some for supper, it was very good and tender it is the first we have seen, dead or alive,—

29th Sunday quite warm, came 15 miles very sandy, and bad traveling for the cattle, it will be 175 miles before we see timber again, we haul a little dry wood along to make coffee and tea,—

30th Monday it has been cloudy and cool to day, and better roads, traveled 23 miles

31st Tuesday evening, travel 25 miles to day, when we started this morning, there were 2 large droves of cattle and about 50 wagons ahead of us, and we either had to stay poking behind them in the dust, or hurry up and drive past them, which was no fool of a job to be mixed up with several hundred head of cattle, and only one road to travel in, and the drivers threating to drive their cattle over you if you attempted to pass them, they even took out their pistols, husband came up just as one man held his pistol at Wilson Carl,[8] and saw what the fuss was, and he said boys follow me, and he drove our team out of the road entierly, and the cattle seemed to understand it all, for they went in the trot most of the way, the rest of the boys followed with their teams, and the rest of the stock, I had rather a rough ride to be sure, but was glad to get away from such a lawless set, which we did by noon. the head teamster done his best by whiping and holloing to his cattle, he found it was no use and got up into his wagon to take it easy, we left some swearing men behind us, we drove a good ways ahead, and stopt to rest the cattle and eat some dinner, while we were eating we saw them coming, all hands jumpt for their teams, thinking saying they had earned the road too dearly to let them pass us again, and in a few moments we were all on the go again. very warm to day, thermomenter at 98 in the wagon at

---

[8]Wilson Carl was a single man, a wagoneer for the Knights. He settled in Yamhill Co., Oreg., an accomplished carpenter. Some say the town of Carlton was named for him, but there is some disagreement about this. On May 26, 1856, he and Mary Stout were married. Joseph Gaston, *Centennial History of Oregon*, II (Chicago, 1912), pp. 906–911. The Knights thought enough of him to name their son, born on September 18, 1853, on their arrival in the Portland area, for him: Wilson Carl Knight.

one oclock,   toward evening there came up a light thunder storm which cooled the air down to 60,   we are now within 100 miles of ft. Laramie,—

June 1st   It has been raining all day long, and we have been traveling in it, so as to [be] able to keep ahead of the large droves, the men and boys are all soaking wet and look sad and comfortless, the little ones and myself are shut up in the wagons from the rain. still it will find its way in, and many things are wet, and take us all together we are a poor looking set and all this for Oregon. I am thinking while I write, Oh Oregon you must be a lovely country,   came 18 miles to day

2nd   Thursday morning. It has cleared off pleasant after the rain and all hands seem bright and cheerful again, we are going along the same old gait. Evening traveled 27 miles to day   passed Court house rock, and chimney rock, both situated on the other side of the river, and have been in sight for several days, we have campt oposite chimney rock—

3rd Friday morn. We had another hard blow, and rain last night, looks some like clearing off this morning, Evening came 21 miles to day and have campt about oposite to Scotts bluffs, water very bad, have to use out of platte most of the time, it is very high and muddy—

4th   Saturday   More rain last night, is raining some to day, the roads are very bad, nothing but mud and water, came 16 m

5th   Sunday   Very warm. Slow traveling, several of the oxen have sore necks, caused by traveling in the rain, came 18 miles to day, and are campt near platte, where we have wood, and plenty of grass for the stock—

6th   Monday. Still in camp, husband and myself being sick (caused we suppose by Drinking the river water, as it looks more like dirty suds, than anything else)   we concluded to stay in camp, and each take a vomit, which we did, and are much better; the boys and myself have been washing some to day, the prickly pear grows in great abundance along this platte river road.—

7th Tuesday. Rained some last night, quite warm to day. Just passed

fort Laramie, situated on the opposite side of the river; This afternoon we passed a large villiage of Siou indians, numbers of them
came round our wagons, some of the women had moccasins, and
beads, which they wanted to trade for bread. I gave the women and
children all the cakes I had baked. husband traded a big indian a lot
of hard crackers for a pair of moccasins, and after we had started on,
he came up with us again, making a great fuss, and wanting them
back (they had eat part of the crackers) he did not seem to be satisfied or else he wished to cause us some trouble, or perhaps get into
a fight, however we handed the moccasins to him in a hurry, and
drove away from them as soon as possible, several lingered along
watching our horses that we tied behind the wagons, no doubt with
the view of stealing them, but our folks kept a sharp lookout, till
they left, we had a thunder storm of rain and hail, and a hard blow
this afternoon, have traveled 18 miles, and are campt among the
black hills, they are covered with Cedar, and pine wood, sand stone,
lime stone, and pure water—

8th   Wendsday   It is a pleasant morning after the rain, every thing
looks fresh and green, we are traveling through the black hills, over
rocks, and stones. there is some splendid scenery here, beautiful val-
lies, and dark green clad hills, with their ledges of rock, and then far
away over them you can see Larimie peak, with her snow capt top;
evening came 16 miles to day, had another shower this afternoon,
and have campt in a lovely spot, plenty of wood, water, and good
grass

9th   Thursday, came 18 miles to day; weather warm, had a slight
shower in the afternoon, campt without wood or water, but good
grass.—

10th   Friday   It has been very warm to day thermometer up to 99
at noon, traveled 21 miles over a very rough road, and have campt on
the bank of the platte river, wild sage brush to burn, which makes a
very good fire, when dry, very poor grass, here one of our hands left
us (Benjamine Hughs)

11th   Saturday, The last of the black hills, we traveled this forenoon
over the roughest and most desolate piece of ground that was ever

made (called by some the Devils grater) not a drop of water, not a spear of grass to be seen, nothing but barren hills, bare broken rocks, sand and dust. quite a contrast to the first part of these hills we reached platte river about noon, and our cattle were so crazy for water, that some of them plunged headlong into the river with their yokes on, travel 18 miles and camp—

12th   Sunday morn, we are traveling on in the sand and dust   it is very dusty, and the road is covered with teams and droves of cattle, the grass is very poor, mostly gone to seed—Evening came about 17 miles and have campt near the bank of platte, the boys have driven the cattle on to an Island where they can get grass, and I have just washed the dust out of my eyes so that I can see to get supper,—

13th   Monday evening. This has been a long, hard days travel came 30 miles through sand and dust, and have campt opposite the old upper ferry on platte, tomorrow we will come to the first poison water, there will be no more good water for about 25 miles, we will also leave platte river in the morning for good—

14th   Tuesday evening we started this morning at day break to travel our long, dry, dusty days travel, the dust and sand has been very bad—passed the Avenue rocks this afternoon, traveled 31 miles and are about to camp, there is not less than 150 wagons campt around us, but we have left most of the droves behind, and no end to the teams, had a great deal of trouble to keep the stock from drinking the poison or alkali water, it is almost sure to kill man or beast who drink it—

15th   Wendsday came 19 miles to day, passed Independence rock this afternoon, and crossed Sweet water river on a bridge paid 3 dollars a wagon and swam the stock across,   the river is very high and swift, there is cattle and horses drowned there every day; one cow went under the bridge and was drowned, while we were crossing belonging to another company, the bridge is very rickety and must soon break down. we are campt 2 miles this side of the bridge near the river.—

16th   Thursday We are now traveling up sweet water valley between two mountains, one of them being covered with snow, sweet water is a clear cool and beautiful stream, and close to its margin lies the road, this morning we passed the devils gate, came 16 miles, and have campt on the bank of Sweet water, no wood, nor grass, on this side of the river

17th   Friday   Concluded to stay in camp and rest the cattle a day or two, swum the cattle and horses across the river where there is plenty of good feed, we also get our wood from the other side, the best swimmers go over, and cut a light cedar log, and swim back with it, have been sewing and cooking to day. the mosquitoes are very bad here   cut the first cheese to day

18th   Saturday   Still in camp, overhauling the wagons, cooking sewing patching, ect, ect, had a very hard blow and a slight sprinkle of rain this afternoon—

19th   Sunday. On our way again, traveling in the sand and dust sand ankle deep, hard traveling, came 18 miles and camp on the bank of sweet water again, and swim the cattle over to feed—

20th   Monday evening. came 22 miles to day, passed good water once, passed a good deal of poison water, and have campt in the mountains   weather warm and pleasant—

21st   Tuesday evening, we have traveled over a very rough rocky road to day, over mountains, close to banks of snow.—had plenty of snow water to drink, husband brought me a large bunch of flowers, which he said was growing close to the snow, which was about six feet deep. travel 16 miles to day, and have campt on the mountains about seven miles from the summit, we are traveling through the south pass, the wind river mountains are off to our right, among them is Fremonts peak, they look romantic covered with snow.

22nd   Wendsday morning, very cold   water froze over in the buckets,   thermometer down to 30, the boys have on their overcoats and mittens, Evening it snowed a little through the day, the road has been very dusty, but smooth and level as a turnpike   came 18 miles and camp about ½ mile from the pacific springs   we left sweet water this morning—

23rd   Thursday, cold again this morning. water froze over, came 27 miles and campt on the bank [of] little Sandy river after dark

24th   Friday noon, came from little Sandy, to big Sandy, 7 miles, and camp for a day or two to rest the stock, good grass, and water here, Henry Miller[9] left us this morning we started with five hands, and have only two left—

25th   Saturday   Still in camp, washing, cooking, and sewing &c. Weather very pleasant—

26th   Sunday morning, we are on our way again traveling in the dusty dust, we must go 17 miles or more without water or grass, evening all hands came into camp tired and out of heart, husband and myself sick, no feed for the stock, one ox lame, camp on the bank of big Sandy again—

27th   Monday morn, Cold cloudy and very windy, more like November than June, I am not well enough to get out of the wagon this morning, the men have just got their breakfast over, and drove up the stock, all hurry and bustle, to get things in order, its children milk the cows all hands help yoke these cattle the d---ls in them, Plutarch: I cant   I must hold the tent up, its blowing away, hurrah boys, who tends these horses; Seneca, dont stand there, with your hands in your pockets, get your saddles and be ready   Evening, traveled 18 miles to day, and have campt on the bank of Green river, and must wait our turn to cross on a ferry boat, no grass for the poor cattle, all hands discouraged, We have taken in 2 new hands to day, which will make us full handed again,—

28th   Tuesday evening, still in camp, waiting to cross nothing for the stock to eat, as far as the eye can reach it is nothing but a sandy desert, and the road is strewed with dead cattle, and the stench is awful, one of our best oxen too lame to travel, have to sell him for what we can get, to a native for 15 dollars; (all along this road we see white men living with the Indians, many of them have trading posts, they are mostly french, and have squaw wives,) have to yoke up our muley cow in the ox's place—

29th   Wendsday morn, Cold and cloudy, the wagons are all

---

[9]Henry Miller was a 21-year-old man from Ohio. He settled on a claim in Coos Co., Oreg., on June 10, 1854. He was still single at that time. *Genealogical Material in Oregon Donation Land Claims*, III (Portland, 1962), #1831, p. 131.

crowded up to the ferry, waiting with impatience to cross, there are thirty or more to cross before us, have to cross one at a time, have to pay 8 dollars a wagon, 1 do for a horse or cow, we swim all our stock, Evening we crossed the river about 3 oclock, then traveled 10 miles, and campt close to slate creek, it is cold enough to sit by the fire—

30th   Thursday evening. Traveled 20 miles to day, and have campt in the mountains, near a clear cold spring of good water, grass plenty, and dry sage brush to burn, the children have climed a mountain to see the sun set

July 1st   Friday, We had a fine shower last night, which laid the dust and freshened the grass, it is cold this morning, almost freezing, We are now ascending a steep mountain, now we are at the top—all around us we can see the snowy mountains, and down below is a beautiful green valley, and a small Indian villiage. Evening travel 18 miles to day, crossed hams fork of Green river this afternoon, and have campt half way up a steep mountain

2nd   Saturday evening we have been traveling up and down steep mountains all day   came about 15 miles, and camp, within 2 miles of Bear river close to a good spring.—

3rd   Sunday   Bad luck this morning, soon after starting one of our best oxen took sick, and in less than an hour he was dead, suppose he was poisoned with alkali water, or weeds. turned out the old ox and started on. crossed Smiths fork of Bear river on a bridge   paid 1 dollar a wagon, it is a very rappid stream, and hard to swim stock over. we then came over some very rough ground, the worst we have seen, nothing but rocks to travel over, close under a steep mountain, water and grass plenty, also wood, we will stay here till after the fourth, two of oxen quite lame.—

4th of July,   Monday   it has been very warm to day, thermometer up to 110 and yet we can see banks of snow almost within reach, I never saw the mosquitoes as bad as they are here   Chat has been sick all day with fever, partly caused by mosquitoe bites, the men have been shoeing one of the lame oxen the first one they have tried to shoe the other ones foot is too much swelled.

5th Tuesday Noon, we are campt on top of a mountain to noon and rest awhile, it is warm, but there is a good breeze up here,   Chatfield is sick yet had fever all night,   Evening crossed 2 creeks to day, one with a bridge over   paid 1 dollar a wagon to cross, travel 15 miles over a very hilly road and camp near the sulpher springs situated in a small prairie, surrounded by mountains

6th   Wendsday evening   traveled 20 miles to day and camp near a spring (in mosquito valley) there is plenty of good grass all along Bear river valley   traded a cow and calf to day for a steer to yoke up with the odd one, and find after useing him half a day, that we have been cheated, as he cant stand it to travel—

7th   Thursday evening, We have traveled 20 miles to day, all up hill and down, it has been very warm and dusty. we have campt about half a mile off from the road close to a splendid spring of limestone water, in a beautiful pine and cedar grove, while I am writing we are haveing a fine little shower, which is a great treat, our poor dog gave out with the heat and sand so that he could not travel, the boys have gone back after him, it has cleared off and I must get supper—

8th   Friday morn. Verry pleasant. found our dog last night; we have just left the Soda Springs, after regaling ourselves and quite romantic, we then come on a few miles and stopt at Steamboat Spring, a great curiosity, situated near the bank of Bear river, it spouts up about a foot and a half, out of a hole in the solid rock   it is about warm enough to wash in, I put my hankerchief in to wash, and it drew it under, in a moment it came up again, and I took better care of it, Afternoon after traveling 14 miles, we have campt near a spring, to rest a lame man, and a sick man, a lame Ox, and a lame dog, ect, grass plenty   left Bear river this forenoon—

9th   Saturday   We passed the forks of the emigrant road yesterday noon, after leaving the California road, we find the grass much better, as most of the large droves are bound for California; Noon came 10 miles and have campt on Shoshanee creek, in this part of the country the water is all hard   not fit to wash with, got our thermometer broke here—

10th   Sunday evening, Travel 9 miles this forenoon, and came to

Port neuf creek, paid 1 dollar for crossing it on a very rough bridge, then we stopt awhile to noon in a small bottom then travel 8 miles up a mountain, and camp near the top close to a very large spring of clear cold water, running from under a snowy mountain,—

11th   Monday morn, We will now descend the mountain, pleasant weather, but the roads dusty, evening we have forded Rosses creek, and one more small creek to day, came 15 miles and camp by a small creek.—

12th   Tuesday Noon, came 12 miles, crossed Rosses creek again this morning, on a bridge, paid 25 cents a wagon and we have just crossed Port neuf river on a ferry boat, paid 2 dollars a wagon, and swam the stock, we are now in sight of the the three Butes, Evening came 10 miles this afternoon, crossed Panack [Bannock] creek, and have campt this side of it, we are now traveling down the bank of Snake river.—

13   Wendsday afternoon, we have just been spending an hour at the American Falls on Snake river, there are several falls on this river, the river is wide, and deep, and very swift in places, we should cross it and keep down on the other side, but there is no ferry boat, and we have no way to cross it, therfore we must keep down on this side, with very little grass, while on the other side there is plenty. travel 22 miles and camp.—

14th   Thursday   It is dusty from morning till night, with now and then a sprinkling of gnats and mosquitoes, and as far as the eye can reach it is nothing but a sandy desert, covered with wild sage brush, dried up with the heat, however it makes good fire wood; evening I have not felt well to day, and the road has been very tedious to me, I have ridden in the wagon and taken care of Chatfield till I got tired, then I got out and walked in the sand, and stinking Sage brush till I gave out, and I feel thankful that we are about to camp after traveling 22 miles; on the bank of Raft river, about dark. river high.—

15th   Friday evening, last night I helpt get supper, and went to bed, to sick to eat any myself, had fever all night, and all day. it is sundown, and the fever has left me, and I am able to creep round and look at things, and brighten up a little, the sun has been very hot to day, remained in camp nearly all day waiting for the river to fall, we forded the river late this afternoon by raising the wagon beds a foot, to prevent the water from running in, we have encamped about half a mile from the same place, the bottom here is full of poison water.

16th   Saturday   evening we came 16 miles over a very rough rocky road, without water, then rested 2 hours, and travel 4 more, and have campt near Swamp creek.—

17th   Sunday, we are traveling through the digger Indians country but have not seen any yet, we crossed Swamp creek this forenoon, and Goose creek this afternoon, goose creek is almost straight down, and then straight up again, several things pitched out of the wagons into the creek, travel over some very rocky ground, here Chat fell out of the wagon, but did not get hurt much. came 26 miles to day, and camp after dark near the bank or Snake river

18th   Monday   traveled 22 miles   crossed one small creek, and here campt on one called Rock creek   it is here the Indians are so troublesome, this creek is covered with small timber and thick under brush, a great hiding place, and while in this part of the country the men have to guard the stock all night. one man traveling ahead of us, had all his horses stolen and never found them as we know of. (I was very much frightened while at this camp, and lie awake all night—I expected every minite we would all be killed, however we all found our scalps on in the morning). there is people killed at this place every year.

19th   Tuesday   came 15 miles crossed Rock creek about noon in the midst of all the dust, we had a nice little shower, which laid the dust, and made the traveling much better, campt about 3 oclock, close to a Canon in Rock creek.

20th   Wendsday evening, dry traveling to day, no grass, water very scarce, stopt at noon to water at a very bad place on Snake river, 1½ mile or more a steep bank or precipice, the cattle looked like little dogs down there, and after all the trouble of getting the poor things down there, they were so tired they could not drink and was obliged to travel back, and take the dusty road again, we are still traveling on in search of water, water

21st   Thursday morn, very warm, traveled 25 miles yesterday and campt after dark ½ mile from Snake river—Crossed Salmon river about noon to day, and are now traveling down Snake river, till we reach the ferry   afternoon came 12 miles, and have campt close to the ferry, our turn will come to cross in the night, have to pay 4 dollars a wagon, cross on a ferry boat, and swim the Stock which is a very hard job, on such a large river, Indians all round our wagons.

22nd   Friday, crossed the river before daybreak, and found the smell of carrion so bad, that we left as soon as possible   the dead cattle were lying in every direction. still there were a good many getting their breakfast among all the fags, I walked of among the rocks, while the men were getting the cattle ready, then we drove a mile or so, and halted to get breakfast; here Chat had a very narrow escape, from being run over, Just as we were all getting ready to start Chatfield the rascal came round the forward wheel to get into the wagon, and at that moment the cattle started, and he fell under the wagon, somehow he kept from under the wheels, and escaped with only a good, or I should say bad scare, I never was so much frightened in my life, I was in the wagon at the time putting things in order, and supposed Frances was taken care of him. After traveling 6 miles, we have encampt for the day, on the bank of a creek, full of springs, a fine place to wash, and rest the cattle, plenty of good grass. afternoon rained some.—

23rd   Saturday,   We took a fresh start this morning with every thing in order, for a good days drive, travel about 5 miles, and here we are, up a stump again, with a worse place than we have every had before us, to be crossed, called Bridge creek. I presume it takes its name from a natural bridge which crosses it, this bridge is only wide enough to admit one person at a time, a frightful place, with the water roarring and tumbling ten or 15 feet below it   this bridge is composed of rocks and all round us, it is only place to cross over and is nothing but a solid mass of rocks, with the water ripping and tearing over them   here we have to unload all the wagons and pack every thing across by hand, and then we are only on an Island there is a worse place to cross yet, a branch of the same, have to stay on the Island all night, and wait our turn to cross, there is a good many campt on the Island, and there are camps on each side of it. there is no chance to pitch a tent, as this Island is a solid rock, so we must sleep the best way we can, with the water roaring on each side of us; The empty wagons, cattle, and horses, have to be taken further up the river and crossed by means of chaines and ropes, the way we cross this branch, is to climb down about six feet on rocks, and then a wagon bed bottom will just reach across, from rocks to rocks, it must then be fastened at each end, with ropes on chaines, so that you can cross on it, and then we climb up the rocks on the other side, and in this way every thing has to be taken across   some take their wagons to pieces, and take them over in this way—

24th   Sunday evening, crossed the river this morning, and got loaded up, then traveled 16½ miles without water, then we came to a creek of poisen water in the bottom, did not dare to stay there, came on a mile and a half, to a spring in the bottom and have campt, the Indians are very bad here, have to keep watch all night.

25th   Monday morning. Bad luck this morning to start with, a calf took sick and died before breakfast, soon after starting one of our best cows was taken sick and died in a short time, presume they were both poisened with water or weeds, left our poor cow for the wolves, and started on, Evening it has been very warm to day, traveled 18 miles and have campt right on top of a high round sand hill, a fine mark for the indians, we have also got on to a place, that is full of rattlesnakes. one of our oxen sick.

26th   Tuesday   very warm, and terrible dusty, we raised a long tedious mountain this forenoon, crossed one little creek about noon, all the water we have seen to day, it is near night, and we are still traveling on, and urging our poor tired cattle on till we find water, it looks as if it never rained in this region, it is so dry and dusty, we have been jumping and jolting over rocks all day, and are now about to camp near a creek of clear cold water   traveled 17 miles—

27th of July   Wendsday,   another fine cow died this afternoon. came 15 miles to day, and have campt at the boiling Springs, a great curiosity, they bubble up out of the earth boiling hot, I have only to pour water on my tea and it is made; there is no cold water in this part,—(This band and myself, wandered far down this branch, as far as we dare, to find it cool enough to bath in, it was still very hot, and I believe I never spent such an unesy, sleepless night, in my life, I felt as if I was in the bad place, I still believe it was not very far off—I was glad when morning came and we left.)

28th Thursday noon Filled all the empty vessles last night with water, to cool for the stock, have traveled 12 miles to day, and have campt in the prairie, 5 or 6 miles from water, Chat is quite sick with Scarlet fever.

29th Friday came 18 miles over some very rocky road and camp by a spring, Chat is some better—

30th Saturday Travel 16 miles over a very hilly, but good road, and camp by a stream of water and good grass, it has been very warm to day.

31st Sunday morning, cool and pleasant, but very dusty, came 12 miles and camp about 1 oclock not far from Boise river, we will stay here a day or two and rest, and recruit our cattle—

August 1st Monday Still in camp, have been washing all day, and all hands, have had all the wild currants we could eat, they grow in great abundance along this river, there are three kinds, red, black, and yellow, this evening another of our best milk cows died, cattle are dying off very fast all along this road, we are hardly ever out of sight of dead cattle on this side of Snake river, this cow was well and fat an hour before she died.—Cut the second cheese to day—

2nd Tuesday noon traveled 12 miles to day, and have just campt on the bank of the Boise river, the boys have all crossed the river, to gather currants, this river is a beautiful clear stream of water running over a stony bottom, I think it the prettiest river I have seen as yet, the timber on it is balm of gilead,[10] made a nice lot of currant pies this aftenoon.

---

[10]This was the black cottonwood, a poplar. See footnote 28, p. 183.

3rd   Wendsday evening, traveled 18 miles, and have campt about one half mile from the river, plenty of good grass.

4th   Thursday evening. We have just crossed Boise or Reids river, it is deep fording, but by raising the wagon beds about a foot, and being very careful we are all landed safe, and about to camp not far from the bank of the river, have traveled 20 miles to day, have also seen a good many Indians and bought fish of them, they all seem peaceable and friendly.—

5th   Friday, We have just bid the beautiful Boise river with her green timber, and rich currants farewell, and are now on our way to the ferry on Snake river; evening traveled 18 miles to day, and have just reached Fort Boise, and campt, our turn will come to cross, sometime tomorrow, there is one small ferry boat running here, owned by the Hudsons Bay Company   have to pay 8 dollars a wagon, our worst trouble at these large rivers, is swiming the stock over, often after swimming nearly half way over, the poor things, will turn and come out again, at this place however, there are indians who swim the river from morning till night   it is fun for them, there is many a drove of cattle that could not be got over without their help, by paying them a small sum, they will take a horse by the bridle or halter, and swim over with him, the rest of the horses all follow, and by driving and hurraing to the cattle they will most always follow the horses, sometimes they fail and turn back; this fort Boise is nothing more than three mud buildings, its inhabitants, the Hudsons bay company a few french men, some half naked indians, half breeds &c

6th   Saturday afternoon, got all safe across the river by noon, and it being 15 miles, and have just reached Malheur river and campt, the roads have been very dusty, no water, nothing but dust, and dead cattle all day, the air filled with the odor from dead cattle,

Augst 8th   Monday morn, we have to make a drive of 22 miles, without water to day, have our cans filled (here we left unknowingly our Lucy behind, not a soul had missed her untill we had gone some miles, when we stopt awhile to rest the cattle; just then another train drove up behind us, with Lucy   she was terribly frightened and so was some more of us, when we found out what a narrow escape she had run. She said she was sitting under the bank of the river, when we started, busy watching some wagons cross and did not know we were ready. I supposed she was in Mr Carls wagon, as he always took charge of Frances and Lucy and I took care of Myra and Chat, when starting he asked for Lucy, and Frances says "shes in Mother's wagon." as she often came in there to have her hair combed.—it was a lesson to all of us.) Evening it is nearly dark and we are still toiling on till we find a camping place   the little ones have curled down, and gone to sleep without supper, wind high, and it is cold enough for a great coat and mittens.—

9th   Tuesday morning early, came into camp last night at nine oclock, after traveling 19½ miles, with enough water in our cans to make tea for supper, men all tired and hungry, groped round in the dark, and got a supper over, after a fashion, we are now on our way to Birch creek, which is 2½ miles from our camp, Halted at Birch creek and got breakfast, then started on and traveled as far as Burnt river 17 miles and camp . . .

10th   Wendsday, traveled 12 miles, crossed burnt river 5 times, and have campt on the bank of it about 4 oclock in the aftenoon, to repare the wagons some—Evening cold.

11th   Thursday, frost this morning, three of our hands got discontented, and left us this morning to pack through, I am pleased as we shall get along just as well without them, and I shall have three less to wait on,—Evening came 10 miles to day, and crossed burnt river 4 times, and have campt near a small spring, about 3 miles from the river.

12   Friday, Came 12 miles to day   crossed burnt river twice, lost one of our oxen, we were traveling slowly along, when he dropt dead in the yoke   unyoked and turned out the odd ox, and drove round the dead one, and so it is all along this road   we are continually driving round the dead cattle, and shame on the man who has no pity for the poor dumb brutes that have to travel, and toil month after month, on this desolate road. I could hardly help shedding tears, when we drove round this poor ox who had helped us along thus far,

and had even given us his very last step. We have campt on a branch of Burnt river.—

13   Saturday   Travel 5 miles this morning, then stopt to water at a spring; it is near night   we are still traveling on, through dust and sand, and over rocks, untill we find water, had none since this morning.

14th   Sunday morn,   Campt last night after dark after traveling 15 miles in a large bottom, near some puddles of very poor water found out this morning that it needed straining   Afternoon, after traveling 10 miles we have campt on the bank of Powder river about 1 oclock   another ox sick, we will rest here untill morning—

15th   Monday. traveled 11 miles, crossed Powder river three times (Powder river is a small clear stream) and have campt on a small creek, about 12 miles from the Grand round Valley.—

16th   Tuesday, Slow traveling on account of our oxen having sore feet, and the roads being very rocky, passed the Silvery springs. traveled 12 miles, and now we have a long steep rocky hill to descend into the Valley   it is a mile long, very steep and rocky from the top of this hill, we could see a band of Indian horses in the Valley below, and being mostly white, they looked like a flock of chickens, after reaching the bottom of this hill with a good deal of difficulty, we find our selves in a most lovely Valley, and have campt close to a spring, which runs through it, there are also two or three trading posts here, and a great many fine looking Kayuse Indians riding round on their handsome ponies.—

17th   Wendsday evening. crossed the Grand round Valley, which is 8 miles across, and have campt close to the foot of the mountain, good water, and feed plenty, there are 50 or more wagons campt around us, Lucy and Myra have their feet and legs poisoned, which gives me a good deal of trouble. bought some fresh Salmon of the Indians this evening, which is quite a treat to us, it is the first we have seen.—

18th   Thursday Morn   Commenced the ascent of the Blue Mountains   it is a lovely morning, and all hands seem to be delighted with the prospect, of being so near the timber again, after weary months of travel, on the dry dusty sage plains, with nothing to relieve the eye; just now the men are holloing, to hear their echo ring through the woods.—Evening travel 10 miles to day up and down steep hills, and have just campt on the bank of Grand round river, in a dense forest of pine Timber, a most beautiful country;

19th   Friday   quite cold morning, water froze over in the buckets; travel 13 miles, over very bad roads, without water   after looking in vain for water, we were about to give up as it was near night, when husband came across a company of friendly Kayuse Indians about to camp who showed him where to find water, half a mile down a steep mountain, and we have all campt together, with plenty of pine timber all around us. the men and boys have driven the cattle down to water and I am waiting for water to get supper, this fornoon we bought a few potatoes of an Indian, which will be a treat for our supper.

20th   Saturday, Cold all day, came 11 miles, and camp about two oclock, in a pine and fir forest close to a small stream of poor water, grass very scarce, 15 miles more and we will leave the blue mountains.

21st   Sunday morn   Cold, after a great deal of trouble to find all our cattle, we got started about 11 oclock and travel 4 miles then stopt to noon, not far from a spring, then travel 3 or 4 miles and turned out to let the cattle feed an hour   feed very scarce, Evening we are descending a long mountain   it is nearly dark   came 12 miles, and still traveling

22nd   Monday morning, I began to think last night we would never get to the foot of the mountain   it was 4 miles long, however we came into camp after nine oclock at night and find ourselves in the Umahtilah Valley, a warmer climate, more like summer, no feed for the poor stock, we are now traveling on the Nez perces plains, warm weather and very dusty, came 12 miles and camp at a spring ½ mile from the Umahtilah river, grass all dead but the stock eat it greedy for fuel willows and some little sage brush.

23rd   Tuesday   very warm, grass all dead, the dust is worse than ever to day. I can hardly see the toung [tongue] cattle

24   Wendsday Morn, traveled 20 miles yesterday and came into camp after dark on the bank of the Umahtilah river, numbers were campt around us, no feed for the poor stock; it is quite warm, came 5 miles this morning, and have just stopt at the Indian agency to fill our cans at the well, Evening after filling our cans with water, we came on and stopt to noon, and let the cattle pick dry grass as it is too warm to travel in the middle of the day then come 10 miles, and crossed Butter creek then came a mile up the creek, and have encampt near a good spring, and as there is no feed near the road, the men have driven the stock a mile and a half out to dry bunch grass.

25th   Thursday   We will remain in camp to day, to wash, and rest the cattle. it is 18 miles to the next water, cotton wood and willows to burn. we will start this evening and travel a few miles after dark it is too hot and dusty to travel in the heat of the day. campt about nine oclock in the dry prairie

26th   Friday afternoon, came 6 miles last night and 12 to day, and have just reached a small spring, where we can only water one ox at a time, by dipping up buckets full, this spring seems to rise out of the ground, and then fall again right off. we will camp here, and drive the cattle a mile to feed, a good many Indians campt around us, bought Salmon of them for supper and breakfast, sage brush to burn,

27th   Saturday, Came 5 miles and stopt at the well spring about noon, and watered the stock, then drove them out to grass, this well spring is not much better than a mud hole. we will remain in camp till evening, our cattle are weak and in order to save them, we travel slowly and rest during the heat of the day. 15 miles to the next water.

28th   Sunday,   Started last night about sun down, and drove 5 miles, and found tolerable good grass, to turn the cattle out to. Started very early this morning and drove as far as Willow creek, 10 miles and camp again till evening, plenty of willows to burn, but no running water it is standing in holes along the creek and very poor. it will be 22 miles before we get water again.

29th   Monday, traveled 10 miles last night, and 12 to day and have campt about 1 oclock on Rock creek   weather very warm, and dust bad.

30th   Tuesday. travel 7 miles this morning, crossed Rock creek 4 times, and have just crossed John Days river, and encampt on the bank of it about 1 oclock, not far from a trading post, here husband sold an ox that was unable to work for 25 do., we will make the best of this river, as it is 25 miles to the next, Our camp is in a very pretty Valley, or glade, surrounded by hills and our cattle and horses are feeding among the hills, a mile or two distant, and close to us lies the river, a beautiful clear stream, running over a gravelly bottom.

31st   Wendsday morn   Still in camp, it was too stormy to start out last evening, as intended, the wind was very high all the afternoon, and the dust a fine sand so bad we could hardly see   thundered, and rained a little in the evening. it rained and blew very hard all night, is still raining this morning, the air cold and chilly. it blew so hard last night as to blow our buckets and pans from under the wagons, and this morning we found them (and other things which were not secured) scattered all over the valley. one or two pans came up missing. every thing is packed up ready for a start, the men folks are out hunting the cattle. The children and myself are shivering round and in the wagons, nothing for fires in these parts, and the weather is very disagreeable. Evening got a late start this morning, traveled about a mile and was obliged to stop, and turn the cattle out on account of rain, at noon it cleared off we eat dinner, and started, came up a long, and awful rocky hollow, in danger every moment of smashing our wagons, after traveling 7 miles, we halted in the prairie long enough to cook supper, split up some of the deck boards of our wagons, to make fire, got supper over, and are on our way again. cloudy and quite cold all day—

Sept 1st   Thursday morn, traveled 8 miles last night, and encampt in the prairie without wood or water—Afternoon after traveling 11 miles and descending on a long hill, we have encampt not far from the Columbia river, made a nice dinner off of fried Salmon, quite a number of Indians are campt around us, for the purpose of selling Salmon to the emigrants—

2   Friday   Came 5 miles this morning, and are now crossing the Fall (or Deshutes as it is called here) river on a ferry boat, pay 3 dollars a

wagon, and swim the stock, this river is very swift and full of rapids. Evening travel 5 miles this afternoon   ascended and descended a long steep hill, crossed Olneys creek and have campt on the hill close to it, cold weather, and no wood, pretty good grass—

3rd   Saturday Morn   cool and pleasant   had a fine shower last night which laid the dust and makes the traveling much better—here husband (being run out of money) sold his sorrel mare (Fan) for 125 dollars, Evening Traveled 17 miles to day   crossed Olneys (or the 15 mile creek) 7 times and have encampt on the bank of it   we are near the timber once more. . .

4th   Sunday Morning   Clear and bright. had a fine view of Mount Hood, St Hellens and Jefferson this evening traveled 15 miles to day without water, after descending a long, steep, rocky, and very tedious hill we have campt in a Valley on the bank of Indian creek, near some French men who have a trading post, there are also a good many indians encampt around us   no feed for the cattle to night. 15 miles more will take us to the foot of the mountains.

5th   Monday forenoon, passed a sleepless night last night, as a good many of the indians campt around us were drunk and noisy and kept up a continual racket, which made all hands uneasy, and kept our poor dog on the watch all night, I say poor dog because he is nearly worn out with traveling through the day, and should rest all night, but he hates an Indian and will not let one come near the wagons if he can help it, and doubtless they would have done some mischief but for him. ascended a long steep hill this morning which was very hard on the cattle, and also on my self as I thought I never should get to the top although I rested two or three times. after traveling about two miles over some very pretty rolling prairie, we have turned our cattle out to feed awhile, as they had nothing last night—Evening traveled about 12 miles to day and have encampt on a bra[n]ch of Deschutes, and turned our cattle and horses out to tolerable good bunch grass—

6th   Tuesday   Still in camp, washing and overhauling the wagons to make them as light as possible to cross the mountains   Evening after throwing away a good many things and burning up most of the deck boards of our wagons so as to lighten them, got my washing and some cooking done, and started on again   crossed 2 branches, traveled 3 miles, and have campt near the gate, or foot of the Cascades Mountains, (here I was sick all night caused by my washing and working too hard)

Septbr   7th   Wendsday, first day in the mountains   came 16 miles to day, crossed Deshutes or a branch of it 4 times and have encampt on the bank of it, bought flour at 20 cts per pound to feed the stock—

8th   Thursday   Traveled 14 miles over the worst road that was ever made   up and down very steep rough and rocky hills, through mud holes, twisting and winding round stumps, logs, and fallen trees. now we are on the end of a log, now bounce down in a mud hole, now over a big root of a tree, or rock, then bang goes the other side of the wagon and woe to be whatever is inside, (there is very little chance to turn out of this road, on account of the timber and fallen trees, for these mountains are a dense forest of pine, fir, white cedar, or redwood, the handsomest timber in the world must be here in these Cascades Mountains) many of the trees are 300 feet high and so dense as to almost excude the light of heaven and for my own part I dare not look to the top of them for fear of breaking my neck—we have campt on a little stream called Sandy, no feed for the stock except flour and by driving them a mile or so, they can get a little swamp grass, or pick brush—

9th   Friday, Came 8½ miles   crossed Sandy 4 times, came over corduroy roads, through swamps, over rocks and hommochs, and the worst road that could be immagined or thought of, and have encampt about 1 oclock in a little opening near the road, the men have driven the cattle a mile off from the road to try and find grass, and rest them till morning. we hear the road is still worse on ahead; There is a great deal of laurel growing here which will poison the stock if they eat it, (there is no end to the wagons, buggys ox yokes, chains, ect that are lying all along this road   some splendid good wagons just left standing, perhaps with the owners name on them; and many are the poor horses and mules, oxen, cows, &c, that are lying dead in these mountains, afternoon, slight shower—

10th   Saturday   pleasant, Noon we have just halted in a little valley at the foot of Big Laurel hill to rest ourselves and poor weary cattle an hour or so   we dare not rest long in these mountains for fear of a storm, which would be almost certain to kill off all our stock, although the poor things need it bad enough, after what they have gone through with this forenoon,   it would be useless for me with my pencil to describe the awful road we have just passed over (let fancy picture a train of wagons and cattle passing through a crooked chimney, and we have big laurel hill) after decending several bad hills, one called little laurel hill, which I thought as bad as could be but in reality it was nothing to this last one called Big Laurel, it is something more than ½ mile long, very rocky all the way, quite steep, winding, sideling deep down and muddy, made so by a spring running the entire length of the road, and this road is cut down so deep that at times the cattle and wagons are almost out of sight, with no room for the drivers except on the bank, a very difficult place to drive also dangerous, and to make the matter worse, there was a slow poking train ahead of us, which kept stopping every five minuits, and another behind us which kept swearing, and hurrying our folks on, and there they all were, with the poor cattle all on the strain holding back the heavy wagons on the slippery road. (the men and boys all had their hands full, and I was oblidged to take care of myself and the little ones as best I could, there being no path or road except the one where the teams traveled, we kept as near the road as we could, winding round the fallen timber and brush, climbing over logs, creeping under fallen timber, sometimes lifting and carrying Chat, at others holding my nose to keep from smelling the carrion.) I must quit as all hands are getting ready to travel again—Evening   came 10 miles to day   crossed Sandy river once and have campt by it about dark   fed the stock flour, and cut down Alder for them to browse on   nothing else for them, poor things, kept them yoked and tied all night. (here I was sick all night and not able to get out of the wagon in the morning.)—

11th   Sunday evening   traveled 12 miles to day, crossed Sandy (or Zig Zag) river once and have encampt close to a spring branch, and drive the cattle ½ mile from the road to feed on swamp grass, the road has been a very little better to day although we came down some very bad hills, also through mud holes—

12th   Monday evening   came 12 miles to day, crossed Sandy once ascended thru very steep hills, passed over the devils back bone, they call it here—We also passed over some very pretty country to day, we stoped to noon at a beautiful spot, it was prairie interspersed with strips of pretty fir timber, with their branches sweeping the ground, to the left of us was a deep ravine, with a clear stream of water meandering through it, (this pretty place was along towards the end of the old *fellows* back bone)   passed one new made claim this evening, and have encampt near a small stream of clear water—it is three miles to the first farm—

13th   Tuesday Noon, ascended three very steep muddy hills this morning, drove over some muddy mirey ground, and through mud holes, and have just halted at the first farm to noon, and rest awhile, and buy feed for the stock; paid 1 ½ dollars per hundred for hay;— price of fresh beef 16 and 18 cts per pound butter ditto 1 dollar, eggs 1 dollar a dozen; onions 4 and 5 dollars per bushel, all too dear for poor folks so we have treated ourselves to some small turnips at the rate of 25 cts per dozen, got rested and are now ready to travel again—Evening traveled 14 miles to day, crossed Deep creek, and have encampt on the bank of it, a very dull looking place, grass very scarse, We may now call ourselves through, they say; and here we are in Oregon making our camp in an ugly bottom, with no home, except our wagons and tent,   it is drizzling and the weather looks dark and gloomy. here old man Fuller[11] left us, and Wilson Carl remains—

14th   Wednesday   still in camp, raining and quite disagreeable

15th   Still in camp, and still raining. I was sick all night

16th   Still in camp, rain in the forenoon, and clear in the afternoon—wash some this forenoon—

---

[11]Several Fullers traveled overland in 1853. The only one, according to land records, who might be termed an "old man" would have been Joel Fuller, born in 1803. His wife was Rebecca. They had been married on Jan. 1, 1824. They brought with them a family of several children and settled on Claim #3148 in Marion Co. *Genealogical Material,* op. cit., II (Portland, 1959), P. 34.

17th   Saturday morning   in camp yet, still raining—Noon it has cleared off and we are all ready for a start again, for some place we dont know where   Evening came 6 miles, and have encampt in a fence corner by a Mr Lamberts[12] about seven miles from Milwaukie, turned our stock out to tolerable good feed—

Oregon T Saturday evening Sept. 17th, *1853*.

---

[12]Joseph H. and Mary Lambert lived near Milwaukie, Oreg., on the west bank of the Willamette, several miles southeast of Portland. He was a noted nurseryman and originated the Lambert Cherry. Howard M. Corning, *Dictionary of Oregon History* (Portland, 1956), p. 140.

Trip for the Colorado Mines, 1862
Ellen Tootle

INTRODUCTION

Grandmother was a very interesting person and her grandchildren were devoted to her. They talked about her continually so that she became real to me even though I was too small to remember her. When she died Grandfather came to live with us and he died in 1908. He was around six feet tall and she was very tiny—little hands and feet. She spoke French fluently and was a voracious reader especially of poetry and the classics. She was a kind person and did a great deal of charity work.

The above words were written in a letter to the editor by Ellen T. Lacey of St. Joseph, Missouri. Miss Lacey is a granddaughter of the Tootles and has been most helpful in supplying information about her grandparents.

Ellen Duffield Tootle's birthplace was Hagerstown, Maryland. Hagerstown is just a few miles south of the Mason-Dixon line in a part of Maryland that experienced seriously divided loyalties during the Civil War. She had been born on November 27, 1832, the daughter of Mr. and Mrs. William Duffield Bell. He was a prominent newspaperman. Her mother, Ellen Bell, was well educated and had been active as a school teacher for a number of years.

On Thursday, June 5, 1862, Ellen Tootle wrote in the overland journal published here, "Seven weeks from the time we were married." Her wedding date had been on April 17, 1862, in her Maryland home town. She had met the groom, Thomas Eggleston Tootle while on a visit to relatives in St. Joseph, Missouri. Thomas Tootle (b. April 4, 1820, Marion, Ohio) was a prosperous banker and businessman in St. Joseph. He ran a well-known dry goods store. The purpose of the delayed honeymoon journey was to scout out the possibility of expanding the business to Denver, Colorado. During the following years the dry goods business was expanded to Denver and to Helena, Montana, in addition to several stores in Iowa and Nebraska.

Over the years of their married life there were several children born to the couple: Mary Armstrong, b. Aug. 9, 1863, who married Judge William Knowles James; Ellen Bell, b. Feb. 10, 1865, who married Graham Gordon Lacey, and Thomas Tootle, who died in infancy. The Tootles were Methodists. they lived out their lives in St. Joseph. Ellen died in April 1904, and Thomas in 1909.

One feature of their journal was the speed of travel. They started from Plattsmouth, Nebraska, on June 4, 1862, and reached Denver, Colorado, on June 21, 17 days later. They visited towns and mines along the face of the Rockies for a number of days, then they turned their backs on Denver on July 14 for the return journey. They arrived back at Plattsmouth 17 days later on July 31. The reason for the rapidity of their journey was that their wagon was drawn by high quality Missouri mules, which traveled twice as fast as oxen.

The only person who accompanied them on their journey was a mule-skinner named Warren. We don't learn his surname. According to family members he was a free black man. We know nothing more about him.

Ellen Tootle's diary was published in the *Museum Graphic* by the St. Joseph Museum, Vol. XIII, No. 2 (Spring 1961). It is here published with their permission and with that of Miss Helen T. Lacey, the descendant, quoted above.

We have also found most useful Sheridan A. Logan's definitive book, *Old Saint Jo,* published in 1979. Mr. Logan has been personally helpful as well.

Ellen Tootle is very explicit in her descriptions of the mines and towns in the gold region of Colorado. As further descriptions of them, the reader will find helpful the following publications: Muriel S. Wolle, *Stampede to Timberline, The Ghost Towns and Mining Camps of Colorado* (Boulder, 1950); Harry Hansen, ed., *Colorado, A Guide to the Highest State* (New York, 1970), revised edn., and, of course, that indispensible publication of the Colorado Historical Society, *Colorado Magazine.*

THE DIARY

Started from St. Joe, May 27th, 1862, on the "West Wind" at 10 o'clock p. m.

May 29.   A storm last night compelled the boat to lay by 4 or 5 hours, so that we did not arrive at Plattsmouth, Nebraska, until 1 o'clock. Were awakened in the night by the rain coming on us and found the berth quite wet in spots and some of our clothes on upper berth completely saturated with water. Though it stopped raining in the morning, it continued cloudy and just before we arrived at Plattsmouth, came down torrents. We had to climb the hill in wind and rain, our feet slipping back every step we took. Staid with Mr. Hanna, Mr. Tootle's partner. Were received cordially by himself and wife, (both Kentuckians) and treated with the greatest kindness.

Plattsmouth is situated on the bluffs. It is much larger than it appeared from any one point. There is but one place from which the whole town is visable. Like all new towns the houses are of board with one or two exceptions which are brick. The location of the place and country around are beautiful. It is one of the principal points from which the emigration and freighting for Colorado, California and those countries start from. It will, after awhile, be the chief route as there are no obstacles on that route which the other roads possess, no rivers to ford and road very fine. That western trade is even now immense and what supports the place. Eggs, potatoes, and butter are very cheap. A farmer went to the store and offered 10 bushels of potatoes for a pair of shoes for his wife, priced $2.50, and haul them to town (10 miles.) In the fall they will not dig them for that price, but in the spring, will sell them for whatever they can get. Nebraska, Iowa, and north Missouri, the farmers raise a great deal of sorgum [sorghum] (Chinese Sugar Cain) and manufacture not only their own molasses, but for sale too. Some farmers, the poorer ones never have sugar in the house during the year, but make their preserves, pies and sweeten their coffee with sorgum. Some of it is as clear as honey.

May 30.   The presbyterians had a "reception" as they termed it for the purpose of assisting in raising funds to build a church. They were entertained by Charades and for refreshments, cake and ice cream. Charges—10 cts. admittance, 10 cts. for a large saucer of ice creem and slice of cake. It rained and there was such a small attendance that the Charades were postponed though the ice cream was all sold. Friday, the evening appointed, though it rained again, it did not interfere. The Charades were well enacted for persons of no practice, indeed some sustained their parts very well and with a good deal of vivacity. It was quite amusing.

May 31st. Saturday.   Went to Sidney. It is in Iowa, southeast of Plattsmouth on the opposite side of the river, but not on it. It was a cloudy day and rained several times, notwithstanding which we had a pleasant ride. The scenery is very beautiful, timber, bluffs, and rolling prairie, nothing monotinous. We passed through 3 quite pretty little towns, Pacific City, Tabor, and Glenwood. Mr. Tootle drove his mules for the first time and though they are very fine ones, he had to be whipping and hollering at them all the time like all mules. Sidney like Plattsmouth, is a small town. Contains about 500 inhabitants. It is situated on high prairie and the houses not so scattered. It looks larger. The houses are nearly all white, gives it a neat appearance. We staid with Mr. Tootle's uncle. He is living in a large house and large rooms. A luxury one appreciates in this new country. Everything had such a home like appearance and the cooking so like home and everyone so kind, I would have liked to have remained longer.

Wednesday, June 4th.   Did not get back to Plattsmouth until late Monday evening. Mr. Tootle could not get through with his business and preparations in time to start before this morning. Did not get off until 10 o'clock. Had to make 35 miles to arrive at a camping place which we reached about 8 o'clock P. M. Were not as comfortable today as we expect to be, things were just put in every way. The inside of the wagon is filled nearly to the top with boxes, trunks, comfortables, blankets, guns, a matress, all the etc. of camp life. As we were so late starting, did not stop for dinner, but ate a rhubarb pie Mr. Hanna gave us. It was very soft and rather difficult to dispose of having no plates to hold it, no knife to cut or fork to eat with. We took our first lesson in the use of fingers as a substitute. By the time we got into camp, the mules and pony picketed for the night, our ham and crackers eaten and the wagon cleared so as to spread the bed, it was 11 o'clock.

June 5th, Thursday.   Seven weeks from the time we were married. At the very hour, we were seated on the prairie eating breakfast. As it was only our 2nd meal, we did not aspire to anything but cold ham and crackers. Mr. Tootle says I cannot do anything but talk, so would not trust me to make the coffee. Boasted very much of his experience. He decided to make it himself, but came to ask me how much coffee to take, for information, I know, but he insisted, only out of respect. The coffee pot holds over 1 qt. I told him the quantity of coffee to 1 qt. He took that, filled the coffee pot with water then set it near, but not on the fire. I noticed it did not boil, but said nothing. When they drank it, they both looked rather solemn and only took one or two sips. I thought it was time to have an opinion upon it. As Mr. Tootle would not volunteer one, I inquired how the coffee tasted. He acknowledged it was flat and weak, but insisted I did not give him proper directions. He consented to let me try it at supper time. Stopped for dinner where we heard there was water, but it was so muddy, even the mules would not drink. Had ham, dried beef, crackers, pickle and syrup for dinner with brandy today. The brandy and whiskey we brought for medicinal purposes, but indulged in a little as we had just started on our journey. The first day, the cork came out of the whiskey bottle and spilled more than half, to Mr. Tootle's great disappointment. Indeed I don't believe he has recovered from it yet. Camped at a beautiful place in the evening. A stream wound round the foot of the hill and the sides of the hill were covered with large trees. Got into camp at 5 o'clock. Mr. Tootle shot three snipes today. Warren cleaned them for breakfast. I was all impatience to try my skill in making coffee. I watched it anxiously until it was boiling and waited with the greatest solicitude and I must acknowledge some misgiving, for them to taste it. Oh, but I was rejoiced and relieved when they pronounced it very good. Warmed some dried beef in butter. As it was my first attempt at cooking, felt a little nervous as to the result. However, everything was cooked very well. Washed dishes in hot water. The first time we had enough and time to warm it. Think we can live quite cleanly. The wagon was arranged more comfortable today, things stored away under the seat in the lower part of the wagon between the mattress and bottom. It did not take but a little time to prepare for bed. Retired at 10 o'clock. Warren wakened us this morning at 3 o'clock. As it was 11 when we retired last night, had rather a short allowance of sleep. I protested against being wakened so early, so we got up at 5 this morning, but find it will be necessary to rise at 4 o'clock, rather more early than agreeable. 12 wagons were camped near us. Two parties, one going to Denver, the other to Washington Territory. Passed wagons today from Denver to St. Joe, ladened with hides. Went 30 miles today.

May [June] 6th, Friday.   Warren awakened us a little after 3 again. Cooked the snipes with Mr. Tootle's assistance. They were delicious. Had soaked crackers for breakfast. My first appempt and I did not soak them enough. Still they were very good and a little change. Dropped the stock of one of the guns. Warren had to ride back after it which detained us ½ hour. Took dinner as yesterday on the open prairie. No water excepting for the mules. Mr. Tootle brought with him a preparation of lemon (as he thought) but it proved to be tartaric acid and sugar, he had been cheated. It was refreshing, though rather a poor substitute for lemonade. Camped at 6½ o'clock. Washed our persons for the first time. There was a house partly built which we went into for the purpose, just a few yards from our wagon. Felt so comfortable afterwards. We undress at night though it is not customary on such trips. Took sheets with us and spread our bed as we do in the mornings at home. A family lives in an adobe house where we camped. They call it adobe, but it is only sod, square pieces ½ yd. square piled upon one another with the grass side down. The outside wall is the thickness of two pieces of sod, or 1 yd. The inside walls only one piece. The chimney and roof is of sod too. It is quite picturesque. Came in sight of the Platte at 5½ o'clock. The scenery was very fine, the country became more rolling, along the Platte. Hills covered with timber and a creek tributary to it. Passed 3 or 4 camps of ox wagons, consisting of from two or three wagons to a dozen. Met a number of wagons returning from Pikes Peak. Retired at 11 o'clock. When we camp, Mr. Tootle and Warren first unharness the mules and pony then picket them. After that build a fire and put the water on to boil. Then either Mr. Tootle or myself make the coffee and get supper together. While they feed and picket pony and the mules for the night, I prepare the bed and wash the dishes. For breakfast we go through the same routine. We have cold dinners.

June 7th, Saturday.   Mr. Tootle put on his traveling suit for the first time. It consists of a flannel shirt, one is blue with a blue and white plaid bosom, cuffs and collar. The other is scarlet flannel with a sulfureous[1] striped with white for a bosom, cuffs and collar. Pants pepper salt cloth. Cold days or mornings and evenings he wears a coat.

My traveling suit is a cotton material brown plaid minus hoopes, dark stockings, brown cambric skirt, brown hat trimmed with brown ribbon and blue veil covering head and face leaving a hole through which I could see and breath. For a change I have a blue calico bonnet with a beaux at least ½ yd. long.

Today we came into Platte River bottom and found the dust very disagreeable, but only for a little while. The road through the Platte bottom is sand from 2 inches to over 1 ft. deep. The mornings and evenings are cool indeed sometimes cold, but through the middle of the day, it is very warm. Saw 3 antelopes at a distance. Flowers like sweet-peas and fox gloves, another that resembles cow-slip exactly excepting the clusters are larger. None of the green leaves resemble the garden flowers. Nearly all the prairie flowers are fragrant. There is quite a variety of colors and shades chiefly blue, pink, red, purple, and yellow.

June 9th, Monday.   We have not seen any snipe since the 2nd day but great numbers of doves, generally in pairs, but frequently in flocks. There are blackbirds too and occasionally we see a lark and some brown birds. I don't know their names. The Platte is now very high and muddy. When it is low, it is clear. The bottom is sand. There is no timber in the Platte valley, all the wood is obtained from the islands in the river. Nearly all the ranches are adobe. Warren talks in his sleep. Last night he said, "Mr. Tootle, I have a black silk lash on my whip 18 yds. long, must I drive until I use it up?"

There was a strong wind when I rode pony this morning. As I had nothing out of my trunk, had to don a black sacque coat—of Mr. Tootle's.

The travel is much greater than the first few days. The roads from Omaha, St. Joe and Atchison come into the road just before and after we pass Fort Kearney. Every few miles we meet trains, some emigants, but generally freight trains. Drove 41 miles Saturday, as we did not intend traveling on Sunday, but the place we camped was a mile

---

[1]Greenish-yellow color.

or more from a house, no wood, no timber, and no water, but at the ranch. We were told that 5 miles over was a ranch where we could buy wood and find water, and 10 miles a ranch with timber and water. When we reached the 1st ranch, found no wood, no good camping place and no water but the river, so we went to the 10 mile place. The timber was on two miles so we camped in the plains. For 10 cts. bought 5 sticks of wood about 3 ft. long, 3 or 4 inches in diameter. We had dinner and supper together as we did not get into camp before 10 o'clock. Had boiled potatoes and fried flitch.[2] Both new dishes, so we enjoyed them very much. By the by I lost a bet on the last. Mr. Tootle bet me a new dress I would eat fat meat before I was half way to Denver. I entirely forgot it, and ate 3 pieces of fried flitch, when he very triumphantly reminded me of it. As we had not been able to wash for two days, both got on pony, (I rode behind Mr. Tootle) and went to the Platte to bathe. The river was so muddy, we were afraid to go in it for fear of holes or quick sand, so we had to content ourselves with a sponge bath. It was a lovely evening, the scenery so fine, nothing could surpass it. The sky was a bright rose color, the Platte flowing beneath it reflecting its rosiat tints and studded with islands of all sizes from 1 yd to 1 or 2 miles long, some covered with high grass and all have trees, some evergreen. That was all the timber in sight. Behind us the prairie was stretched out for miles bounded by the bluffs. The Platte though from 1 to 1½ miles wide is nowhere more than 1 to 4 ft deep. It had more islands than any river in the world. We counted 7 just in front of us in a few hundred yards. In other places I counted 40 or 50 in a small distance. They contributed very much to the beauty of the river.

When we got back to the wagon, we lunched on canned peaches, then retired. Peaches were never more relished. We rose early this morning about 3 o'clock. I ride every morning and evening on pony. The trains we pass are for Pike's Peak, California, and Washington Territory, mostly ox trains, some mules occasionally a horse train. There are ranches every 5, 10, 12, 15, sometimes 20 miles. Every ranch is a sort of house of entertainment, has a bar room, and little store attached to it. There are with few exceptions, wells at them and the only places good water can be obtained, so the trains always camp

---

[2]Cured and salted side of bacon.

near them and stop to water at least. At every ranch from 2 or 3 to 6 or 8 trains were camped, some trains consist of 2 or 3, some of 10 or 12 wagons. Yesterday did not seem much like Sunday. Read a few chapters in the Bible, the only way I could observe it.

June 10th, Tuesday.   Warren wakened us this morning 15 minutes of three, telling us it was going to rain. To our great joy it rained but a few moments. Met a stage from St. Joe just where the road comes into the main road. Met it at the first town on the road after leaving Plattsmouth called Nebraska [City] and consists of the stage office, which is of boards, one other board house, 1 log, 2 adobe, one of the last is a sort of bank "Stock of Exchange" is the sign. The woman that kept the stage office house was quite genteel in her manners. Mr. Tootle asked her if I could have a glass of milk. She brought each of us a plate with a glass of milk and two slices of fruit cake (molasses cake with raisins in it) very nice and I enjoyed it extremely. A man came in from Pike's Peak. He had 4 apples in his hand, gave one to the woman, one to her sister, one to a widow and handing the other to Mr. Tootle said he never liked to slight a lady and asked if I would not take it. I was most glad to get anything that looked like fresh fruit. The house the stage stopped at or "Station" as they are termed, had 4 or 5 large rooms. The land lady told me it was not completed, that they had to ship everything either from the Missouri, 200 miles, or Denver, 400 miles. That the timber all came from Denver. They could get it much finer and cheaper and transportation was less. Arrived at Fort Kearney 2 o'clock P. M. Found a letter from Eddie. Never was a letter more welcomed. Camped in the square of Kearney City, 2 miles from the Fort. Mr. Tootle bought 2 loaves of bread. Never enjoyed anything more in my life.

June 11th. Wednesday.   It had every appearance of a storm last night, so we camped in front of an old adobe house. It was uninhabited. It did not rain, but was such a dirty spot that we concluded next morning to ride until 8 or 10 o'clock. Then take breakfast. There were two ranches a few yds from us and the men seemed to be intoxicated so Mr. Tootle did not like to retire until they went into their houses and it became quiet. It was 12 o'clock before he came to bed. Warren called us at 2. I could not get to sleep again. At 4 we started.

Warren commenced hitching at 3. At 9 we camped for breakfast. Mr. Tootle bought a quart of new milk for my breakfast. My but I did enjoy it. We will take a lunch as we ride along and not stop until evening. We prefer this arrangement as we have the coolest part of the morning to travel in, have worked up an appetite for breakfast and I can sleep as long as I wish. There are dead mules, occasionally a horse and great numbers of oxen lying along the road. It is caused chiefly by the alkali which is in the soil and impregnates the water. Persons that are ignorant of it let their cattle drink at the pools of water. The wells are so little impregnated as not to be injurious. Many cattle die from fatigue. The sand is deep and the hills long, it is very hard on them. Until today the water has been good. I would not drink it, but Mr. Tootle and Warren did and it made them sick. Wood sells 5 cts. a stick, 3 ft. long and 4 inches in diameter. Corn sold at Plattsmouth 25 cts. per bushel. 30 miles from there, Mr. Tootle paid $1.00. Here it sells for $2.40. Saw two ducks in the road yesterday, but they would not let Mr. Tootle get near enough to shoot them.

June 12, Thursday.   The ranch we camped at last night was a greater distance than we had been told. Then we had to drive 1 mile farther for grass so that it was 10 o'clock before we got into camp and 12 before we retired. It was so warm and I had slept so much during the day that I could not get to sleep. There was a young antelope at a ranch. We watered and an Indian man and boy drove up. While we were at breakfast, a filthy, dirty squaw and papoose came up. Fortunately we were done. The Papoose had a little dirty yellow flannel, (something between a sacque and shirt) on, nothing else and it hardly came to its waist. It ran about where it pleased. The squaw had drawers and skirt with a buffalo robe wrapped around her. Skirt, drawers and robe were all the color of dirt. We had sardines for breakfast. Mr. Tootle remarked "Indians will eat all the grease they can get." Gave her the box with the oil and some pieces of sardines. Then offered her the fat from the fried flitch. She held out her hand for it. He motioned her to hold the box and poured it in. She then began dipping the crackers we had given her in it and drinking it with great gusto. It made me sick. Came upon a wigwam consisting of 6 or 7 lodges. They are made of a dozen or more poles 12 or 15 ft. long, 5 or 6 inches in diameter at the bottom, tapering up. The larger end is put in the ground, and the small ends all together stick out of the hole at the top. The hole is at the top in one side for the smoke to escape and triangular, each side ½ or ¾ yds. long. There is another similar hole at the bottom for ingress and egress. The lodges are made of buffalo skins sewed together and there is a piece the size of the holes hanging to one side so they, can close them up when they Wish. They look picturesque in pictures, but to see them dispels the romance. The Indians are all filthy looking creatures. The ones we meet now are Sioux. They are uncivilized. Some few are dressed in citizens clothes, nearly wrapped in blankets or robes. Some boys even 10 or 14 years old with nothing but a dirt colored shirt to their waist.

June 13, Friday.   Passed Cotton Wood Springs at 5 o'clock A. M. Came upon another Indian camp, they are at every ranch we pass now. We seemed to have come into mosquito region last night and this morning. They swarmed the wagon. We could scarcely eat supper for them.

June 14, Saturday.   Last night camped at a station. Mr. Tootle got a pitcher of delightful buttermilk. The house was very clean and neat, of log, the door, walls and ceiling covered with coffee sacques. That is the case with all the houses when they make any pretensions to comfort. There was no timber in sight all day yesterday and this morning until we passed "O'Fallons Bluffs", then we saw bushes and occasionally a tree on an island. We have been travelling since Thursday on the bluffs. The road is very rough up and down hill so that we travel about 3 miles an hour. Since we passed O'Fallons Bluff, we are travelling through the bottom. Yesterday passed the place where the river forks. We travelled along the South Fork of the Platte. The scenery this morning was unsurpassed. To the left were level plains spread out for miles, bounded by bluffs. To the right were the bluffs, lonely broken, rugged, with a gap through which we could see the South Fork of the Platte bordered on both sides by prairie so level that they look like the meadows of Maryland. Beyond them the bluffs of the farther side of the South Fork of the Platte, and in the distance the bluffs of the North Fork at a short distance have the appearance of ranges of mountains in the distance. Pony was so nearly well that I resumed my riding yesterday evening.

The Indians we meet are Sioux, uncivilized, filthy, degraded race. Mr. Tootle bought the ham of an antelope from them. It took him more than ½ hour to wash it clean. We fried some in butter for dinner. It was so tender and nice, so delicate and pleasantly flavoured, much nicer, I think, than venison. After washing it, it destroyed Mr. Tootle's appetite, he never could relish it. We occasionally see the graves of some Indian chief or braves or their wives. 4 or 6 poles 6 or 8 ft. long are put erect in the ground, the shape of an oblong square. The upper end is generally forked. Then other are laid across them on the tops, to support the corpse which is wrapped in a blanket with a piece of buffalo robe or vermillion colored cloth spread over them. Northwest of Denver is a stream called Vermillion creek where they get a vermillion clay they color with. There are camps of Indians at almost every ranch. We meet numbers travelling, some walk, some ride on ponys. It is chiefly the men who ride. They carry their tents on ponys. They tie the poles in two bunches, one on one side the other on the other side of the pony, put the tent, (folded up) on his back near the upper end of the poles. The large ends of the poles are exact side of the pony's head, the small ends drag on the ground. Sometimes they have their baggage or papoose tied between the poles just below the horses tail. They are tied to both sides of the poles and hold them together. Until 2 o'clock today the wind blew terrifically. Blew the dishes off the table (boxes) capsized the table, almost blew me over.

June 16th, Monday.   Came to Julesburg or Overland City about 4 o'clock. It is the most important point on the road. All the crossing of the Platte for California, Utah, Oregon, and Washington on this road is done here excepting a very little at the "old California Crossing" about 25 miles below. The city consists of 2 stables, 1 blacksmith shop, wagon shop, one station, all the property of the stage company. A hunting dog followed us today from a ranch. The Indian dogs are nearly all half wolf. Saw a prairie dog yesterday at a station. Some men caught it away from its hole and run it down. It was about the size of a Gray Squirrel and looked much like one of a yellowish gray color. Its ears are so small as scarcely to be perceptible. Its head is perhaps more like a rabbit. They are more of the nature of a ground squirrel than any other animal and what is called their bark is nothing like the bark of a dog more like the noise a squirrel makes, indeed I thought at first it proceeded from a bird, and frequently mistook it for the noise of the creaking of the wagon wheels. They are so quick in their motions that it is almost impossible to shoot them. Mr. Tootle fired at several, but they dropped in their holes before the shot could reach them. At least he did not think he hit them, but he could not tell. The prairie for hundreds of miles is covered with their holes. The soil is so sandy beyond Fort Kearney they do not attempt to cultivate it. They told me at a station that they heard of some one trying to raise potatoes. The islands can be cultivated and sometimes are. I find I cannot sleep after they commence preparing to start, so I get up at 3 o'clock with Mr. Tootle and ride from 4 or 4½ to about 7, then take a siesta when I return to the wagon. It is so pleasant riding early in the morning. We only take 2 meals now. We found we lost too much time having breakfast before we started, the heat of the day would come on by the time we were through. By rising at 3 o'clock, starting at 4, we can travel 12, 15 or 20 miles before breakfast, stop for it at 8, 9, or 10 o'clock, we do not require but two meals, then lay by 12 or 1 o'clock, the mules are resting during the warm part of the day, and fresh for the afternoon. Yesterday had to ride 15 miles to a station. The place we camped Saturday night was so disagreeable that we could only find time to read a few chapters in the Bible. Had to brown coffee, our coffee had given out and did not know how soon we could find a ranch clean enough or if the proprietors would permit it.

June 17, Tuesday.   Yesterday evening the cactus commenced for miles and miles. Almost all the way to Denver the prairie is covered with the Prickly-Pear Cactus. The flower is generally straw color pale or deep. Sometimes it is crimson. There are a few other cactuses all grow low. Excepting the prickly pear, all are round. The flowers of them are pink and very pretty. Mr. Tootle killed one of the large rabbits this morning. It was immense for a rabbit. They are very light grey on their backs, white underneath. Their ears are very long. The sand which was black has become yellow. There are nettles of a beautiful straw color. Pony deliberately laid down with me this morning.

The sand was very deep and he got tired. We will be through the deep sand in a few days. The Platte is so high that in several places it has overflowed the road. Came into Colorado Territory only yesterday near the "old California Crossing". Saw more dead oxen than usual yesterday and today. The Sandhills are very hard for them to pull up and there is a great deal of alkali in the soil here. Mr. Tootle found two beautiful pink cactus. He planted them at a station so we could get them when we returned.

June 18th Wednesday.   Two antelope crossed the road about ¼ of a mile ahead of us and disappeared over the bluff. This is not the season for buffalo and this road is two much travelled to see many. They told us at a station that the Indians had driven them to the Arkansas to prevent the whites from shooting them. In coming up the sand hills today about every 100 yds passed a dead or dying oxen. The hills are very long and sand 1 ft. deep. Met a number of trains returning from Denver without freight. Two or three wagons are fastened together. All the oxen that are not required for use are driven along. It is done for economy, not half the hands are necessary. One man can drive three or four wagons and one of the loose oxen. They sell wood now for 10 cts. per lb.

June 19th, Thursday.   We see but few birds now. Oh, Occasionally doves, and a large bird with long neck and legs. Mr. Tootle thinks it is kingfisher. Denver is about 600 miles west of St. Joe. If I remember correctly about the computation of time, here (500 Miles west) would be nearly ½ hour behind St. Joe time, but strange to say, they are ahead of St. Joe. They are very fast people. 300 miles from St. Joe, they were 30 minutes before St. Joe time. 400 miles, 35 minutes. By the watches here the sun rises at 5, sets at 8 o'clock.[3] See great numbers of prairie dogs. Came in sight of the Rocky mountains today about 12 o'clock. Mr. Tootle saw them two hours before he pointed them out to me. 115 miles from the mountains and 100 from Denver. They present the appearance of white painted clouds,

---

[3]Before what we know as "standard time," people went by "sun time." They set their time pieces at noon as they traveled westward. If there was a town clock, it was set every day at noon. It was in 1873 that Dr. C.F. Dowd, principal of Temple Grover Seminary for Young Ladies, Saratoga Springs, N.Y., proposed the idea of "standard time," i.e., four time zones across the United States. It was adopted by the railroads on Nov. 18, 1883.

excepting they are more decided than clouds and their outlines more distinct. Pictures of the Alps are correct representations of them. Have seen mirages frequently, but today saw finer ones than ever before. The representation of water was perfect of a large lake with rushes growing in it and timber on the border and in places where the timber opened, the water ran through as perfectly as in a natural lake. The clouds were reflected in it as in real water. I believe the greatest curiosity we have witnessed since we left home was two whirlwinds today. The large one was at such a distance we could not have as fine a view of it. The other was only a few yds. from us. Its connection with the ground was almost severed. It looked like a little cloud of dust for 6 or 8 ft, then for 50 or 60 or more it formed a distinct tube or pipe, a perfect sand spout from 9 to 12 inches in diameter. We could see the sand draw up on the inside and descend upon the outside. It was a perfect and distinct hollow tube. After awhile the wind curved it and it gradually dissipated, but not until at least 15 minutes after we first saw it. What seemed strange was that there was so little wind as scarcely to be perceptible.

June 20th Friday.   Came to Bijou Creek [Colorado] this morning and found the first timber for 8 days. Saw a number of antelope today, and hundreds of prairie dogs. Their houses on the outside are like large ant hills from 1½ to 3 ft in diameter, made of gravel they throw up out of the ground.

Nothing could be more grand than the mountains today. Only their tops are covered with snow, down half the distance visible today. A greater extent of range came in sight than yesterday. Were in a storm today the most severe part passed by us.

June 21st, Saturday.   Arrived at Denver about 8 o'clock P. M. It is real luxury to live in a room and sleep in a bed again. Cheyennes and Arrapahoes came into town yesterday with the trophies they had taken in battle with the Utes. The Utes are the mountain Indians, the others are plains Indians. The Indians of the mountains are always on terms of deadly hostility with the Indians of the plains. The party that came into town had some trophies from the war, scalps, a few prisoners aned some ponys. They had war dances all night and during Sunday, but left Sunday evening. I regretted so much we could not witness the dance. Attended the Episcopal church in the morning. Bishop Talbot,[4] the Episcopal Bishop of the northwest preached. He is a native of Virginia. At night we went to the Methodist. The Catholic is the only other church. The Episcopalians have no church, but use a room. Denver is situated on the Platte about 18 miles from the base of the mountains. It is but 5 years old.

June 25th Wednesday.   Gov.[5] took a company of Artillery and followed the Indians that were in town because they stole horses and furniture from the whites. They are a part of a tribe that would not sign a treaty with the U.S. Government. They promised him to leave the territory in a few days. Started at 9 o'clock for the mountains. As we approach, the first range looks like immense sand bluffs covered with short grass or pine trees of immense size. From the time we leave Denver until we get to the mountains, the road descended. When we get into the mountains we ascended ridge after ridge and descended but little. There is a long, long hill and so steep in going down one feels that they are never coming to the bottom or rather you think all the time you are coming to the foot but it is only the base of one of the long hills that compose the very very long one. Just after we entered the mountains we came upon Golden City. It is almost deserted. A very small town about 2 miles from Golden Gate. When we arrived at the Gate, I thought it was the terminus of the road. Nothing but mountains rising up in every direction. The road after passing through the gate turns off at a right angle around the base of one of the ridges of mountains and continues at the base, the mountains rising at each side of it. There are the most beautiful wild flowers richer in color and larger than the ones on the plains. A flower like our blue cultivated columbine, but 3 or 4 times as large, Larkspur and several flowers the same as our wild flowers. We saw one field of quite fine wheat and

---

[4]The Right Rev. Joseph Cruickshank Talbot of the Protestant Episcopal Church was consecrated Bishop of the Northwest in 1859. His giant diocese was composed of Nebraska, Colorado, the Dakotas, Utah, Montana, and eastern Idaho. He liked to call himself "Bishop of All Out Doors." He was also to look in on conditions in New Mexico and Arizona. "Joseph Cruikshank Talbot," *Appleton's Cyclopedia of American Biography* (New York, 1889) VI, pp. 21–22; Myra Ellen Jenkins, "New Mexico—1863," *Historical Magazine of the Protestant Episcopal Church*, XXXII, No. 1 (March 1963), pp. 221–23.

[5]Governor John Evans of Colorado Territory had been appointed by President Abraham Lincoln. Marshall Sprague, *Colorado, A Bicentennial History* (New York, 1976), pp. 36ff.

quite a number of gardens. The toll gate man had a magpie. It was the shape of a crow. Its head and neck black, its wings and tail blue. The first gold found was in Cherry Creek which runs through Denver. There was so little, it did not pay for working. My sacque dropped out of the wagon coming down the very long hill. It quite distressed me. Because it belonged to my travelling suit and it will be spoiled. There are two hotels on this road very well kept. We thought we could get to Central City and would not stop, but the mules were so jaded that we stopped at a little log cabin. Everything looked clean.

June 26th, Thursday. The log cabin we stopped at had two rooms and the garret or loft was divided by a partition into two rooms, that to my joy and surprise we had a room to ourselves. We could only stand upright in the middle. There is so much competition on this road that they are obliged to have good fare. For supper we had worked biscuit, boiled ham, fried potatoes, a large dish of green peas (the first we have seen this season) and eggs. Peaches and elegant rich cream. Tea and milk. For breakfast, we had the same. We enjoyed the peaches and cream though an outre dish for breakfast. They cannot raise vegetables on the mountain. There is too much frost. All those tender vegetables are raised in the valleys of the mountains. Radishes, turnips, and those hardy vegetables only, are raised on the mountains. Wagons pass every day from Denver to Central City and over the frequented mountain roads, very frequently with fresh meat and vegetables raised in the valleys, and canned fruits and vegetables. A great quantity of the latter are used. The only way in which I was conscious of the rarity of the air was by becoming fatigued when walking a very short distance. It is extremely hot here in summer in the middle of the day and frost every night. They gave us a feather bed to sleep upon, but it contained so few feathers we could feel every slat in the bed. But everything was so much better than the appearance outside led us to expect that we were delighted. Came down a hill 3 miles long, but not so steep as the one yesterday. Arrived at Central City about 9 o'clock A. M. the livery stables here is on the lower floor of the hotel. Our room was immediately over it. The Verandah and Metropolitan are the fashionable hotels of the place, both kept by the same man. Our room was in the Metropolitan, very rude and indifferent accommodations. The whole

Gregory diggins[6] is a very rough looking place. They are continuations of little towns each bearing different names. When a man discovers a lead, he builds near it and as others come to work it, they build up along it, thus forming a town. The most central and important is Central City. So we stopped there. As we entered the city we met wagons loaded with quartz and others with sand, going to the mills. The first and largest mills are the Black-Hawk. There are no locks on the doors out here, nothing but a latch. Visited the mines this afternoon. Went upon golden hill. The Gregory mines, the richest here in the mountains, as is the custom, have adopted the name of the discoverer. He is from Georgia. He would work a lead until the presence of gold became certain, then sell it. In that way he made his fortune. First visited Mr. Martin & Leir's mill. Mr. Leir visited the mines with us, but gave us some very fine collect all fine ones and you can only obtain them from them. Of course there are different qualities of gold and different qualities of quartz. The purest gold found in the quartz is of a bronze color. The finest quartz, I mean the quality, that yields most abundantly and the finest quality of gold is a prussian blue. The gold is found in veins of quartz, very light and porrus, lying on the surface. The rock at each side of the lead or vein of gold quartz is white or light greyish quartz, called wall rock. (They term everything quartz out here). The veins of gold in this part of the mountain are confined to a belt about ½ mile wide and makes its first appearance at the base of a hill east of Central City and runs west about 3 miles. Out of that belt, little or no gold is found. In it, if you take up a pan full of dust in the street or anywhere, it will contain at least 3 or 5 cts. worth. The richest part of the Gregory mines is called the "patch" and is about ¼ mile square. The whole of it is covered with holes, piles of sand and quartz, sluices and every spot of it worked. Here I saw the cradle or rocker in use. It is used in sluice mining. It is set under the trough. As it rocks, the water runs off the sides and the weight of the gold sinks it to the bottom. It is the shape of an old fashioned child's cradle, wider and the sides more sloping. Has a sheet iron bottom with larger holes through

---

[6]Two fine references to the Colorado Gold Rush, its miners and mining camps, are Phyllis Flanders Dorset, *The New Eldorado: The Story of Colorado's Gold and Silver Rushes* (New York, 1970), and Muriel S. Wolle, *Stampede to Timberline: The Ghost Towns and Mining Camps of Colorado* (Boulder, 1950).

which the gold falls to a second bottom. The sluice or gulch mining is done by a continuation of troughs, the lower end resting on the trough below it. That is what gives them the inclination. The troughs are about 1 yd long, have strips across the bottom to arrest the gold, or two bottoms, the upper one with holes. The water running such a distance the weight of the gold deposits of course with sand which is washed from it, in pans generally, sometimes cradles. They clean the troughs every Saturday, generally, and take out the sand and gold, wash the sand away. The gold found in this way is called gulch gold, It is the purist. The nuggets are all found in this way. Surface gold or that found on the surface has less foreign matter than quartz gold. Quartz gold is that found in the quartz rock. That found 200 ft down is called lead gold. In the sluice mines here, the richest is found in yellow earth. Here they dig down the banks. Down at Terryall, Pikes Peak, it is done by a hydraulic machine, the pipes play with water upon the banks, just as fire engine pipes play upon a building and wash it down. The quartz rock and sand is hauled to a mill, shoveled into a trough over which iron pounders of different weight, (in the mills we visited, they weighed 800 lbs.) 10 or 12 pounders. They are so arranged that the falling of one, raises the adjoining one and visa versa, so that half the number are raised at one time. They fit into a die of metal upon which they crush the quartz into very fine powder. Water runs through the trough all the time, carrying the quartz after it is pounded, upon plates spread with mercury with which the gold forms an amalgamate and the quartz dust runs off. As 1/10 of the gold (or rather quartz powder containing 1/10 of the gold) runs off in the water before it leaves the mill, just as it runs out of the trough, it runs over two rows of plates 1½ or 2 yds long or ¾ or 1 yd wide, covered with mercury. Once a week, generally Saturday, the plates outside the trough are cleaned and put into a cradle, the mercury evaporated by heat and thus the gold obtains a comparative purity. The pounded quartz after all the gold that can be taken from it is extracted. It is called tailings and contains about $40 to the cord this imperfect mode of extracting does not enable them to get. When a miner discovers gold his right is paramount to all other claims. If he discovers it under a house he digs thus undermines the house and lets it tumble over or else tears it down previous to commencing work. All that is necessary is to give the occupant notice of an hour or two to leave. I saw a number of houses tumbled over. The discoverer of a claim has a right to 300 sq. ft. Any one else to only 50 sq. ft. All their expenses is the recorder's fee of 60 cts. In working mines when they get too deep to pitch out the earth and rock, it is drawn out in buckets by a windlass, but when it gets too low, it is done by horses. Ropes are attached to the buckets and run over pulleys around a large wooden drum which has a shaft to which a horse is attached to turn it. They are introducing steam engines as a substitute. The lands of gold here runs east and west and what is singular all the leads point to a certain knob in the mountain. The sluice mining pays about an average of $8 a day to a man, that is, a man finds that much gold in a day. Quality averages from $7 to $15 per day. The Black Hawk mills do a more extensive business than any other mills, average $3200 per week, but only about ⅓ is clear. The other mills average but $200 per week. Mr. Leir said their expenses were $100 per day. They pay $1.50 a sqare inch for 24 hours. It is brought from the Snow Range, 12 miles. As it enters the mills it runs through a square box which has the grades to measure it. Silver and copper are both found in the quartz that contain gold, but iron, chiefly in the form of pyrite. In the leads of very fine gold here, opal is found. It is a milky white with the colors of the rainbow. In the George Gulch, rubies are found in abundance. Wages vary from $1.00 to $15.00 per day and even more. To bore through 1 ft. of rock costs from $15 to $40. At Pikes Peak, there are other mines discovered since these, yet have not proved so rich. Got back to Denver 6 o'clock this evening. The Black Hawk mills payed out $3200 before they cleared one ct.

Monday, June 30th.   Started this morning for Pikes Peak via Colorado City. The scenery is finer than any we have witnessed since leaving home. The different ridges of the mountains and hills are of every shape. Numbers of them have the appearance of having the tops cut off and are perfectly level, some for two or more miles in extent and are cultivated. Some have rocks on the top. One large conical hill, seemed to have the apex cut off and an immense rock, 65 ft. high set down upon it. The roads are splendid, as smooth as a floor and superior to any gravel walks in private parks. They are all gravel hard smooth and level, the finest in the world. We have not got into the mountains, but seem to be between some outside ridges and spires of the mountain. The flowers since we have got into the mountains are much richer colors and more numerous. They are of bright scarlet, crimson, purple, and blue of different shades and yellow and a few white.

July 1st, Tuesday. The roads are more hilly though just as smooth, still gravel. Came today upon the head waters of the Arkansas. They are Monument Creek and La Fontain Quebouil[7] or fountain of the boiling waters. Monument Stream empties into La Fontain Quebouil. It derives its name from the white monuments on its banks. They are composed of quartz held together by a cement of lime and sand, seems to have been washed into the shape they now are, which is every variety, pyramids, spires, columns, square monuments, some of the columns decrease in size towards the top, others increase in size towards the top. They are generally in groups and at a little distance have the appearance of a cemetary. Several of the columns had a large, flat, square slab of limestone on top like the cap on a pillar. They were 3 to 6 inches thick and extending beyond the column about 6 or 8 inches on all sides. The monuments are from 3 or 4 ft. in height to 40 or 50 ft., in height. Some at a distance resemble cabins so much that we wondered at persons building on such high mountains, such inaccesible places. Others were perfect representations of pieces of architecture. At a distance, we could not get near them, they seemed to have pillars, cornicing, entablature and all the parts of architecture.

July 2nd, Wednesday.   Arrived at Colorado City. It is the capital of the territory. It has about 50 houses, but not more than a dozen have the appearance of being inhabited. The inhabitants of the city and southern part of the territory wish to retain the seat of the government there, but the citizens of Denver want it removed there, and I expect will eventually accomplish their object as they have more influence. Pikes Peak is 1½ or 2 miles from Colorado City and is

---

[7]Here she comes pretty close to the name given to Fountain Creek, which early French explorers had dubbed La Fontaine Qui Bouille (The Spring That Boils), so called because of bubbling springs at its head. It is now Fountain, El Paso Co. "Place Names in Colorado," *Colorado Magazine*, XVIII, No. 1 (Jan. 1941), p. 33.

12,000 ft. to 12,500 ft. high above the level of the sea. The ascent is both difficult and dangerous and the air so rare and cold that some who have ascended have had their health permanently injured. One man died immediately or within a few days after having ascended it. In the valley it is very healthy. A citizen who has resided their 2 or 3 yrs. said she knew of no sickness or not one death from disease during that time. Several persons that had come there in delicate health had recovered. The springs in which the fontain rises are soda. They are not hot, but are called boiling because that escape of the gas causes the water to bubble up as if it were boiling. The taste of soda is very perceptible. They possess also a strong acid taste. With tartaric acid and sugar, they told us it made good soda water. We had no tartaric acid but took some vinegar off of pickles. It effervessed and would have been quite palatable, but as Mr. Tootle remarked "it was too pickly" Very nice soda biscuit can be made with the water. There are 3 soda springs and one chalybeate.[8] Some pretended to detect the taste of iron, but all of the springs tasted alike to me excepting the smallest one was the strongest. Where ever a hole is dug near it fills with water and bubbles up just as the springs. The bottom of the springs are white from the deposit of soda. The Indians and Spaniards and all the inhabitants from New Mexico and Colorado Territory who are sick resort to it for their health. It is said to accomplish some wonderful ones, cured inflamatory diseases. I was told a woman who had been confined to her bed for years with rhumatism was entirely cured in a few weeks. They certainly are a great and very interesting curiosity. Another place of interest was the Garden of the Gods. It is an opening between two ridges of the mountains and entirely surrounded by them, containing numbers of red, pink, white and lead colored rocks of immense size, indeed all sizes from a few ft. to 300 & 400 ft. high and as many in bredth. Others are columns and of every shape. The red ones are old red sandstone and a concrete sandstone. The bluish white and lead color limestone and the lead white gypsum. The entrance is not wider than 16 or 18, between rock from 200 to 400 ft. high. At one side is a pure white one of gypsum and beside it a greyish white limestone. The

---

[8]Iron salts.

other side of the entrance is a red one. Some resemble the ruins of castles and the pink and white beside the red ones bring out the different colors so distinctly that the effect is much more beautiful and imposing. After you enter is an immense old red sandstone one 3 or 400 ft high and as broad. A few ft. in front is a pink one about half the size, in a line north is another immense one light-greyish limestone with veins of pink and red; a few yards from it another the same size, red sandstone; and in front of it a gypsum one of lead white color and so they are, over the whole garden; small ones interspaced between the large ones. It is most aptly named, just such a place as one would suppose the Gods might once have inhabited, but now in ruins. The most beautiful flowers in it too. In one of the red sandstone rocks there is a cave. The stratum of old red sandstone must be at least two miles wide extending north and south, sometimes upheaved in long ridges just like a wall along the ridges of the mountain 10 or 12 ft. high, other times in isolated rocks or in clusters. One the party killed a rattlesnake at the mouth of the cave. We returned to the hotel, took dinner, and left for Denver by the same route we had come there. We had intended taking the road that led through South Park, visiting the Buckskin Tan, Tarryall, and Idahoe mines and returning by Clear Creek, the scenery being represented as very fine. On account of our time being limited, we were compelled to abandon it and return by the road we came. When we got to Colorado [City] one of our mules was so much fatigued as to alarm us and Mr. Tootle feared travelling through the mountains might unfit them for the journey home as soon as he was compelled to take it. It was with great regret we turned around. Another circumstance that had considerable weight in deciding us was the number and kind of flies. They were so large and had annoyed the mules so very much causing them to bleed a great deal. A Mexican that came down the mountain, the road we had intended taking, said they were much worse up there and had nearly killed his pony, the blood was dripping from all over it.

Left Colorado 3 o'clock P. M., Thursday, 3rd of July. Stopped at a house where an old acquaintance of Mr. Tootle lived and staid all night. In the morning his daughter went with us to the top of the highest mountain in that neighborhood. We could look down upon the others and over the prairie as far as the eye could see. It was grand. Many of the mountains were level on top. As we came down, we gathered some beautiful specimens of quartz and other stones. I never enjoyed anything so much in my life. Over the whole side of the hill, around all the trees for yards were laying these beautiful stones, crystals as clear as glass, pure white, yellow, red, green, brown, black, all colors and all sizes, polished smooth as glass and bright by friction. They looked more like french candies than anything I could compare them to. I gathered first my dress skirt full, then my under skirts, so heavy I was loaded under the weight. Mr. Tootle gathered great many too, but he was satisfied with fewer, or rather he knew we could not carry all the stones on the mountains home, so we selected the most singular looking and threw the others away. It almost made the tears come to have to leave them behind. Started after dinner and travelled to within 20 miles of Denver. So passed the 4th of July. More real pleasure than any 4th ever brought to me before. Yesterday evening saw a porcupine. It was very large. In running, curved its body up and down like a measuring worm. It ran so fast, Mr. Tootle could not get his gun in time to shoot it.

Saturday, July 5th.   The man at whose ranch we stopped took us to where there were two petrified trees. The trunk where it broke off from the root was lying just where it was broken. The whole tree was not petrified, but just 3 or 4 yds of it in different places, yet just in the line it fell. The ground was covered with pieces of wood you could not tell were petrifacations until you took them in your hand. The second tree was more beautifully petrified, where there was more pitch in it. It was petrified harder, of richer colors and parts of it where there was a good deal of pitch was crystalized. The tree was broken off about a yd from the ground, there was the old trunk and the fallen tree laying for 2 or 3 yds with the splinter sticking up and broken just as a live tree. Both were fine. We brought a number of specimens away. Mr. Tootle sent in an old chunk which must have weighed 60 or 70 pounds which you could not distinguish from an old chunk of wood, but by the weight and touching it. Reached Denver Saturday evening perfectly delighted with our trip. The grass in the mountains is a peculiar kind containing so much nutriment that it is not necessary to feed the cattle even in winter when the snow is on the ground. They get at it through the snow. The soil is sandy so the snow does not lay long. In the mountains the climate is very mild in winter excepting on the elevated parts. Persons generally locate between the ridges in the gulches. The country is very healthy and but little disease. The air is so rare even at Denver people feel sleepy all the time and in place of rising in the morning refreshed feel languid. I was told by some persons that in the period of 3 or 4 years, ones become seriously debilitated and others contradicted it. In the Rocky Mountains besides gold are silver and lead mines. In the South Park, salt is made from the salt lakes. The mountain ranges are 250 miles. When emigration first commenced here and before roads were made, they went over the tops of the mountains, up one side and down the other. Frequently it was so steep they would have to cut down the largest trees they could find and chain them to the wheels of their wagons to hold them back. I was told all the houses of Golden City (which is at the base on the Plains) was built of these trees. Men were at the foot of the mountains ready to seize them directly they were loosened from the wagons, would hew them into logs, then sell them. Learned a new and appropriate name for Yankeys. A servant of all departments at Colorado city, a wild, harum-scarum, kind-hearted girl, they called Texas because she came from there, though born in Mississippi, said "I would die for a Southerner, but would not give a cent for a *Pinch back Yankey*".

July 14. Reluctantly and after a most delightful visit turned our backs on Denver and the Rocky Mountains. The wind blew terribly for several hours so that neither veil or goggles protected us from the dust. Indeed, Mr. Tootle could not see to drive, but had to turn off of the road and stand still for 10 minutes at a time. It was short fortunately. They told us at the first station they seldom had such severe storms. Here they said it hailed and the hails were the size of a hen's egg. Cut to pieces everything in the garden. It was very cold during and after the storm.

July 15. Camped at Bijou station.[9] They were going to tear it down

---

[9]Bijou Station, Colo., was one of the best known stopping places on the Overland Stage Line. Ben Holladay had just taken it over in late 1861. Bijou was 20 miles from the next station to the east, Beaver Creek, the longest distance apart of any of the stations. Frank A. Root and William E. Connolley, *The Overland Stage to California* (Topeka, Kan.,1901) pp. 70, 102, and passim.

the next day. All the women had left. The men offered us the use of the kitchen so we cooked supper there.

July 16, Wednesday.   Camped at Bijou Creek. Passed the Junction at 4 o'clock. Camped at a ranch 6 miles beyond in Alkali Bottom. Winged ants collected in swarms on the top, front and back of the wagon just like bees when they swarm. Mr. Tootle forgot to bring the meat he bought in Denver, so we had or could not buy any fresh meat. We got very tired of salt meat. We depended upon buying butter and potatoes along the road, and did not succeed in purchasing any meat.

July 17.   Breakfasted at Beaver Creek Station. Have been annoyed by gnats. They sting severely though not larger than the point of a pin. At first I mistook them for a speck of black sand. A storm came up and we stopped at the American Ranch Station[10] until it was over. Got our supper there.

Saturday, July 19th.   Mr. Tootle shot a wild duck. We are going to have it for dinner tomorrow. Last night came into mosquito region. They were in the thickest swarms I ever saw. Flocks of black birds follow the horses and cattle, settle on the backs, fly around them to catch the mosquitos and flys.

Monday, July 21st.   Camped Saturday night on the river. Had no drinking water, so Sunday had drive to a ranch 6 miles ahead. Did not start until 6 o'clock as we had so short a distance to travel. We had no light bread, no butter, or milk, nothing to fry the duck in. When we got to the ranch, no one lived there, but a man, and we could get nothing but water, and that was no good. They told us the next ranch was 8 miles, so we concluded to drive there. There we could not even get water, so had to drive 5 miles farther to the Animal Springs. It was one o'clock when we got there. Cooked our duck and enjoyed our dinner. Tried to make soup of the legs and wings but failed. Though I watched it closely, the water boiled away and the duck burnt. Breakfasted at Gills Station.[11] No one lives there but a Frenchman. His house was so clean and neat that we cooked our breakfast there and ate it in the room.

---

[10]American Ranch Station in Colorado was also known as Kelly's Station. Ibid., pp. 102, 222.

Thursday July 24.   Camped near a ranch. A rain storm came up. The first we were in. We went into the house to make milk soup just as it commenced to rain. Went back to the wagon before 9 o'clock and it was still raining and dark as Egypt. I had just that evening spread clean sheets on the bed. When I stepped over the seat my foot went into a puddle of water. I put the other down. It went into another puddle. Every place I put my hand was either wet or in water. The matches were so damp they would not light. Mr Tootle and Warren had gone to feed and fix the mules for the night. It seemed an age before they came back. The fleas were devouring me, so all I could do was to stand or sit in the puddles of water and catch and murder fleas until they came back. I felt savage enough to murder anything even myself. When Mr. Tootle came back and lighted the lamp, we found everything wet, excepting his blanket shawl. Not a very pleasant prospect for the night, however, we got things arranged more comfortably than I had any expectation, thanks to Mr. Tootle's ingenuity. We turned the wet side of the matress down, spread some soiled clothes for a sheet (we had but 2 pairs of sheets, one was soiled and I had put it to the side of the wagon to keep out the air, the others were on the bed when the rain commenced). We used Mr. Tootle's shawl for a cover.

July 25, Friday,   Had a storm in the middle of the night. It thundered and lightninged terribly, rained very hard. Mr. Tootle arranged the wagon so we did not get wet. Arrived at Fort Kearney a little after 3 P. M. Bought some meat, tough and not nice. Took supper at the last house on the stage road.

July 26, Saturday.   Saw a fine field of corn about 20 miles east of Kearney. The man said it was put in with the plough and had not been touched since. A little Frenchman had a bed of melons the other [side?] of Kearney, they looked flourishing, but he said they required a great deal of attention. He had to water them every day. The soil beyond Fort Kearney they do not attempt to cultivate excepting upon the islands of the Platte which are more fertile. Along the sand hills wild cherries grow on bushes from 1 ft to 1 ½

---

[11]Here she probably means Gilman's Station in Nebraska, another important stage stop, Ibid. See especially the fold-in map at the end of Root and Connelley's book.

ft. high. They are the size of our common sour cherry, but taste exactly like our wild cherry. They have plumbs that grow in the same way, some on bushes as high as 5 or 6 ft. both red and yellow. At Colorado City, they have a blue plumb that grows like these cherries.

July 28 Monday.   It is intensely hot today, warmer than yesterday which was the first day we experienced any inconvenience from the heat. The mosquitos swarm around us at night and the fleas almost devour me. Last night, Mr. Tootle made a fire in the frying pan and smoked the mosquitos out of the wagon and me too. I did not know which was more disagreeable. Yesterday, swarms of winged ants settled upon our wagon. There must have been millions. they were smaller than the ones that visited us before. Rode 25 miles yesterday. We thought it 10 or 12 miles to the next station and concluded it would not be more unprofitable riding a short distance than loll around and sleep when we got tired reading. To ride awhile would be a little variety and rest us, but the station was twice the distance we were told.

July 29, Tuesday.   Travelled 50 miles yesterday from 4 o'clock in the morning until 10 at night, stopping only 2½ hours for breakfast. We took our supper in the wagon as we rode along.

July 30, Wednesday.   Arrived at Salt Creek, 3½. Our first camping place as we went out. Salt Creek rises in salt lakes. Within the last year a quantity of salt has been made from the water of the lakes. Last Sunday, Mr. Tootle resolved not to chew anymore. He had been breaking off gradually for the last 3 or 4 months. For a few days he felt nervous and badly, but now feels better ([Insert:] June 14, 1863, has been smoking ever since he returned).

Thursday, July 31st   Mr. Tootle smoked one pipe yesterday, another today, the first since we have been married. Arrived at Plattsmouth about 4 P. M.

Monday, Aug 4th.   Left Plattsmouth for Sidney [Iowa]. Had to cross the Missouri in a row boat. Felt a little nervous. Returned to St. Joe from our visit to Pikes Peak Monday, August 11th, 1862.

A Letter from the Oregon Trail, 1863
Elizabeth Elliott

INTRODUCTION

"Poignant" is a word which would characterize many documents appearing in this series. This is especially true of this letter. It was sent to us by Mrs. Elizabeth Kay-Pitts of Medford, Oregon, who had seen a notice of our project in the Medford *Mail-Tribune*. We are grateful to her for the use of the letter and for her furnishing information about the Elliott family.

Traveling with a large company of 1863 overlanders from Marshall County, Iowa, the Elliott family planned to settle in Benton County, Oregon. They began their journey with three little children: Maria, age 7, and twin boys, Dayton and Fremont, age 3. The poignancy of her letter lies in her reporting of the deaths of children along the way, including one of her own, Fremont.

Henry Elliott and Elizabeth were both Ohioans, having been born and married in that state. Elizabeth, born May 18, 1836, in her letter refers to herself as "Libbie." They moved from Ohio to Indiana just after their marriage, and their first child, Maria (pronounced Mar-EYE-a) was born in Indiana in 1856. They then moved to Marshall County, Iowa, where in 1860 there were born twin boys, Dayton and Fremont.

Henry was a diligent farmer, and the rich farming land of the far-away Willamette Valley in Oregon was like a magnet drawing them even farther west. They were spurred on by correspondence from Henry's brother, William H., who had settled in Benton County, Oregon, with his wife and three children. The mother of this family was another Elizabeth Elliott. The two wives with the same name, living in Benton County, adds difficulty in searching out their records. Henry and Elizabeth lived near Monroe.

Elizabeth Elliott lived a long rich life. The date of her death was July 26, 1927. The following obituary appeared in the Corvallis, Oregon, *Gazette-Times* on July 28:

Body brought to Benton County—A dispatch from Salem says Mrs.

Elizabeth Elliott, 91, who had lived in Oregon 45 [sic, actually 64] years, died instantly Tuesday night at the home of her daughter, Mrs. Kay, of Salem, when she tripped over a porch rug and fell headlong to the sidewalk, five feet below the porch. She received a fractured skull and deep lacerations. . . The aged woman was well known as one of the leaders in the fight for educational progress in the Willamette Valley. Mrs. Elliott will be buried in Monroe. She is survived by two daughters, Mrs. W. H. Kay of Salem and Mrs. Edgar Grimm of Nome, Alaska.

Families who traveled in the same wagon train as the Elliotts from Marshall County, Iowa, were mentioned by Elizabeth. They were the Logsdons and the Howells. She misspells both names.

The U.S. Census of 1870 lists two families of Logsdons and one of Howells. These people were all Benton County neighbors, named in the census as follows:

Charles Logsdon, age 34, and his wife, Margaret, age 29, both born in Illinois. Two children, Mary, 3, and Margaret, 1, were born in Oregon. Charles Logsdon was a farmer.

Thomas B. Logsdon, age 40, and his wife, Mary O., 27, both born in Illinois, and one child, Leona, one year old. Thomas was also a farmer.

George Howell, age 47, and his wife, Margaret J., 43, were both born in Ohio. Their children, all born in Iowa, were William A., a school teacher, age 21; Mary, 15; George P., 13; Rachel, 10; and Jesse, 5. This, too, was a farm family.

THE LETTER

Camped at noon on little Sandy
June the 12th   1863

Dear neglected Parents   through a multitude of troubles and cares I have neglected answering your kind letter which we received at Ft Laramie   I will in the first place tell you about the sickness we have had in our company   there has been 44 cases of measles in the company from Marshall Co [Iowa] and our own family   I mean, there was 3 deaths in about 3 weeks, Mr Howal lost a babe about 8 months old   it died a few miles the other side of Laramie so they got a very nice coffin for it   Mr Logestons babe was the next   he was about 2 years old,   the next was Mr Logestons boy about 5

years old, they were not in reach of any place to get a coffin therefore they buried them in boxes, the mother of the 2 children will
be confined in a few weeks, any one would think so much trouble
would kill her but she bears it well, I will now tell you about our
own family, Fremont & Dayton took the measles about the same
time, but they did well, as we supposed but just as they were getting
over them, they took the whooping cough, the diseases both work
on the lungs you know and their lungs were naturally rather weak so
they have had a dreadful time, we thought several days ago we
would have to leave his body on the plains, but they are both now a
little better, if they do not take cold I think they will get along,
just as they were getting over the measles Maria took them she was
pretty sick for several days, before she got real stout I took them I
was confined to the wagon several days, and before I got so I could
cook or do anything Henry was on a mountain viewing the Devils
gate and when he went to come down he jumped from one rock to
another and sprained his ankle so you can see we have had a terrible
time

July 2nd

My Dear Parents since I commensed this letter our family circle
has lost one of its members Freemont is no longer a sufferer on this
earth, he died Sabbath afternoon June 21st. we had a Physition
at Ft Bridger he pronounced his worst disease dropsy, he had
been terribly bloated for 2 weeks, the doctor gave medicine for him
but it did not seem to do him any good, his disease was of such a
nature that he could not lay down to sleep for over 2 weeks he set
up day and night, well he suffered along until 3 or 4 days after we
left the Ft, Sunday afternoon about 2 oclock he was taken with fits
he had 7 or 8 very hard ones about 4 he died in a fit he was sens-
able to the last minit when he took the fit he died in he tried to
straiten his little fingers and said oh dear ouch, while one hard fit
was on his dear little eyes and mouth jerked as though it would kill
him he looked at me and reached his dear arms out to me and said
Oh Libbie. he was so sensible, Oh dear I never shall forget that
pleading look, it seemed as though it would break my heart I could
not ease his pain, but he is gone his suffering is over. we laid him
at the foot of a mountain by a splendid spring, we was not where we

could get a coffin so some of our company took 2 cracker boxes nailed them together lined it with bleached muslin so it looked very well, I had had his red stockings his shoes his linen coat and pants put on him and his light hat in his hands Oh he was such a pretty corpse, he looked very natural Some of our co said they never saw such a pretty corpse Oh how I wanted his likeness taken and sent it to you he did look so sweet with his summer suit on and his hat in his hands, little did his Aunt Maryann or his Aunt Sarah think when they made his coat and pants they were making his burying clothes little did any of us think of the like or how different we would off talked and acted, but I suppose he is better off but it is so hard to part him and Dayton but the day he died we thought they would be buried in one grave for Dayton was taken worse the same time Fremont was and some thought D would die first, well we watched over him all night while Fremont lay a corpse expecting every moment to breathe his last until about day he began to get better he has been gaining very slow since untill last night he was taken worse, we was up pretty near all night with him and today he is very sick, if we save him it will be with the utmost care he has become so very weak and poor I dont know as I ever saw as poor a child, we have had so much sickness and trouble on the road I have fell away very fast, I was weighed while at Ft Bridger and I had fell away 21 ½ lbs, and I have such heart rending trouble since I presume I have fell away a good deal more,

William Howels lost his youngest the 20 of June a little girl about Fredies age, she was buried the 21 and Fremont the 23rd they lay side by side, it was a great satisfaction that we did not have to leave him alone

there has been 5 Children died out of our co since we started Fremont talked a week or so before he died so much about going to Grandmas to get some bread and milk, poor little sufferer he did get so tired jolting along in the wagon Dayton talks so much about him Oh how we all miss him he was so lively, allways saying something cunning how dreary our wagon looks without him tell his little cousin he used to have so much pleasure and sometimes some difficulty with he had not forgotten them he often talked about them and their plays it seems to me now that I can never get reconsiled to his death   it is a loss that cannot be made up   I would like to write something about the natural curiosites we have seen on the road but my mind is not settled enough now   maybe before we get a chance to send it I will write more   after we left Ft Bridger we took the old Oregon road   Fremont was buried 60 miles from Bridger on this road   we have had no trouble with the Indians since we started but there has been trains attacked this season   we have saw a great many graves of persons killed by the Indians last season, I have not lost one hour sleep on account of fear from them since I left home,   we are now in a train of 34 wagons   we are now 800 miles from Benton Co Oregon

We are now on the fery boat crossing Snake River
    you must write to Oregon

Libbie   Father   Mother

GRAVE MARKER OF MARTIN RINGO
NEAR GLENROCK, WYOMING
Courtesy of Randy Brown, Douglas, Wyoming

The 1864 Journal
Mary Ringo

INTRODUCTION

When Mary Ringo on Wednesday, May 18, 1864, began the entries in her overland journal she was expecting the birth of her sixth child. Not once did she mention this fact in the record of her journey. It was on this date that the Ringos left family and friends in Liberty, Missouri, for the long trek to California.

This is a very special diary written by a woman of remarkable inner strength. A daughter, Mattie Bell, wrote years after the event, "I think she was the bravest woman I ever heard of. . . ."

Mary was the wife of Martin Ringo (b. Oct. 1, 1819), a Kentuckian who had served during the Mexican War as a mounted infantryman at Fort Leavenworth, Kansas.[1] He was discharged on June 21, 1847, and settled down as a farmer near Weston, Missouri, just across the Missouri River from Leavenworth. He met a young woman named Mary Peters (b. Nov. 13, 1826) and on Sept. 5, 1848, they were married. Immediately after the marriage ceremony the Ringos moved to Washington, Wayne County, Indiana.

Their first two children were born in Indiana: John Peters (b. May 3, 1850), and Martin Albert (b. Jan. 28, 1854). The family later moved to Gallatin, Daviess County, Missouri, where three more children were born, all girls: Fanny Fern (b. July 20, 1857); Mary Enna (b. May 2, 1860); and Mattie Bell (b. April 28, 1862).

At the time of the first entry in her journal, May 18, 1864, the ages of the children were John, 14 years; Albert, 10; Fanny, 7; Mary Enna, 4; and Mattie Bell, 2. Mother Ringo had a very busy journey.

That first entry (May 18) in the diary was made in Liberty, Cass County, Missouri. They had relatives in that town just north of Kansas City, and there was a tearful parting for the start of the journey. The next day, May 19, they were ferried across the river and camped out near

---

[1]Much of the detailed information about the Ringo family has come from *Ringo Family History Series,* Volume V, *Line of Descent from Major Ringo* (Alhambra, Calif., 1980), pp. 11–34.

Leavenworth on the Kansas side. They followed the Leavenworth Trail, as it was called, across northeast Kansas, to join the main trail along the Platte at Ft. Kearney, Nebraska. From there they took the usual trail along the Platte, turned south to Salt Lake City on the Mormon Trail, then they went on westward by the stagecoach road to Austin, Nevada, on the Reese River. They eventually continued west to San Jose, California, where they were met by Mary's sister, Augusta, and her husband, Coleman Younger, a well-known breeder of fine cattle. Mary and the children settled down to live in San Jose. The 1870 Census listed their address as "Santa Clara Co., California, Alviso P.O., City of San Jose, 1st ward."

There are two dreadfully tragic events that marked the Ringo journey.

The first of these is summed up in Mary's diary entry for Saturday, July 30: "And now Oh God comes the saddest record of my life for this day my husband accidentally shot himself and was buried by the wayside and oh, my heart is breaking. . . ."

We have published as an "Epilogue" to Mary Ringo's journal a letter written by a fellow traveler, William Davenport, to the Liberty, Missouri, *Tribune*. Davenport was mentioned many times by Mary, once, even, as "Dr. Davenport." His letter is dated August 1, 1864, sent from "the Platte River." It was published in the *Tribune* on September 16. Here are some of the key lines:

> Just after daylight on the morning of the 30th ult. Mr. Ringo stepped on top of the wagon, as I suppose, for the purpose of looking around to see if Indians were in sight, and his shot gun went off accidentally in his own hands, the load entering his right eye and coming out the top of his head. At the report of his gun I saw his hat blown up twenty feet in the air, and his brains were scattered in all directions.

Martin Ringo was buried alongside the overland train. Aubrey L. Haines in his book, *Historic Sites along the Oregon Trail*,[2] tells of the site as having a marker of native stone incised with the words, "M. Ringo." He says the location is two miles west of Glenrock, Wyoming, 150 feet north of the old U.S. Highway 26/87. A new marker was set up by the Oregon–California Trails Association at the behest of Randy Brown of Douglas, Wyoming, who has given much help to the editor of this series, with verbal and photographic information about the setting. The

---

[2](Gerald, Mo., 1981), p. 178.

new marker was set up in the summer of 1987. It has a quote from William Davenport's letter to the *Tribune*: "He was buried near the place he was shot, in as decent a manner as was possible with the facilities on the plains."

But there was a second tragic event that marked the exodus of this family. On October 8 Mary Ringo wrote, "We remain in Austin, Nevada." This was her last entry in the diary. There is appended to the journal a conclusion written by the youngest of the three daughters, Mattie Bell (Ringo) Cushing, saying that in Austin a son was born. She writes, "Fortunately it was still-born for he was terribly disfigured from mother seeing father after he was shot. Even my brother [John] who was fourteen years old noticed it and said he looked just like father did."

After "a week or ten days," Mattie says, they went on with one wagon pulled by mules over the Sierra to San Jose, where they settled permanently. They were welcomed by Mary's sister, Augusta, and her husband, Coleman Younger.

Now as to the diary itself. We learned that Frank Cushing, son of Mattie Bell Cushing, and a printer by trade, had published the diary of Mary Ringo, his grandmother, in 1956. We learned also that Frank Cushing had died, but had given a copy of the diary to several friends, among them Herschel C. Logan of Santa Ana, California. Mr. Logan sent us his copy of the book, and we were able, with his permission, to make a photocopy of it. Of the rare journal Frank Cushing had printed only 45 copies, and had copyrighted it so that it could not be copied promiscuously. There is a note at the beginning of the book saying that it had been copied from the handwritten original which had become almost illegible over the many years since 1864. In this note Frank Cushing said, "We have followed the original spelling, punctuation and capitalization."

We wrote the Register of Copyrights in Washington, D.C., and learned that under the law as it was used in 1956, the copyright had run out fourteen years after October 24, 1956. The book is now in the public domain. We hope the present publication of the precious diary in *Covered Wagon Women* would have met Frank Cushing's approval.

Note on John Ringo

There was one person mentioned by Mary Ringo from time to time in her journal. That was John, her oldest son, age fourteen. She fondly called him "Johnny" or "Johnnie." Johnny spent most of his time as a cowboy, handling the oxen and horses and mules. He observed the two traumatic experiences of the family's long journey: the death of his father, and the stillborn child with the disfigured face, born in Austin to his mother.

Now it is known for a fact that this young man grew up to become the notorious cattle rustler, Johnny Ringo.[3] There are songs about him, movies, television programs, and countless western articles and books. He was the man behind the myth. To sort fact from fiction is virtually impossible.

He was listed by the census taker in San Jose in 1870 as John Ringo, age 20. Some time after that date he made the long journey on horseback to Mason County, Texas, where he worked driving cattle. He was supposed to have been involved in several killings during his Texas years, but the historical record is quite confused. He did serve for a period as sheriff of Mason County in the late 1870's.

He made his first appearance in Arizona in 1879, and lived out his life in the Tombstone area. There he was involved in cattle rustling, both from American ranches, and from Mexicans just across the border. A major problem for John Ringo was that he often drank too much to assuage times of moodiness and despondency. This led him into quarrels with other cattlemen. One day early in July 1882, Johnny Ringo's body was found near the side of a road leading to Tombstone. There has been much disagreement as to how and why Ringo met his death, whether he had been murdered, or was it suicide?

A statement of a coroner's jury dated July 14, 1882, seems to solve the problem.[4]

> The undersigned reviewed the body and found it in a sitting posture facing west, the head inclined to the right. . . There was a bullet hole in the right temple, the bullet coming out on top of the head on the left side. . . . Several of the undersigned identify the body as that of John Ringo, well known in Tombstone. . . . His revolver, he grasped in his right hand, his rifle rested against the tree close to him—He had two cartridge belts, the belt for the revolver cartridges being buckled on upside down.

We agree with Jack Burrows, the major authority on the life and death of Johnny Ringo, that death was by suicide. Gunfighter buffs have

---

[3]Much of the material on Johnny Ringo we have gleaned from an excellent study of both the man and the myth in Jack Burrows, *John Ringo: The Gunfighter Who Never Was* (Tucson, 1987), passim. Burrows' study is a definitive biography of John Peters Ringo.

[4]This coroner's report on the death of John Ringo has been published in several sources. We have used the version published in Allen A. Erwin, *The Southwest of John H. Slaughter, 1841–1922* (Glendale, Calif., 1965), pp. 203–4.

a term, "man-tally," to describe the number of deaths that could be attributed to gunfighters as they drew on each other. Burrows succinctly says of Ringo, "For the record, his man-tally stands at one: himself."[5]

THE JOURNAL

May 18, Wednesday. Left my family and started on my long trip across the plains, went 10 miles, had some trouble with the oxen and camped for the night and here I took my first lesson in camp life, cooked my supper and went to bed but couldn't sleep until after the chickens crowed for the day and after a short nap I awoke.

May 19, Thursday. I got up and prepared breakfast and started again. We traveled two miles and come to the Missouri river at Leavenworth[6] and here the children have the pleasure of seeing a steamboat. We were detained a short time waiting for the Ferry-boat being on the opposite side we got across in safety. A gentleman by the name of Owen drives the mules up in the city for me while Mr. Ringo helps Johnny with the oxen here. We get our groceries and other necessities for our comfort and then drive about four miles and camp for the night, prepare our supper and go to bed and slept much better than I did last night, we got a stable for our mules and both the oxen for which we pay fifteen cents a head.

May 20, Friday. We remain here waiting we have our family wagon tires cut and by noon Mr. Tipton and Mr. Cirby's families overtake us, we then hitch up and travel out as far as the eight mile house and camp for the night. Mr. Tipton was so unfortunate as to get their wagon wheel broke which will detain them a short time and just after we get into camp Dr. Moores family came up.

May 21, Saturday. Still in camp repacking and repairing. Nothing occurred worthy of note.

---

[5]Op. cit., p. 197.

[6]Merrill J. Mattes, in his *Great Platte Road* (Lincoln, 1969), describes one of the "Jumping-off Places" as Weston-Fort Leavenworth. The Leavenworth Road lay from Leavenworth, Kansas, to Fort Kearney, Nebraska. Mattes' section on "The Fort Leavenworth Road and the Pony Express Route" (pp. 149ff) is of inestimable value to students of the overland trail.

May 22. Sabbath morning   we hitch up and travel through Mount Pleasant—eighteen miles.

May 23, Monday.   Travel 20 miles and have a hard storm near Lancaster a small town in Kansas.

May 24, Tuesday.   Travel 5 miles   could not go any farther on account of the mud.

May 25, Wednesday.   Still at Clear Creek waiting for D. Gatty.

May 26, Thursday.   We started again and got to a little town called Kinnekuck   stayed their most of the day having the wagons repaired. In the evening we moved out two miles and camped on a creek called Grass Hopper.

May 27, Friday.   Our cattle scattered,   we only traveled 7 miles and camped at Walnut Creek.

May 28, Saturday.   Started early this morning and traveled 18 miles and passed through a little town called Grenado and camped 4 miles this side.

May 29, Sabbath.   Start to travel 20 miles today and would have done it had we not stopped at Senica—traveled 15 miles and camped on a little trail.

May 30, Monday.   We traveled 20 miles and camped quite early, we passed through a town. I knew no name so called it Uncle John's store.

May 31, Tuesday.   Traveled 13 miles today and camped at Maryesvill.

June 1st, Wednesday.   We laid by today on account of the rain. The gentlemen went fishing and caught a great many fish. We have quite a nice evening,   some gentlemen who are camped near us came and played on their violins, which is quite entertaining to California travelers.

June 2, Thursday.   We travel 17 miles and camp and have very poor water.

June 3, Friday.   We travel 20 miles and camp at Rock Creek,   here we have such a beautiful camp,   large rocks are here with numerous names, some of them handsomely carved and conspicuously on a nice little square is a Seces [Secesh] Flag. I know by this southerners are ahead.

June 4, Saturday. We camped at Big Sandy traveled 20 miles today, nothing worthy of note transpired.

June 5, Sunday. We travel 18 miles and camp at Little Blue Lay by to wait for Mr. Guthry, while here I washed up all of our dirty clothes, at night our camp friends came and we had some more music. (Stayed here two nights)

June 7, Tuesday. Left and traveled 18 miles. Today Johnnie got his foot hurt quite badly by the wheels running over it, it seems to have been a day of accidents, a little boy was run over by a wagon and killed and a wagon master by the name of Hase killed one of his teamsters, shot him through the head. The murdered man leaves a wife and children.

June 8, Wednesday. We lay by for the gentlemen to go buffalo hunting, they stay all day and until one o'clock at night, they came back very much elated having killed a nice buffalo, the meat is very tender. Johnnie goes along not withstanding his foot is very sore, he says they saw a great many Elk and Antelopes.

June 9, Thursday. We travel 18 miles over what is called the "Nine mile prarie" it has been the hardest drive for our cattle that we have had, some places you could hardly see the men in the wagon for the dust, I was glad indeed to camp, we had good water and plenty of wood.

June 10, Friday. We traveled 22 miles and camped on thirty-two mile creek, we had a very refreshing shower while camped here that settled the dust and cooled the air.

June 11, Saturday. We traveled 15 miles and camped three miles from Platt river, we have to drive our stock to the river, this place is almost destitute of grass, the soil is sandy, we find the cactus and prickly pears grow here and we see numerous little lizzards sliding through the grass and one extremely long snake gliding down in a hole. Our camping neighbors again give us some nice music.

June 12, Sunday. We travel 10 miles and camp at noon, we pass through a town called Doby Town, most all of the houses are built of dirt, the prarie here is very level, we have excellent grass for the stock. In days gone by it must have been a great place for Buffaloes as we see a great many skeletons some of them extremely large. From here I write a letter to my sisters Mrs. McCown and Mrs. Miller.

June 13, Monday. Start early and travel 19 miles. We pass by Fort Kinney [Kearney], we are not allowed to go through the Fort. Mr. Ringo walked up to see if we had any letters from our friends and was disappointed as we did not receive any, mailed my letters here and go on. About two miles from this place is a small town called Kerney City. It is a right promising town. I buy myself a dress here, we find the goods about as cheap as they are in the states. We camp tonight on the Platt River, it is very wide here, we think a mile and a half. The wind is very high and tonight is quite rainy.

June 14, Tuesday. It is still raining, we hitch up and travel 5 miles and camp as it will not do to drive our oxen while it is raining. Johnnie has a chill when we stop and now seems quite sick I hope it may not be anything serious. Johnnie remains quite sick tonight. This evening Dr. Guthries train over take us. I am glad they have as they seem to be very gentlemanly.

June 15, Wednesday. This morning is cloudy but we are going to drive some 19 miles, we find the road very muddy, camp about 5 o'clock, make a corrall with Dr. Guthrie. We find some beautiful cactus in bloom today.

June 16, Thursday. Its a foggy, misty morning—we drive 17 miles, camp late this evening but on account of having stopped on Plumb [Plum] Creek so as to lay on a supply of wood—nothing of note today.

June 17, Friday. We start late and drive 19 miles and camp about sun-set. I do not like to travel so late.

June 18, Saturday. We get an early start this morning, we pass fewer ranches than any day yet, stopped at one and got some excellant water. Near this place is a dead Indian Scaffold. We drive up near so as to see how it is fixed, it is not straightened as we straighten our dead but the feet are doubled round most to his head and it is tied up in blankets its a strange looking way to put away the dead. We travel some miles and camp near the river, some of the cattle give out almost and fall down. We ladies wade over a slough and go over to the river and we have a nice time. There are some ducks swimming, the Dr. killed one and gave it to the children, we saw another large snake.

June 19, Sunday. This is a beautiful day and I am glad to say we lay by and this evening we have a good sermon by the Rev. Mr. Hodge and an exhortation by reformer by the name of Ewel. We are all thankful to have a preacher in our outfit.

June 20, Monday. We are up very early make a cup of coffee and start and travel 25 miles. We pass through a small town called Cotton Wood Springs, this is a military post, they stopped every wagon to examine if we had any United States goods, horses and etc. We think they would have taken Mr. Tiptons horse as he had a U.S. brand on him but thought he was too old to be of much service. We camp about two miles from town and have most excellant water.

June 21, Tuesday. We lay by here so as to lay in a supply of wood. Mr. Ringo, John and Allie take the wagon and go up a canyon some 2½ mi. and get plenty of good dry Cedar, they tell me it is a most beautiful place in those mountains, every variety of flowers. We hitch up at noon and travel 10 miles and camp on a lake called Fremont, it is a beautiful place to look at it you would not think any ways deep but it was over the cattles back, we had a laughable time driving them across the lake, some of them would jump in and go under as though they enjoyed it very much.

June 22, Wednesday. We traveled 21 mi. and camped where there was good grass, at noon we watered in Fremont lake and now leave it and are near the North and South Platt. To day for the first time I see some Antelope, they are beautiful. We are getting along very well.

June 23, Thursday. This morning the cattle are scattered very much and we get a late start. Nothing of note today except we cross what is called Offallins Bluff and have a heavy, sandy road. We see some

Indian Wigwams and two Indians came and offer two ponies for [space]   travel 17 miles.

June 24, Friday.   We only travel 10 miles and camp at noon so as to make enquiries about the boat.

June 25, Saturday.   Several outfits going in and buy the boat and this evening we camp some 4 miles from where we camped last night and its now raining hard,   I hope we will not be detained here long—the rain increases and we have quite a storm but not near so severe as it was some two or three miles up,   it blew so hard there that it turned wagons over that were heavily loaded.

June 26, Sunday.   We are still in camp,   I was in hopes we would have a sermon but Mr. Hodges was helping to cross over the boat, as we are anxious to get away and it was essential to be crossing.

June 27, Monday.   It is a bright morning so I wash all our dirty clothes and in the evening have a headache. We have another light shower. Nothing of interest today.

June 28, Tuesday.   A very warm clay and am getting very tired of lying by, would much rather be traveling. I made myself a bonnet today and am quite tired this evening.

June 29, Wednesday.   I walked with Mr. Ringo down to the river, the water does look so swift, they are crossing wagons quite fast. Several Indians came to camp this morning,   one of them had a saber,   we asked him where he got it,   he said he killed a soldier and took it. I have cut myself a dress and am going to try and make it this week.

June 30, Thursday.   I did very little work today—we have a shower this evening.

July 1, Friday.   We do nothing,   we are getting so tired of camp and tonight we had quite a storm,   such vivid lightning and loud thunder.

July 2, Saturday.   We hitch up once more and start,   we have quite a time for the first few miles, three teams mired down,   we travel some eight miles and camp for the night.

July 3, Sunday.   The boat has been towed up to this point and we are crossing slowly, very slowly,   today we cross seven wagons and as it is cloudy we think best not to cross any tonight. Today Mr. Forbuses train came up,   they are to have the boat 6 hours and we are to have it at noon and use it 6 hours.

July 4, Monday.   Mr. Forbus is crossing wagons and we are resting, the day is very pleasant but no one is talking of celebrating Independence Day—this evening we continue crossing our wagons. Nothing worthy of note transpires today.

July 5, Tuesday.   It is very warm,   we ladies walk up on the river and have a nice bath and this evening the mosquitoes just swarm all over the prarie,   no one can sleep for them scarcely and we are all getting very tired—we have been lying by now some 12 days and nearly all the emigration seems to be going on ahead of us.

July 6, Wednesday.   We cross over the South Platt quite safely,   got on a sand bar and had hard pulling for awhile to get off,   the river is over a mile wide but it is not swearving many places. We are so glad to get over.

July 7, Thursday.   It is a beautiful morning and as we expect to start early I wash all of our dirty clothes this evening. Mr. Moors and Mr. Tiptons families came over and at night we have some more rain with a great deal of wind.

July 8, Friday.   We get up our cattle and hitch up and once more start on our journey,   we are all so glad to get off of this river as we have been lying by on this river 14 days,   we traveled 10 miles today and camp at the old California crossing. We have another slight shower with wind enough to blow our wagons on like as if they were pulled by mules.

July 9, Saturday.   This morning we leave the river and cross over to North Platt and I had such a nice walk over the bluffs and through the canyon and gathered mountain currants and we saw some beautiful flowers and when I came up with the wagons we were on the top of a very high hill and when we went down we had to lock the wagons and then the gentlemen had to hold back on the wheels and when we got down in the valley we are in what is called Ash Hollow, here we find the road very sandy. We travel some 25 miles today, most of the road is very good.

July 10, Sunday.   The morning is warm and sultry, we hitch up and after having gotten up enough wood to last us some two weeks we travel some 14 miles and this is the hardest day we have had on our cattle,   there is so much sand on this route and some such jump offs that it makes it dangerous. Mr. Moors wagon wheel was crashed in coming down a hill,   we travel some 14 miles and camp.

July 11, Monday.   This morning we have to mend the wagon and I take a long walk and climb to the top of the highest bluff,   on one of them is the grave of a man by the name of W. Craner who was shot by accident. We have several Indians to come in our camps and trade for buffalo robes and antelope skins,   there were also two gentlemen from Clay Co. who are returning to the states and who live near my uncles,   one of them, a Mr. Johnson says he will tell them of seeing us and I was glad to have an opportunity of sending them some home messages. This evening we hitch up and start and have quite a storm,   only travel some 5 miles and camp. In the night the wolves come in and howl and scares me a good deal at first. I hope we will not have the plagues to visit us again.

July 12, Tuesday.   We get an early start and travel some 20 miles and camp at a large spring of as good water as I ever drank. Nothing else of note today.

July 13, Wednesday.   It is eight weeks today since we left home and we ought to have been 200 miles farther on our way but we have been detained some 22 days since we left Missouri. Well today we pass the great Courthouse rock and its certainly a great curiosity. I would have been delighted to have gone up close to it but it is some 3 miles from the road at the nearest point. Some of the gentlemen rode up there and said it was surrounded by mountain currants of the largest size—near the rock is another large rock called the Clerks Office,[7] tis certainly a grand natural curiosity. We camped

---

[7]This was one of the terms used for a smaller formation near Court House Rock, now called Jail Rock. It was occasionally called "The Clerk," meaning probably the clerk of the court.

late, traveled 22 miles, had a stream called Laurence Branch of North Platt, this is a bad crossing on account of quicksand, three wagons mired down in it, we have had a tiresome day.

July 14, Thursday. Last night Mr. Tiptons horse and our Kate mule run off and Mr. Ringo was out all day hunting them and found them some eight miles down the road, going back the picket pin had stuck in her leg and she is quite lame. Today we pass Chimney Rock this is another grand edifice, you can see it for some 20 miles, it is a 150 feet high, the chimney or cone being some 70 feet in heighth. The young ladies walked up to see it and brought me some specimans of the plants, they describe it as being beautiful. I have been riding behind the ox wagon all day as we had to tie our wagon tongue under our large wagon. Its much pleasanter than I thought it would be but not like having our mules. We travel some 18 miles today and camp on the river where there is plenty of fish.

July 15, Friday. Our mule is too lame to work today and we will have to ride tied to the other wagon—we traveled about 10 miles and reached a telegraph office, here they tell us that the Indians were committing depredations on the emigrants but we did not think much of it and had gone on some 2 miles when they attracted two of our wagons. Mr. Gouly and one other gentleman had turned out at the wrong road and we drove on knowing that they could see us and would cross the prarie and come to us, whilest we were looking at them we saw the Indians manouvering around them and then rode close enough to shoot the arrows through their wagon sheets just missing their heads, they fired at them and the Indians ran as fast as their horses could go, they crossed the river and attacted another emigrant train killing one man and wounding another. As soon as they attacted we went back to the ranch, correlled, and prepared for a fight but they will not fight if they think you are prepared for them. I do not think I ever spent such a night for I could not sleep a wink. All of the families in the train stayed in the telegraph office and anxiously waited for the morning. We sent back for another train to come up with us and here Mr. Morrices train join us and we now have in our train 62 wagons and are very careful to keep out our guards.

July 16, Saturday.   We hitch up and travel some 18 miles crossing the Scotts Bluff,   this is a bad road but grand scenery. I could have enjoyed it very much but I was so afraid the Indians would attack us but we got over safe and camped at a beautiful place on the river, there is an alkali slough here and some of the cattle drank of it and it killed them. Mr. Hoge loses some of his best oxen.

July 17, Sunday.   We travel 18 or 20 miles and camp near the river, nothing of note transpires today.

July 18, Monday.   We travel 19 miles and camp,   our correll is very large as all of Mr. Forbuses has fell in with us tonight. Mr. Hoge lost another ox.

July 19, Tuesday.   We got an early start and travel 10 miles by noon, we have quite an exciting time, correlled twice thinking the Indians were going to attack us but we mistook friendly Indians and one of our train fired at them,   we are fearful that it will cause us more trouble as the Indian has gone to the Fort to inform against us,   tis noon now and we have stopped for the purpose of having some blacksmithing done,   while here Mr. Davenport[8] came around to see me,   he and the Mr. Morrisons are in our train and I am very glad as they are very excellent men,   several persons from Clay Co. are here. Rock Stone, Lincoln and Beachem and I am partial to Missourians. I write a short letter home.

July 20, Wednesday.   We travel 13 miles and would have gone farther but were detained at the Fort on account of having shot at that friendly Indian and had to recompence them by paying them some flour, bacon, sugar and coffee and were glad to get off on those terms. We camp late,   had quite a shower and ate our supper in the rain. Today I received a letter from sis Mattie, the first I have had since I left Mo.

July 21, Thursday.   We do not start early and only travel 9 miles over a very bad road and stop at a good place to grass the stock. I wash some clothes today. Nothing of importance transpires.

---

[8]This was William Davenport whose letter is published at the end of Mary Ringo's journal. She calls him "Dr." in her entry for August 22, below. He was of great assistance to the Ringo family during the journey. He was from Liberty, Missouri.

July 22, Friday.   We get in to what is called the Black Hills and no one ever saw such bad roads as we have traveled and this is only the beginning of what we will have for the next 75 miles,   our stock gave out and two belonging to the outfit died. We travel 20 miles today and camp after night. I am very tired and we only make a cup of coffee and go to bed.

July 23, Saturday.   We remain in camp and I gather such nice currants and make some nice tarts for dinner,   there is no grass here and they drive the cattle over the river where they get good grass.

July 24, Sunday.   We start at day break and travel some 6 miles to a ranch and here we leave the train that we have been traveling with and join Calon Morrices. I hated to leave the family but they are traveling with freight trains and only go ten miles a day and have camped now to remain some days and Mr. Guthrie advised us to go on,   their cattle are dying so fast, the road is strewn with dead cattle. We travel some 14 miles and camp near a spring and do not herd the cattle,   we have not the men to spare from camp so we only keep camp guard.

July 25, Monday.   This morning early some emigrants came to camp who had a man killed by the Indians last night,   they report sad times ahead. I pray God we may get along safely. Today we discovered our ox was sick and bleeding at the nose,   we turned him out and he was dead in about an hour after we unyoked him. Dr. Davis cut him open to find out what disease was killing off so many cattle and pronounced it bloody murrin [murrain],[9] all the entrails were full of blood and no one can tell of anything that will cure them. Salt is said to be good but they will not lick salt in an alkalie country. I am sorry to lose him but hope we wont lose anymore. Today we travel 15 miles and camp on a creek. I do not know the name of it. It is very brushy,   the grass is scarce and we drive the cattle out to the bluffs. Some of the gentlemen kill a black tail deer and we have very nice steaks.

July 26, Tuesday.   The cattle are scattered in every direction and we

---

[9]Murrain was the name applied to several cattle diseases, the most likely one being anthrax. See the disussion of this disease and cattle deaths on the trail in Holmes, *Covered Wagon Women*, v. 5, pp. 15–16. The cause of death could also have been foot and mouth disease.

will get a very late start—we only travel some 5 miles and correll and send the cattle some 2 miles where they get good grass. We have a large spring but the water is callaciate. Mr. Forbs called to see me this evening and several gentlemen from the States came around. Mr. Summers from Platte. I think we are all going to travel together through this Indian country.

July 27, Wednesday.   We got up at two o'clock and got breakfast and travel some 15 miles and stop on a creek,   plenty of good water and fine grass. We find posted on a tree a notice that the Indians have killed six men near here. We hear they have had a fight ahead of us. I do hope and pray God that we may get through safely,   it keeps me so uneasy and anxious.

July 28, Thursday.   We do not get an early breakfast as we only think of traveling 10 miles to reach this place, a nice creek and correll and have good grass and water. Nothing of importance transpires today,   above here 3 miles the Indians killed some men and took the ladies prisoners.

July 29, Friday.   We do not get an early start and after traveling some 5 miles we see the corpse of a man lying by the side of the road, scalped, had been buried on top of the ground and the wolves had scratched it up. I think we ought to have buried him. We pass the Durlock ranch and camp some two or three miles this side on a beautiful grassy spot and about dark Mr. Ravel went out to bring in his horses when a man shot him through the arm,   in a short time all lights were extinguished and every man to his post expecting to be attacked by Indians but we do not think it was the Indians but a band of robbers.

July 30, Saturday.   And now Oh God comes the saddest record of my life for this day my husband accidentally shot himself and was buried by the wayside and oh, my heart is breaking,   if I had no children how gladly would I lay me down with my dead—but now Oh God I pray for strength to raise our precious children and oh— may no one ever suffer the anguish that is breaking my heart,   my little children are crying all the time and I—oh what am I to do. Every one in camp is kind to us but God alone can heal the breaking heart. After burying my darling husband we hitch up and drive some 5 miles. Mr. Davenport drove my mules for me and Oh, the agony of parting from that grave, to go and leave him on that hillside where I shall never see it more but thank God tis only the body lying there and may we only meet in Heaven where there is no more death but only life eternally.

July 31st, Sunday.   We are up and start early. I could not sleep but rested tolerably well. I and Allie drive our mules   they are very gentle and go so nicely. This has been the longest day I ever spent. We travel about 14 miles and camp—we keep out a strong guard but I was uneasy and afraid all night.

August 1, Monday.   We travel 10 miles and cross Platte River bridge, it is a nice bridge. There is a company of soldiers here who seem to be very fearful of an attack from the Indians. We camp about 2 miles from the Station.

August 2, Tuesday.   We remain in camp having some wagons repaired. I am so anxious to be moving,   time seems so long to me. This morning quite early a good many of the Rappahoes tribe came in to camp but seemed quite friendly. Several ladies called to see me and every one is very kind but I am so lonely and tonight Fanny has an attack of cholremorbus and after she gets easy I rest better than I have any night since the death of my dear husband. Oh God help me to bear this hard trial.

August 3, Wednesday.   We travel 10 miles over a hilly country and camp on Platte River,   tolerably good grass. We meet a good many returning to the States who report no grass ahead. I fear we will make slow progress through. Nothing of note transpires.

August 4, Thursday.   We are detained in camp waiting for some young men who got their wagon wheel broke and had to go back to the bridge station and buy them another and when they came up we start and go about 200 yards and break another wagon,   we correll and remain in camp for the rest of the day. Late in the evening Bovey's [Beauvais] train pass us. I was sorry to see them leave as they had some such kind friends   among them is a Mr. Kella and Mr. Summers, they were particularly kind.

August 5, Friday.   The cattle were scattered so it takes all day to get them together,   we keep them in correll all night so as to get an early start in the morning.

August 6, Saturday.   We get an early start and go some 10 miles— correll and grass the cattle,   there is no water here,   we do not tarry longer than to get dinner. Travel on some miles to find a good cool spring. Today we make some 14 miles and camp at Willow Spring. We find good springs here,   our cattle scatter very much. I feel so sad and lonely.

August 7, Sunday.   We get a late start on account of the cattle scattering. The Mr. Morrices leave our train and are traveling by themselves. I feel sorry for any one to leave as I feel safer in a large company. We noon at what is called Fish Creek and tonight we correll on Home Creek,   the water is very clear and full of fish. We drive the cattle 1½ miles to good grass. We have no wood but sagebrush. The wolves howl all around our camp even after daylight. We travel 14 miles.

August 8, Monday.   We start at five o'clock and drive to Sweet Water by noon where we are now nooning. There is a great deal of alkalie through this section, many places the water is crusted all over with beautiful white crust. We cross Sweet Water and camp at a sandy camping place. We passed Independence Rock and it is a grand sight, many names are carved there, some few of them I knew. We have good grass for our stock but there is a great deal of alkalie here.

August 9, Tuesday.   We get a late start and drive to a point called Hell's Gate (I do not think it an appropriate name for the grand and sublime scenery). The pass is very narrow and perpendicular walls on either side. We heard that a gentleman had fallen from the top of them and was killed instantly. We travel 14 miles and camp at Plantes Station,   have a nice camp.

August 10, Wednesday.   We travel 12 miles and camp below Split Rock,   nothing of importance transpires today. Some of the cattle die and we travel slowly.

August 10, Thursday.   We travel 13 miles and camp near three crossing at a beautiful place but everything seems lonely to me. I hate to see night coming and do hope we will soon get through to Salt Lake.

August 12, Friday.   Our cattle scattered and we get a late start and traveled some 10 or 12 miles by noon. We hitch up and start at 4 o'clock and travel till 9 o'clock at night and camp at Ice Spring,   its very cold,   we keep our cattle in the correll so as to get an early start in the morning.

August 13, Saturday.   We start early and come some 14 miles and rest our stock and then travel some 4 miles and camp on Sweet Water. The stock have good grass tonight.

August 14, Sunday.   We pass a ranch at the foot of Rocky Ridge. We leave Sweet Water here and travel over a hilly country with scarcely any grass,   we rest our cattle till late and then travel till 9 o'clock. We make some 20 miles and camp on Strawberry—the night is beautiful. We pass several trains and their campfires look so cheerful.

August 15, Monday.   We start by sun-up and travel some 3 miles here. Mr. Morris train passes us. Mr. Davis comes to see me   I am always glad to see him for he is the last one Mr. Ringo ever talked to. Oh God thou hast sorely afflicted me—give me strength to bear this heart tryal. We traveled about 11 miles and camp on Sweet Water near a ranch. Nothing of importance transpires today.

August 16, Tuesday.   We come over South Pass and camp at Paciffick Springs,   these springs are very cold and its quite mirey. We travel 15 miles today.

August 17, Wednesday.   We get a late start and noon on dry Sandy—here the cattle have no water and but little grass. We travel some 6 miles and camp where there is neither grass or water,   correll our cattle and horses.

August 18, Thursday.   We start very early and travel to a station on Little Sandy where we have fine water but little grass. We are nooning now—we hitch up and travel some 7 miles farther and camp on Big Sandy—grass very scarce and one of my oxen gives out and we unyoke him and let him rest.

August 19, Friday. We get breakfast and start—have traveled 10 miles and are now nooning, tis very windy and we have a sandy camping place—we travel very slowly and camp 4 miles from Big Timbers and our camp is far from water, we correll our cattle to keep them from scattering.

August 20, Saturday. We start early and drive to Green River some 16 miles and correll after dark. I do not get any supper for I am too tired—we have had a sandy hilly road. Mr. Dewey drove down some of the long hills for me.

August 21, Sunday. We remain in camp today, our stock are on good grass and they are going to let them recruit for a few days. This is the most beautiful river I ever saw—tis very rapid and the water looks green and is very clear. I have not spent my Sabbath as I would like to—I have been cooking and first one thing and then another. I did not read any.

August 22, Monday. We cross Green River and camp on this side. We separate here from Forbuses train and we go with Mr. Davises, Mr. How and Mr. Campbells train. We only have seven wagons in all and I am afraid to travel with so few but no one seems to apprehend any danger but me. Dr. Davenport stays in our correll and writes a letter to his wife. He has been very kind to me since the death of my husband and I am sorry to separate from their train. Mr. Forbus and family were more than kind. I hope they may do well.

August 23, Tuesday. This morning we start our train for Salt Lake and have traveled some 16 miles and camp on Black Creek Fork. I do not think we have much grass and its raining and very disagreeable, do not get any supper as its raining too hard.

August 24, Wednesday. We start our train out at ten o'clock and noon on Black Fork, we then start again and travel some 11 miles by traveling in the night, our mule is a little alkalied and seems quite sick and I walk several miles pass Church Buttes, the sand hills are grand looking domes—we find tolerable good grass for our stock and camp near a mail station, I am glad we are once more in the mail line, it seems more like civilization.

August 25, Thursday. We passe Millesville and camp some three miles this side, have good water and grass. Tonight we keep up a guard as we are in Indian settlement.

August 26, Friday. We get a late start this morning and have only come 6 miles are now nooning in sight of Fort Bridger. My ox team has come and I am going some three-quarters of a mile beyond the Fort and camp. I go to the Post Office and mail one letter only there is no Eastern Mail, the Indians are too bad for the coaches to run. We camp this side of Fort Bridger and have fine grass.

August 27, Saturday. We travel 13 miles today, are traveling the new cut-off, so far the road is very good, we are camping on Muddy Creek we find the government corrells here, a Mr. Bently comes and takes supper with us. Mr. Donly also comes round to see us. I am so lonely and sad and I wish I was at my journeys end.

August 28, Sunday. We lay over today as it is the Sabbath. I am glad that we do. I do not think it is right to travel on the Sabbath. I have the headache today Mr. Buell and family leave our party and go back to the Fort, they were very pleasant people.

August 29, Monday. We start early and travel 19½ miles and camp on Willow Creek, here we see potatoes growing and buy some turnips for 25 cts. a dozen, we also get some cheese at 50 cts. a pound, it is very nice. This is a good camping place and I sleep better than I have for a long time.

August 30, Tuesday. We travel on 8 miles and correll for the night. It is rainy and we do not cook supper, have crackers and cheese.

August 31, Wednesday. We start tolerably early but fall in behind the Government train and have to travel very slowly. At noon we pass them and travel but a short distance as tis raining. We stop for the night having made only 6 miles today.

September 1, Thursday. We lay by and wash. I wash most all of my dirty clothes, we have another shower, it has rained every day this week. I was quite tired but rest very well tonight.

September 2, Friday. We start late and have come 4 or 5 miles, have passed Huffs ranch where I see the first corn growing I have seen this year. I sent Johnny to see if he could buy some potatoes and he has not caught up with us yet,   he does not get any potatoes but gets some nice turnips.

September 3, Saturday.   We travel some 18 miles and correll on Silver Creek where the canyon is so narrow that we hardly have room for our wagons.

September 4, Sunday.   We lay over till afternoon and would not travel now but we have no place for our stock so we hitch up and travel some 6 miles where we have a good camping ground and nice grass.

September 5, Monday.   We travel some 20 miles and camp near a station where a Missouri lady comes to see us,   she is stopping here for the winter, her name is Hueston.

September 6, Tuesday.   We start early and have reached the great Salt Lake City. I have not been up in the City   are camping on the Emigrants Square. Expect I will go up in the morning. I received two letters from sister Mattie and one from Mr. Halliday and no tongue can tell how sad I feel for each letter was written to my dear husband for they know not that he is dead.

September 7, Wednesday.   I wait for Major Barron[10] to come down and as he does not   I go up to see him and present my letter of introduction,   he receives me very politely and promised to assist me in selling my outfit and procuring me a passage in the coach for California but took good care not to come down. I am at a loss what to do. Mrs. Belt called down awhile this evening to see Mrs. Davise. This City is handsomely laid out, every house has an acre of ground ornamented with trees and flowers but I would not live here if the whole city belonged to me among such a class of community. I haven't seen a handsomely dressed lady since I have been here. Morman communities are poor excuses to me and there are more dirty children running around begging than a few,   we buy some nice peaches but they are 25 cts. a dozen. I tell you you have to pay high for everything you get here.

---

[10]We checked all of the soldiers named Barron listed in J. Carlyle Parker's *Personal Name Index to Orton's "Records of California Men in the War of the Rebellion, 1861 to 1867,"* (Detroit, 1978), and found only privates. A careful check with Orton's original work (Sacramento, 1890) listed no officers by that name.

September 8, Thursday.   I sent up for Major Barron to come down as I did not know what to do,   he came down looked at my wagons, oxen and mules and seemed to think they were worth so little that I thought I had better not try to sell them and have hired a Mr. John Donly to drive my oxen and am going to try to go through in my wagons. We leave Salt Lake City about noon and travel some 15 miles and camp near a ranch where they have a large spring but the water is salty and makes us all sick.

September 9, Friday.   We lay over all day.

September 10, Saturday.   We hitch up and travel some 12 miles and camp at a village called E. T.   here the water is very salty as well as the grass,   our mules come very near dying from the effects of it.

September 11, Sunday.   We leave Mr. Davises family and travel on to a small town,   I do not know the name of it and here we get some hay for the stock and buy some nice peaches. We drive out about a mile from town and Mr. Davises family come on and correll with us.

September 12, Monday.   We drive some 10 miles and camp by some fine springs and our stock has fine grass,   we stay here for the rest of the day.

September 13, Tuesday.   We hitch up and go through a settlement where we buy some excellent Irish potatoes. We drive some 21 miles and my mules give out,   we have poor grass and I buy hay and oats for the mules for which I pay $6.00.

September 14, Wednesday.   We travel some 5 miles and camp near a mail station and we have to drive our stock 6 miles to grass,   we stay here the rest of the day and I buy some most excellent mutton. Mr. Davises overtake us again.

September 15, Thursday.   We go some 10 miles to a station called Look-out,   stay here all night.

September 16, Friday.   We travel 12 miles and camp at Government Springs and have excellent grass for our stock.

September 17, Saturday.   We lay over here and I wash our dirty clothes,   they cut some excellent grass for the stock as we will soon cross the great desert and will need all the feed we can haul for them.

September 18, Sunday.   We lay over here as our stock is improving so much.

September 19, Monday.   We leave this place and travel some 10 miles to Indian Springs, here we again lay over for the rest of the day so the stock may all fill up.

September 20, Tuesday.   We remain here until one o'clock and then start for the desert. We travel all this evening and all night and have come some 36 miles and are now resting in the desert.

September 21, Wednesday.   We travel some 10 miles and noon at Fish Springs Station, our Bet mule is a little sick and we fasten our wagon under the ox wagon and go to the next station   from here we move up some 2 miles to a fine spring and camp for the night. The grass and water here are quite salty.

September 22, Thursday.   We hitch up and start again, the stock seem rested and we have traveled some 10 miles and are now noon-ing but there is not a sprig of grass for our teams. We travel some 24 miles and camp at Willow Springs—good water and grass.

September 23, Friday.   We start before day and travel some 30 miles and camp at Deep Creek,   this is a narrow stream but very deep, grass good.

September 24, Saturday.   We remain here until noon and then travel some 6 miles and camp as this is the last good grass we will have for some miles.

September 25, Sunday.   We start early this morning and travel 28 miles and camp but find very little grass,   our mules are very tired as well as the oxen and we camp for the night,   it rains very hard and is very windy.

September 26, Monday.   We start early and travel 16 miles,   we find some good bunch grass and stop and let the stock grass.

September 27, Tuesday.   We travel 16 miles and camp near a station and have good grass,   the water here is quite warm.

September 28, Wednesday. We travel 25 miles and pass through Egan Canyon, here we see a good many emigrants stopping here for the winter to try their luck in the mining process, tis thought that these are rich mines. At night when we camp we have a fine camp fire, near us is camped a woman who is confined and gives birth to a son, her name is Richardson.

September 29, Thursday. We travel 27 miles and have a very tiresome drive our mules and cattle both give out and we do not get into camp till almost midnight. I am very tired.

September 30, Friday. We start as early as we can and go some 10 miles to Ruby Valley, we stop here and rest our stock, we find everything very dear, I buy some coffee at one dollar a pound and give them my tin can to pay for it.

October 1, Saturday. We start early, travel 24 miles and camp at the foot of Diamond Mountain, this is a very high peak, the highest I have seen yet—our mules give out again and we haul our wagon with the oxen, it is a very cold night.

October 2, Sunday. We hitch up and climb the high hill, we get up safely and then descend to a beautiful valley and remain there the rest of the day and night and have a very windy evening and night.

October 3, Monday. We get an early start and have traveled very well but our mules are tired and I am getting so tired traveling. This evening we have a great time climbing to the top of a high hill and are very glad to get to the top, we then camp near a ranch and buy some hay for our oxen—we taveled 24 miles today.

October 4, Tuesday. We travel 20 miles have no grass and poor water.

October 5, Wednesday. We travel 22 miles and have good grass and water—camp in a canyon.

October 6, Thursday. We travel 20 miles over a very bad road, had a very bad hill to climb and a worse one to descend. I walk down which brings on a spell of sickness for tonight I am very poorly. We camp in Simpson's Park.

October 7, Friday.   We travel 10 miles and reach Austin,[11] Nevada, where I have the pleasure of seeing cousin Charley Peters and my old acquaintance Mr. Ford from Liberty, Mo. They are very kind to me and assist me to dispose of my oxen and wagon.

October 8, Saturday.   We remain in Austin, Nev.

IN CONCLUSION: Written by Mattie Bell (Ringo) Cushing, daughter of Mary Ringo.

That is the last Mother wrote in her diary so I will have to finish the best I can from things she told us at different times. I think she was the bravest woman I ever heard of—left as she was with five children to look after and to have everything else to attend to and in the condition she was in. In Austin she had a son born, fortunately it was still-born for he was terribly disfigured from mother seeing father after he was shot. Even my brother who was fourteen years old noticed it and said he looked just like father did. On the way out when we reached Fort Laramie, Wyoming, the government offered her an escort of soldiers to go back to Missouri but she said she was as much afraid of the soldiers as she was of the Indians and besides it wouldn't seem like home without father.

I don't know how long we stayed in Austin, probably a week or ten days and I don't know how we made the rest of the trip. We took the mules and one wagon to San Jose and she told of stopping in San Francisco, California, and how high up the beds were, my sister had to climb on a chair to get in it.

We finally reached San Jose where Mother's sister lived. My aunt and her husband had a very large place and Mr. Younger raised blooded cattle. They had a small house on the place that had formerly been a carriage house and had been made into a house. We lived there a year as mother was not able to do anything for some time but she paid our living expenses as of course she had some money but it was confederate money and she lost 36 dollars on the hundred.

We moved to San Jose and lived on Second Street where mother began the task of providing for her little family, the way was rough but with her sheer determination she raised her family unaided.

---

[11]The best reference to this silver mining town is Oscar Lewis' *The Town That Died Laughing, The Story of Austin, Nevada* (Reno, 1955). We have used the 1986 edition with a new foreword by Kenneth N. Owens.

EPILOGUE: LETTER OF WILLIAM DAVENPORT

From the Liberty, Missouri, *Tribune*, September 16, 1864

From the Plains

Platte River   Idaho Ter.

August 1, 1864

Mr. R. H. Miller—Dear Friend. I write to give you the melancholy information of the death of Martin Ringo. Owing to some difficulties we had with the Indians below Fort Laramie at Scott's Bluffs the emigration formed themselves into large companies. Our company consisted of the Morris brothers and Jas. Reed of Clay county, Forbes, Irvin, Lucas & Co., from Platte and Buc[h]anan counties—Beauvais & Co. from St. Joseph with Mr. Ringo and family and others, making in all about 70 wagons, have been traveling together for mutual protection. We passed through the Black Hills, where the Indians have committed most of their depredations this season without being molested, and camped the night of the 28th July about three miles this side of Deer Creek, and about twenty five miles from this point. Shortly after dark a gentleman by the name of Davis, from Kansas, went out about fifty yards from the camp to look after his horses that were picketed out, and an Indian shot and wounded him in the right arm and side, making a painful tho' not dangerous wound. The Indian succeeded in stealing three horses—one from Mr. Davis, one from Mr. Irvin and one from David Morris. There was only one Indian seen, and I think his only object was to steal horses. The shooting of Mr. Davis created considerable excitement in camp, as we expected to be attacked by Indians in force. The whole company stood guard during the night so as to be prepared in case we were attacked. Just after daylight on the morning of the 30th ult. Mr. Ringo stepped on top of the wagon, as I suppose, for the purpose of looking around to see if Indians were in sight, and his shot gun went off accidentally in his own hands, the load entering his right eye and coming out at the top of his head. At the report of the gun I saw his hat blown up twenty feet in the air, and his brains were scattered in all directions. I never saw a more heartrending sight, and to see the distress and agony of his wife and children was painful in the extreme. Mr. Ringo's death has cast a gloom over the whole company, and his wife and children have our sympathy. The ladies in our company are very kind and attentive to Mrs. Ringo, and every gentleman in the company is disposed to do anything in his power to make her comfortable, or promote her interests. Mr. Ringo was a very mild, pleasant and unassuming gentleman, and was duly appreciated by our company—all of whom esteemed him highly. He was buried near the place he was shot in as decent a manner as possible with the facilities on the plains.

Mrs. Ringo thinks of going to Salt Lake and of disposing of her outfit at that point and taking the stage from there to California. There is a portion of our company that are going to California via Salt Lake, the larger portion are going to Idaho via the South Pass, and a portion of them are going by Bridger's Cut Off, sixteen miles from here.

We do not anticipate any further Indian troubles on our journey, as there is no report of their committing any depredations beyond this point. We are going to travel in sufficiently large companies to protect ourselves, and by keeping strict guard we do not expect to be molested—their only object being to steal horses.

Our company are all enjoying excellent health.

Your friend,
Wm. Davenport.

Index